HISTORIC...

1.(Site of) ... House Ass...
3.The Hous... Great Synagogue 5.(Site of)...
6.(Site of) The Greek Church/present St Martin's school of Art 7. Chinatown (whole of Gerrard St). 8.(Site of) Newport Market. 9.(Site of) John Dryden's House 10.(Site of) Leicester House 11.(Site of) Hogarth's house. 12.(Site of) Burford's Panorama/present Roman Catholic church of Notre Dame De France. 13.(Site of) Sir Joshua Reynolds' house. 14.(Site of) Shaver's Hall. 15.(Site of) the Chevalier d'Eon's lodgings. 16.(Site of) Angelica Kauffman's house. 17. Roman Catholic Church of Our Lady of the Assumption and St Gregory. 18.(Site of) Broad Street pump. 19.(Site of) William Blake's birthplace. 20.(Site of) Carnaby Market. 21. Marshall Street Baths. 22.(Site of) The Pantheon. 23 (Site of) Carlisle House. 24.(Site of) Miss Kelly's Theatre. 25. Karl Marx's lodgings/Leoni's Quo Vadis 26. French Protestant Church. 27. St Anne's Church. 28. Raymond's Revue Bar.

SOHO

To Gerry
Merry Christmas '89.
Love. David.

SOHO

A HISTORY OF LONDON'S MOST
COLOURFUL NEIGHBOURHOOD

JUDITH SUMMERS

BLOOMSBURY

First published in Great Britain 1989
Copyright © 1989 by Judith Summers

Bloomsbury Publishing Ltd, 2 Soho Square, London W1V 5DE

A CIP catalogue record for this book is available from the British Library
ISBN 0-7475-0384-2

Typeset by Hewer Text Composition Services, Edinburgh
Printed and bound in Great Britain by Butler & Tanner Ltd, Frome and London

FOR DANIEL

PICTURE CREDITS

Barnaby's Picture Library: pages 17, 18 *right*
BBC Hulton Picture Library: pages 15, 18 *left*
Guildhall Library, City of London: pages 1, 2, 3, 5, 6, 12, 13, 14 *bottom*
Westminster City Archives: pages 4, 7, 8, 9, 10–11, 14 *top*, 16
John Whitfield: pages 19, 20, 21, 22, 23, 24, 25, 26, 27, 28, 29, 30, 31, 32

Endpaper map by Andrew Farmer

'If you get Sohoitis . . . you will stay there always, day and night and get no work done ever. You have been warned.'

Tambimuttu, the editor of *Poetry London*, to writer Julian McLaren-Ross

The author would like to thank the following:
Unwin Hyman, for permission to reproduce the translated letters of
Jenny Marx from *Red Jenny* by H. F. Peters; the Estate of the late Arthur
Machen, for permission to reproduce extracts from *My Life and
Adventures* by Casanova, translated by Arthur Machen; Michael Joseph
Ltd, for permission to reproduce an extract from *Soho in the Fifties*
by Daniel Farson; Century Hutchinson Publishing Group Ltd, for
permission to reproduce an extract from *Georgian London* by John
Summerson; David McLellan, for permission to reproduce a translated
letter from *Karl Marx: His Life and Thought*; William Heinemann, for
permission to reproduce letter translations from *Angelica: Portrait of an
18th Century Artist* by Adeline Hartup; Reg Davis Poynter, for
permission to reproduce extracts from *Absolute Beginners* by Colin
MacInnes (Allison and Busby); Longman Group UK Ltd, for permission
to reproduce letter translations from *The Enigma of the Age* by Cynthia
Cox; Macmillan Ltd, for permission to reproduce letter translations from
The Letters of Mozart and His Family edited by Emily Anderson.

CONTENTS

ACKNOWLEDGEMENTS

'You don't know what you're taking on,' Kathleen Gibson, Secretary of the Soho History Group, warned me when I first approached her with the news that I intended to write a book about Soho. Luckily, she was right, for had I realized what a huge task I was undertaking I would probably have been too daunted to begin. A big thank-you to her for her constant encouragement, help and interest; to Bryan Burrough, Chairman of the Soho Society, for being an inspiration; to Roy Harrison of the Westminster City Archive for his invaluable help; to Philip Beckworth of the Blake Society; and to Ralph Hyde of the Guildhall Library.

I would also like to thank the many Sohoites who generously shared their thoughts and memories with me, and without whose co-operation it would not have been possible to write the end section of this book, including Palmina Alalouf, Peter Anderson, David Barton, Ronald Batty, Bill Bean, Charles Beare, Bessie Dowse, Gaston Berlemont, Gordon Bray, Zinna Bulmore, Jean Brown, Ennio and Alberto Camisa, Stephen Chamberlain, Stephen Clackson, Paul Crocetta, Sadie Feigen, Carolyn Ford, Christina Foyle, Ettie Gontarsky, Bunty and Derek Hand, Peter Heath, Mary Honeywill, Michael Klinger, John Koiza, Nick Lander, Joan Mander, George Melly, Christine Mo, Nancy Pierce, Lois Peltz, Laura Phillips, Paul Raymond, Bill Rest, Wagih Saleh, Edna Sherman, Sohing Pang, the Rev. Fred Stevens, Rica Teagno, Michelle Wade, Louis and Lily Walters, Bruce Welch, Caroline White and Ngook Ching Wong.

The inspiration for this book came from Barclays Bank, whose long association with the area and its people has led it to encourage the creation of a permanent record before the pace of change might make that impossible.

Introduction

First, the name. It is not so much a word as a short, wistful sigh.

It is known from Harrogate to Hemel Hempstead and from Helsinki to Alice Springs, and to each person who hears it it conjures up a different image. An out-of-towner will picture topless girls in fish-net tights, and red lights, and dangerous dark nights, and they will mutter disapprovingly, 'Never go there.' A group of male American tourists will snigger, and their women blush. A Liverpudlian football fan will leer wanly at the remembrance of hangovers past, of beer cans kicked along a gutter, of rubbish sacks overturned and bottles crushed, and a night spent dozing miserably in a damp doorway. An advertising executive will think lunch, the style-conscious of drinks in the Soho Brasserie. But the 2,000-odd residents of Soho will think only of the place where they belong, probably of the streets in which they grew up, and they will smile and breathe that simple, explicit four-letter word – home.

Soho! 'An Anglo-French hunting call, probably of purely exclamatory origin', according to the *Oxford English Dictionary*. A rallying call used by the hunt when a hare has been discovered. The 15th-century vocabulary *Promptorium Parvulorum* defines this most succinctly: 'Sohoe, the hare ys founde.'

Next, the place, which is harder to define. It is a small island land-locked in London's West End, where for 300 years it has held sway, on and off, as the centre of social and creative life. Barely half a square mile in size, it is cut off from the metropolis by the fast-moving traffic of Regent Street, Trafalgar Square, the Charing Cross Road and what opium-eater Thomas De Quincey called 'the great Mediterranean of Oxford Street'. The explorer penetrating these shores will not escape quickly. Soho is a place to linger in. Except for the buses that grind down Shaftesbury Avenue – a Victorian afterthought, not an indigenous Soho street – there is no public transport across it. Underground stations surround it warily. Drivers enter it at their peril, blood-pressure rising in inverse proportion to their speed. Pedestrians trying to hurry along its busy pavements are impeded by a hundred sights, sounds and scents which assault the senses and all but stop them in their tracks. A pungent and seductive breeze blows through Soho which smells by turns of soy sauce, dust, exhaust fumes, lust, strong coffee and cheap perfume, good wine and old beer, urine, ripe melons and rotting cabbage leaves.

Soho may not always be pleasant, but it is never dull. One might die there of despair or overindulgence, but one can never be bored or miserable for long. Only one man in history managed it – Daniel Finch, the swarthy and uncompromisingly moral Earl of Nottingham, who in the 1680s became one of its first residents. Not content with the large mansion he occupied in Gerrard Street, the moaning Finch moved to more fashionable Soho Square, where he was so consistently gloomy that he earned himself the nickname 'Don Dismallo'.

Soho is always arid, often dirty and sometimes sordid, yet it is never intimidating. It is a humane place, built on a human scale. There is no grandeur to live up to and, give or take the odd incongruous tower block, there is nothing to look up to, either, for the average Soho building is a mere five or six storeys high. Even Charles II, whose statue once peered down regally from atop a high fountain in Soho Square, now looks *hoi polloi* straight in the eye from a modest plinth. The spirit of Soho, as of the king in whose reign it was conceived, is distinctly humanitarian. It has always been generous, providing shelter, hope and opportunity for generations of immigrants. Even at its poshest it was egalitarian, with rich and poor living side by side. It is not a place that stands on ceremony. For the past 48 years, its parish church has been a bomb-site; for the past 126 years its one remaining palatial building has been a hostel for homeless women, the House of St Barnabas-in-Soho in Greek Street.

Soho is a place for individuals, as its residents and work-force will tell you. There is no pressure on its people to be the same. 'You can do what you like in Soho, you come and go as you want to,' they say. 'You can be yourself in Soho.' And, 'You could walk naked in Soho and no one would care.'

Soho is Cosmopolis, and its residents are cosmopolitan by birth and in outlook. They include Italians, French, Cypriots, Greeks, Poles, Sicilians, Chinese, English and, nowadays, Bengalis. They are as down-to-earth, as hard-working, as unpretentious and as uncomplaining a group of people as one could wish to meet. They are neither City people nor suburban people. They are, above all, working people, and, whatever their origins or religions, they are all Sohoites and so get on very well with one another. They are at the same time worldly and innocent. Their tolerance of other people is unlimited. And, as the headmaster of the local parish school will tell you, their children are remarkably bright.

More things happen in Soho every day than a person can easily imagine. Priceless violins are split apart like oysters. Music is composed, recorded and played. Films are bought, sold, processed, cut, dubbed and printed. Epaulettes for high-up colonels are embroidered in spun gold thread. Suits and dresses are sketched, cut out, sewn, finished and pressed in scores of small factories and workrooms. People buy and sell everything, from designer sofas to strawberries to sex. Business deals, most of them legal, are clinched over drinks, meals and handshakes. Fortunes are made and lost at gaming tables and in corner betting shops. The cream of British youth is held to ransom by shrieking video games and one-armed bandits in numerous smoky arcades called, inexplicably, names like Family Leisure. Since its very beginnings, Soho has been a gamblers' place.

Soho's restaurants have always been famous. In the late 18th century the painter Sir David Wilkie used to dine at a local 'ordinary', the King's Arms in Poland Street. There, he wrote, 'about a dozen gentlemen meet at 2 o'clock, and have a dinner served up that only costs 13*d*. a head, which I am sure is as cheap as any person can have such a dinner in any part of Great Britain: besides, we have all the advantage of hearing all the languages of Europe talked with the greatest fluency, the place being mostly frequented by foreigners: indeed, it is a very rare thing to see an Englishman; while there are Corsicans, Italians, French, Germans, Welsh and Scotch.'

Apart from the prices, things have not changed. It is impossible to calculate how many meals are prepared and eaten in Soho each day. It is almost impossible to count how many restaurants there are, for new ones open and close with alarming speed. At a rough estimate they currently number 265, including the sandwich bars in

Berwick Street market and the tea-houses of Chinatown. One can eat Italian, Indonesian or Indian, Cantonese or Turkish Cypriot, Kosher or Korean, Mexican or Malaysian, Spanish, Middle Eastern or Moroccan, English, French or Greek. There are Japanese *sushi* bars and American hamburger bars, Italian sandwich bars and French coffee bars. One can choose from pasta and pizza unlimited, cream cakes light as *cappuccino* froth, or steaming slabs of salt beef. One can eat fast or slow, sitting, standing or on the move, healthily wholemeal or heavily Hungarian, fancily *nouvelle* or basically and greasily egg, bacon and chips.

People get drunk in Soho. The district is remarkably well-equipped for this. Its most infamous institutions are its private drinking clubs. It has more than 50 pubs. Wine bars are currently multiplying. Yet however many drinking establishments there are, their walls cannot contain the number of customers, who spill exuberantly out on to the pavements clutching glasses of beer or Kir and talking volubly. Numerous off-licences sell exotic aperitifs, wines, champagnes or aged malt whiskies to the cognoscenti, and strong cider or fortified wine to the growing number of destitute down-and-outs who crouch in shop doorways or hover around the groups of more prosperous drinkers, cadging money or cigarettes.

To some, Soho's watering holes are its *raison d'être*. But Soho is all things to all people. It is corn-on-the-cobs being auctioned off on a Saturday night in Berwick Street market. It is the theatres of Shaftesbury Avenue and the supermarkets of Chinatown. It is a row of well wrapped-up and Trilbyed foreign gentlemen, gossiping the afternoon away on a Soho Square bench. It is a group of Italians in sheepskin coats and sunglasses standing outside the Bar Italia gesticulating with cigarettes.

Soho is the wall of British cheeses behind the counter in Camisa Fratelli. Home-made ravioli parcelled up with infinite care in Lina Stores. The Algerian Coffee Store on Old Compton Street, where the staff speed on espresso, and the merchandise includes 27 varieties of coffee and 120 different teas. The news-stand outside Moroni's, where the latest issue of *The Caterer, Broadcast* and *Screen International* are on sale next to *Die Welt, Le Figaro, El País, Svenska Dagbladet, Il Giornale,* numerous and indecipherable Arabic and Chinese titles, the *Independent* and the *Irish Times*. A dusty hallway where the panelling is veined with new wires and old gas-pipes, like the back of an ancient hand. Breakfast coffee and croissants in the plain dark depths of Patisserie Valerie, a place famed as much for its illicit lovers' trysts as for its cakes.

Soho is a tired chef having a quick smoke in an open doorway. A shop window hung with a lethal display of kitchen knives. A black leather harness studded with steel, better suited to a horse than a person. A politician stepping out of a taxi and straight into the Gay Hussar. A woman in thick make-up and thin clothes enticing a man down some dimly-lit cellar staircase. Ronnie Scott's Jazz Club at any time of the night. A Chinese nun saying a prayer in St Patrick's church. School gates sandwiched between a kebab restaurant and a hostess bar.

Soho is one hundred printed or handwritten signs: 'Non si fanno panini – Sorry, we don't make sandwiches'; 'Warning – Articles of Value Should not be left on seats while receiving Holy Communion'; 'This House offers a temporary home for women who have the necessary recommendations'; '4000-year-old Taoist Secret Technique for men. Conserve Life-force. Increase Virility. Guaranteed Effective'; 'Tina, Swedish Model, 2nd Floor', scrawled in red felt-tip on a scrap of paper and hastily pinned up inside an open door.

Soho is a place of dazzling contrasts. It is both homely village and red-light district, a place of work and a place to forget it. It will take you from rags to riches, from the night before to the morning after and on through the next day. Its boundaries contain everything from Garrards the Crown Jewellers to its own branch of Marks & Spencer, which stands on the site of a building that was 'the wonder of the 18th century and of the British Empire' – the Pantheon, one of the most important entertainment palaces of its day.

Soho is infinitely varied. Pick a Soho street at random and examine it. A quick glance at, for instance, Poland Street, reveals the following: two sandwich bars, three restaurants and three pubs; two bookshops, two printers and two publishing firms; eight fashion wholesalers; 15 film production companies and two film-processing plants; one creative consultancy; Marks & Spencer; one designer furniture store; one recording company; one shop selling office equipment, and another selling artists' materials; five travel agents; an advertising agency; a car showroom and a multi-storey garage which occupies the site of the old workhouse; a betting office; a costume jewellery wholesaler; five chartered accountants' and one solicitor's office; a night-club (for members only); a name-plate engraver's; a newsagent, where, in the window, cards offer French Lessons by Miss Cain, Drama Lessons by a Kinky Mistress and the services of a 19-year-old Bossy Boots; a timber yard; and the London office of the Royal Wanstead School. In the past Percy Bysshe Shelley lodged here, and before him singer Elizabeth Billington – popularly known as the 'Poland Street Man Trap' – novelist Fanny Burney, architects William Chambers and Giacomo Leoni, and sculptor John Flaxman and his good friend, Soho's home-grown genius, William Blake.

An impressive list. Yet Poland Street is not unusual. Every street has its ghosts and celebrities. For Soho's past is even more dizzyingly diverse than its present. Go back 10 years and it was the porn capital of England. Go back another 10 and it was the birthplace of British pop music. Before World War II it was a melting-pot for Italian, Jewish and French immigrants. In the 19th century it was one of the metropolis's worst slums – which did not stop Horatio Nelson spending his last night in London in Dean Street, after visiting his coffin-maker Peddieson. Back in the 18th century it was the home of two kings, the burial place of a third, and the centre of London's aristocratic, intellectual and artistic life.

Soho has had a hard life. It kicked off with delusions of grandeur which it very soon realized were just that, whence it got on with the more mundane task of making a living. Since then it has been the residence of artists, con-artists, artistes and artisans, a place of grandiose schemes that ended in spectacular failure, of chameleonic names and muddled sexual identities. It has attracted the bizarre, the outlandish and the wildly eccentric.

No other district in London has a history to match it. Let us begin.

I

The Hare ys Founde

In September 1562 the Lord Mayor rode out from the City of London one morning, in the company of the aldermen, to make his annual inspection of the water conduits in the fields to the west of town. After hunting hare, they dined at the Mayor's country banqueting house on the north side of Oxford Road, the main route from the City of London to the triple gallows at Tyburn. On their way back to the City, the party found and killed a fox in Hog Lane, an ancient track leading south from the 12th-century leper hospital of St Giles-in-the-Fields to the monument to Queen Eleanor of Castille at Charing Cross.

With the exception of a few small privately owned freeholds, these hunting fields were Crown property which had been acquired by Henry VIII during the dissolution of the monasteries. Previously they had belonged to the Abbot of Westminster, who had leased them out to three tenants: the Mercer's Company in the City, the Abbot of Abingdon, near Oxford, and the Master of the Hospital of Burton Saint Lazar in Leicestershire, who was also custodian of St Giles's hospital.

Apart from a small hamlet which had grown up around the leper hospital, and the Royal Mews at Charing Cross – a large walled yard first built for keeping falcons during Edward I's reign and later rebuilt as stables – there were few buildings in the fields where the local parishioners of St Martin-in-the-Fields and St Margaret's, Westminster had the right to lay out their clothes to dry and to graze their cattle in the weeks after 1 August, Lammas Day.

Yet this rural place was already under threat. The City had outgrown its medieval walls, and, in an early form of ribbon development, houses had been built along all the main routes out of town. Though the south bank of the Thames was still open land, given over to bear-baiting circuses, orchards and pleasure gardens, the northern strand was an unbroken line of mansions which stretched from the City walls to the ill-planned jumble of Court buildings in Westminster and Whitehall.

The City itself, with its old medieval buildings, narrow streets and primitive open sewers, was distinctly unhealthy. Smallpox and plague broke out with such alarming frequency that escaping disease became an obsession of the age. The parish of St Martin-in-the-Fields had been subdivided from the parish of St Margaret's, Westminster in April 1542 expressly in order to avoid the 'danger of infection which might happen to our Court by the carrying of dead bodies past our royal palace to be interred at St Margaret's'. Well-founded fears of illness had driven a growing number of people out of the City, and many more wanted to follow them.

Yet building new houses on the outskirts of London was forbidden by law. On 7 July 1582, in the first of three royal proclamations against the illegal erection of tenements within three miles of the City, Elizabeth I cited the reasons for this in no uncertain terms: 'Firstly, the difficulty of governing a more extended multitude, without device of new jurisdiction and offers for the purpose; secondly, the improbability of supplying them with food, fuel and other necessaries of life at a reasonable rate; and thirdly, the danger of spreading plague and infection throughout the realm.'

In practice, the growth of London, like the behaviour of the people, was hard to control. The gradual enclosure of the Soho hunting and Lammas fields by Crown tenants led to riots – almost exactly 10 years after this proclamation was published – when 40 parishioners, determined to exercise their summer grazing rights, descended on them on Lammas Day (1 August), and broke down the offending fences with pickaxes. And despite repeated royal proclamations against building or taking in lodgers, by the early 17th century so many houses had been illegally constructed outside the City walls that James I is said to have remarked that 'the growth of the capital resembled that of a rickety child's head, in which an excessive influx of humours drained and impoverished the extremities, and at the same time generated distemper in the overloaded parts'.

By 1606 so many people were living near the church of St Martin-in-the-Fields that the parish complained to the King that 'the church is not of sufficient bigness to receive the parishioners and the churchyard is so little as there is no room to bury the dead'.

Additional land granted by the King to be used as a graveyard was defiantly built over, and within two years, as a result of the dreadful lack of sanitation in the area, St Martin's Lane had degenerated into an open drain. Reluctant to cause too much trouble, King James closed his eyes to the illegality, held his nose and granted £100 towards the building of an underground sewer in order to make his journeys through the area more pleasant. Not that this cured the problem: as late as 1625 it was reported that 'St Martin's Lane is now full of great muckhills . . . neere 300 loads wch upon every Rayne is brought down before the King's Pallace.'

Nevertheless, all the smartest courtiers were now moving out west, where despite the stink of dung the air was still sweeter than it was in the City, and from where access was easy to the three royal palaces of Whitehall, Westminster and St James's. By the 1630s a number of grand houses had been constructed along the edge of St Martin's Field, on the west side of St Martin's Lane. Most of them were built there illegally, but nobody seemed to care very much. The King's own physician, Sir Theodore Mayerne, had moved into one of them in 1613, and during the next few decades he was followed into the area by many other notables, including Sir Ralph Freeman, the dramatist and the Master of Requests, and Sir John Suckling, who later made his name as a Royalist poet.

Suckling, who wrote of himself that he 'priz'd black eyes, or a lucky hit/At bowls, above all the trophies of wit', was less famous for his poetry than for being one of the best bowlers in England and a great gambler who 'did use to practise by himself abed, and there studied the best way of managing the Cards'. His new home in St Martin's Lane was ideally placed for reaching a gambling club nicknamed Shaver's Hall, which had recently opened on land behind the Royal Mews and where, much to his sisters' dismay, Suckling was frequently to be found.

The proprietor of Shaver's Hall was Simon Osbaldeston, formerly the Lord Chamberlain's barber, who in 1634 had bought a sizeable plot of land in the Windmill Field from the estate of one Robert Baker. Baker, a tailor and property speculator, had made money by selling 'piccadillies' – frilled collars – after which his own house, Pickadilly Hall, had been named. Osbaldeston, who purchased a three-and-a-half-acre plot, pulled down the existing water conduit house and the gunpowder store, and put up a large, brick-built banqueting house with gambling rooms, an indoor tennis court and a wide first-floor balcony overlooking ornate terraced gardens, shady orchards, and two bowling greens. George Garrard, who visited Osbaldeston's soon after it opened, estimated that the venture had cost 'above 4000*l*.; a dear undertaking for a gentleman barber'.

How much of a gentleman *was* Osbaldeston? Garrard accused him of entertaining gamblers and bowlers 'at an excessive rate' and of charging three times the licensed price for a meal. As to the name of the establishment, Garrard wrote in a letter to Viscount Conway, 'Simme Austbiston's house is newly christned, It is calld, Shaver's Hall, as other neighbauring Places thereabout are nicknam'd Tart Hall, Pickadell Hall; At first noe conceyte ther was of the builders beeing a Barber; but it came upon my Lord of Dunbarres loosing 3000*l*. at one sitting; whereon they said a Northerne Lord was shaved there.'

Despite this, Shaver's Hall was extremely popular with the nobility and the gentry, who went there not just to gamble but to loll around under the trees talking and getting drunk. Although it was suppressed by the authorities on one or two occasions when festivities in the garden got out of hand, Shaver's Hall stayed in business until Cromwell clamped down on such trivial pursuits.

Hunting and gambling were not the only forms of recreation on offer in the Soho Fields. The Military Company of Westminster, a band of volunteer soldiers formed in 1615 with the support of the Privy Council, had acquired three and a half acres of land behind the Royal Mews in 1616. Under the captaincy of a professional soldier named Thomas Holcrofte, the Military Company built a two-storey house containing an armoury, a library, a meeting room, a kitchen and a parade ground. The Military Ground (or Garden, or Yard, as it was also known) was surrounded by a nine-foot wall, which may account for the fact that little is known about the actual military activities of the Company members, even during the Civil War. From an inventory of the house contents – which included banners, suits of armour, drums, Spanish javelins and 'clothes for Pyoneeres', as well as five tables and four dozen leather chairs – it seems that the members spent much of their time dressing up and cutting and thrusting their way round the parade ground, or else preparing for their annual feast – a tradition they had adopted from the Artillery Company in Spitalfields, on whom they modelled themselves.

In the 1620s and 1630s, two large mansions went up nearby. The first belonged to Sir William Howard, who built a house to the east of the Military Ground. The second, and more important, was built near Shaver's Hall by Robert Sidney, the second Earl of Leicester, in a part of the Soho fields known as Swan Close. Leicester House, as Sidney's mansion was called, was destined to become the home of two kings and two queens, and to be the most illustrious house in Soho.

Swan Close, a seven-acre plot of gently sloping pasture in St Martin's Field, backed on to the south wall of the Military Yard, and formed part of the Lammas land pledged to the citizens of the parish by Henry VIII. Hugh Audeley, the Registrar of the Court of Wards and Liveries and a wealthy financier, had leased it from the Crown in 1626, and four years later sold it to Robert Sidney for the princely sum of £160.

Sidney was a scrupulously law-abiding man so, unlike most of his neighbours, he actually applied to the Crown Commissioners for permission to build a house in the close. This permission was duly granted, but with two provisos: first, that he pay £3 annually to St Martin's parish to compensate for the Lammas grazing rights that would be lost; and secondly, that the best part of the garden, where the parishioners had traditionally laid out their clothes to dry, be landscaped at his own expense with paths and trees, and planted in such a way that there was still room for the tradition of drying clothes to continue. In addition, there was to be free access to the garden for all the local people, and the continuing existence of footpaths across the land was to be guaranteed.

Sidney agreed to all of this. A diplomat by profession and by nature, he was a quiet, intellectual man – 'very conversant in books, and much addicted to the mathematics', according to the Earl of Clarendon – and given the choice he always preferred his country seat of Penshurst Place to London. He was in his thirties when he started building Leicester House, and married to Dorothy, one of the Earl of Northumberland's daughters. They had two sons – Philip, Viscount Lisle, with whom Robert always had deep personal and political differences, and Algernon, his younger brother, who got on well with his father but who was destined to be executed for his part in the Rye House plot. For this small ménage, the Earl spent over £8,000 in building what he called a 'little House; which was not built for a Levie, but only for a privat Family' – a modest description, considering that it had 55 fireplaces and was for many years one of the largest private homes in London.

Building probably began in 1632, when Sidney returned from a stint as Ambassador Extraordinary to the King of Denmark. Faithhorne and Newcourt's Map of London, drawn up in 1658, shows it as a large gabled house built around a central courtyard, owing more to Jacobean architecture than to the Renaissance style it later resembled. Around the house are the formal gardens and terraced walks laid out to fulfil Lord Leicester's promises to the parishioners, and planted with a great number of pines, cypresses and apricot, peach and cherry trees.

When Sidney was appointed Ambassador to France in 1636, the mansion was still unfinished, and Dorothy stayed behind in England to supervise the interior decorators. From Penshurst and London she wrote a stream of letters to her husband describing their progress. In return, Sidney sent home 'many things of good valew as beds, divers peeces of rich sylver plate as flowerpotts, plaques for candles, basins, basquets etc, and many peeces of stuffes, wrought velvet, damaske etc.'. This was apparently not good enough for the gout-plagued Sir Thomas Wentworth, Lord Lieutenant and first Earl of Strafford, who rented the house for four months from April 1640, at a time when Dorothy had joined her husband overseas. Lady Carlisle, Dorothy's sister, wrote that Wentworth 'desiers most to have his beads [sic] of damaske', and two beds were duly sent over from Paris, one 'green wrought velvet lined with satine, garnished with gold and silver; thother of red damaske garnished with silk'.

The Sidneys returned to their fabulously decorated mansion in 1641, but Robert's lack of sympathy with the Royalists led to his falling out of favour at Court, and three years later he moved back to Penshurst for good. Leicester House was kept on as a rather grand family *pied-à-terre*, and though Sidney received many requests to rent it out, he usually refused, writing on one occasion that 'old as I am, I do a little consider my innocent Pleasure, and I think that a pretty, pleasant Place. I consider my Health and the Ayre of the House. I consider my little privat Business, and the convenient

Scituation [sic] of the House for it. I consider the Honour of wayting on the King sometimes, when his Majestye will give me Leave; and the Nearnes of the House to the King's Pallace.'

On this occasion the would-be tenant was a tragic figure: Elizabeth, Queen of Bohemia, Charles II's aunt and the so-called 'Queen of Hearts', who arrived in England in 1661, penniless and extremely ill. The King put in a good word for his aunt, after which the Earl agreed to rent Leicester House to her for three months. However, as if sensing that she was unwelcome there, the Queen of Bohemia died after only one week in residence. A widow for 30 years, she passed away on 13 February, the eve of her wedding anniversary on St Valentine's Day.

Not surprisingly, the Civil War and Commonwealth period saw a lull in building development around London. Because the fields to the west of London were a vital approach to Westminster and the City, several forts were sited there, with the result that by the end of the war much of the farmland had been ploughed up and ruined. Consequently, by the time of the Restoration the countrified atmosphere of the Soho Fields had not changed all that much, even though the development of Covent Garden by the Earl of Bedford in the 1630s had brought London to their borders. Still, by 1660, smart houses formed an unbroken line along the west side of St Martin's Lane, stretching all the way to Charing Cross, where the Royal Mews had also become a popular place to live. As early as 1637 Garrard had written that 'Dwelling-houses are daily erected in every corner of the Mews fit only for Stables.' Cleared of the illegal residents of these houses during the Civil War, the Mews was subsequently used for holding prisoners – 4,000 Royalists were kept there after the battle of Naseby – and for housing soldiers, and at one point it was cleared 'For the Protector's use'.

Slowly but surely, the district of Soho was struggling to be born. There had been references to it as early as 1632, when the name of So-Hoe first appeared in the rate book of the parish of St Martin-in-the-Fields. In 1633 Charles I granted four Crown tenants – the Earls of Bedford and Salisbury, Sir Edward Wardour and Sir Oliver Nicholas – a licence to make a watercourse from 'a spring in Colman Hedge, alias Soe Hoe, across to the King's highway' to a waterhouse near the Military Yard, from where the water was to be pumped into homes in St Martin's Lane and Covent Garden. This is probably the same 'watercourse of spring water coming and rising from a place called So-howe' mentioned in the rate books in 1634. Two years later, people were recorded as living at the 'brick-kilns, near Sohoe'.

No matter how the name was spelled, it already spelled trouble. In 1641 a 'lewd woman' called Anna Clerke was bound over to keep the peace after 'threteninge to burne [sic] the houses at So:ho'. And in September 1642 Noah Cliffe, the parish constable of St Martin-in-the-Fields, was sworn at by a yeoman called William Colley, whom Cliffe accused of 'threateninge to burne the houses at Sohoe'. Just why the place should have attracted these would-be arsonists is unclear; perhaps the hamlet was so primitive that setting fire to it was the only damage anyone could possibly do.

The most important development in the fields during the Commonwealth was a line of 'cottages, Cutts, Shedds or meane habitaçons' now existing on land leased from the Crown by the Pulteney family fronting on to Colman Hedge Lane – present-day Wardour Street. One of these dwellings was described in a parliamentary survey of 1650 as a tenement consisting of three rooms below stairs, a chamber above, a garret and 'a small backside', and it was 'commonly called or knowne by the name of So:ho'. It is very likely that this tenement was a hunting inn, standing between present Meard Street and Bourchier Street, for this stretch of Wardour Street was soon to be called 'Old Soho'. The inn probably took its name from the hunting cry 'Sohoe!', and, like Pickadilly Hall down the road, it may well have given its name to the street and to the surrounding neighbourhood.

Many of the noble families who had stayed out of London in Cromwell's time came rushing back following the Restoration of the monarchy in 1660, re-creating the pre-Commonwealth market for grand houses near Whitehall and St James's. But the authorities still seemed determined that the Soho Fields, so important for their springs of fresh water, should not be built over. Yet another royal proclamation, published in 1661, complained that earlier laws against development near the City had been disobeyed, and forbade any further building within two miles of the City walls, except on the foundations of old houses.

However, in the exhilarating climate of freedom that had returned to the country with the monarchy, few people took any more notice of this proclamation than they had of past ones. Speculators leased large parcels of land in the fields from Crown tenants such as the Salisbury, Newport, Leicester and Pulteney families, and illegal buildings continued to spring up like mushrooms. In 1664 even the law-abiding Lord Leicester granted an illegal 31-year building lease in the south-west corner of his land to one Anthony Ellis, a mason of the parish. But though Ellis was to build six houses in Leicester Field within the next five years, the market for new housing soon collapsed as suddenly as it had inflated. For late in 1664 an event occurred just outside the parish boundary that, for the next few years, was to halt the development not only of Soho, but of the whole of London.

There had been bubonic plague in England during the 1630s and 1640s. But no one was prepared for the magnitude of what was to come. The Great Plague, as it came to be known, spread to England from Holland, where it had broken out in the late summer of 1664. It first took root not in the overcrowded walled City of London, as one would have expected, but in the relatively sparsely populated parish of St Giles-in-the-Fields, where two men, said to be French, were taken ill in late November in a house at the upper end of Drury Lane. Their families tried to hide the disease, but the authorities heard about it, and two physicians and a surgeon were sent out through a frost-gripped city to inspect the corpses. According to Daniel Defoe's fictionalized account, *A Journal of the Plague Year*, published in 1722, the doctors went to the house and, 'finding evident tokens of the sickness upon both the bodies that were dead, they gave their opinions publicly that they died of the plague. Whereupon it was given to the parish clerk, and he also returned them to the Hall; and it was printed in the weekly bill of mortality in the usual manner, thus –

Plague, 2. Parishes infected, 1.'

These figures, looking as innocent as football results, were but the first of a growing number. Over the next 18 months, it is estimated that 70,000 to 100,000 Londoners died of plague. Panic spread as fast as the contagion. Parliament was prorogued in the early months of 1665, and the Court fled to the safety of Oxford. Many of London's rich citizens sacked their servants and took refuge in their country estates, leaving the medieval streets deserted but for the poor, the unemployed and the sick.

Infected houses were marked with a red cross and boarded up for 40 days – with all the inhabitants, healthy or sick, locked inside. Sometimes they starved to death before disease got them. Death-carts rattled through the empty streets, their drivers ordering the healthy to 'Bring out your dead.' Corpses were buried by drunken grave-diggers in vast mass-burial pits. Businesses went bust. The shuttered houses of those who had left town or died were broken into and looted.

In the belief that dogs and cats might be responsible for spreading the disease, the Lord Mayor ordered that all pets and strays be exterminated. Tens – maybe hundreds – of thousands of animals were destroyed within days. Their corpses were left to rot in the streets along with the piled-up unburied human remains. As it turned out, the Mayor had been very wrong, for the real carriers of plague were fleas who lived on rats. Now, without cats to keep down the rat population, and with all the rotting animal flesh to feed on, the rats multiplied, making the situation even worse.

In the unusually hot summer, the death toll increased. Soon 700, 800 and 900 people were dying every week. By mid-July, the weekly death toll had reached 1,000, and by August it was over 2,000. The official death toll for the third week of September was 8,297. It began to seem as if the entire population of London was doomed.

Quacks and profiteers stayed around to make what they could out of the desperate situation. So did a few public-minded citizens who took it upon themselves to bring some kind of order to the chaos. A commission was appointed to work out the best way of stopping the plague. One of its most notable members was the Earl of Craven, who, using his Drury Lane house as a base, walked through the streets every day, handing out money to those who needed it, and visiting the sick.

During an outbreak of plague in the 1630s a pesthouse had been built in the Soho Fields on the west side of Colman Hedge Lane, in a close of land owned by Sir Edward Wardour. But this hospital was far too small to cope with the huge numbers now sick and dying. Realizing the urgent need for more graveyards and for another pesthouse, Lord Craven rented a plot from the heirs of Robert Baker of Pickadilly Hall, and on it he built '36 small Houses for the Reception of poor and miserable Objects', as the victims were pathetically called. The site of Craven's hospital, which was situated just east of present-day Carnaby Street, later became known as Pesthouse Close. It was the last piece of the Soho Fields to be developed: because of the thousands of plague victims buried in the mass graves there, until the 1730s it was not thought safe to build on the land.

The plague died down in the winter of 1665/6, and in February the Court returned to a depopulated London. Metropolitan life could start up again – but not for long. Just seven months later, the City itself disappeared.

The Great Fire of London started on a particularly windy night, 2 September 1666, in a City bakery in Pudding Lane. The Lord Mayor, Sir Thomas Bloodworth, was woken up in the early hours of the morning and told about it. 'Pish!' he said. 'A woman might piss it out!'

By daybreak a large section of the City was on fire, as was London Bridge. Fanned by the gale, the flames continued to spread along the labyrinthine lanes of closely-built, predominantly wood-framed medieval houses. During the next four days 44 livery halls, 87 churches, and 13,000 homes were reduced to smouldering rubble. Miraculously, only a handful of people were killed.

The bewildered citizens salvaged what they could from the charred remains of their homes and workshops, and camped in the fields on the outskirts of town while the streets were cleared and London was rebuilt – this time of less combustible materials, but to the old street plan, designs for a new-look City having been rejected.

It was a boom-time for builders and bricklayers, who flocked to the disaster-struck capital from all over the country to lend a hand with the reconstruction work. By 1672, most private homes in the City had been rebuilt. But many rich citizens had had more than enough of living in a densely packed area where they were constantly threatened by outbreaks of pestilence and fire, and after a few months under canvas in the Soho Fields, they decided to settle there for good. Building had already shot ahead in answer to the new demand for homes, particularly in the Windmill Field, which had been sold to speculators when Robert Baker's widow died in the plague year.

However, most of these new houses were so badly planned, so sordid and so poorly built that Sir Christopher Wren, the Surveyor General of Works, complained to the King about them in the early months of 1671. The King responded by issuing this royal proclamation on 17 April:

Whereas in the Fields commonly called the Windmill Fields, Dog Fields, and those adjoining to Sohoe and several other places about the suburbs of London and Westminster, divers small and mean habitations and cottages have been lately erected on new foundations, and more are daily preparing, not only without any allowance from the King, but some against his express command signified by the Surveyor General, which are likely to prove common nuissances [sic] by being used for the most noisome trades, and becoming a receptacle for a multitude of poor, to the damage of those parishes already too much encumbered, and by rendering the government thereof unmanageable, but especially by choaking [sic] up the air of the King's palaces and parks, and endangering the infection if not the total loss of all those waters, which by many expanseful conduits are conveyed thence to the Palace at Whitehall, whereof some decay is already perceived by the Sergeant-Plumber and more is feared; the King charges all persons to forbear building any more new buildings in the suburbs of London and Westminster, or to finish any already begun without licence under the Great Seal, and if any disobey, all such buildings shall be abated and thrown down, and the offenders proceeded against with the utmost rigour of the law.

These were strong words, but empty ones, for as it turned out, this was to be the last royal proclamation against building in the suburbs. Charles II was getting fed up with playing King Canute to the surging tide of development. By the end of that year, all efforts to enforce what amounted to over 100 years of restrictive building policies in the Soho Fields had stopped. Lord Leicester was pardoned for having granted an illegal building lease on his land, and with royal permission he contracted with 10 builders to put up rows of houses along the other sides of Leicester Field, his front garden. Shaver's Hall and the land north of it were already being developed by Colonel Thomas Panton, a gambler and speculator who had shrewdly acquired a lease on Osbaldeston's place two years before the Great Fire. By 1673, the Surveyor General himself was drawing up plans for houses in Gelding Close (Golden Square), a field just south of Craven's pesthouses. And in 1675 so many people were found to be living in the district that a special Soho rate book was opened up by the vestry of the church of St Martin-in-the-Fields.

Realizing that if he couldn't stop the development, he might as well profit from it, the King sold the freehold of the Military Yard to Baron Gerard of Brandon, a well-known Royalist who had leased it just after the Restoration. In addition, he granted Gerard full permission to erect 'in or upon all or any part or parts . . . any houses or buildings whatsoever'. With the official go-ahead now given, speculators all over the area breathed a sigh of relief, and called in their workmen.

Building went ahead at breakneck speed. Within the space of seven years the fields south of Oxford Road and east of Shugge Lane (later Regent Street) disappeared under a network of building sites, finished houses and half-completed streets. By the early 1680s, most of the district as we know it today had appeared, none the worse for its prolonged, illicit birth.

The brand-new suburb was at first still part of the parish of St Martin-in-the-Fields, and the vestry soon began to complain under the burden of all the new parishioners. As a result, when, in 1676, an unknown lady bequeathed £5,000 to Henry Compton, the Bishop of London, to be used to build a new church where it was most needed, Compton considered 'the Greatness of our parish & the littleness of our Church', as St Martin's vestry commented afterwards, and offered the money to St Martin's. A one-and-a-half-acre building plot was chosen as a site for the church between Colman Hedge Lane, now called So Ho, and Dean Street. A nearby road – Compton Street – was named in honour of the Bishop. Two years later, the new parish of St Anne – named after the Duke of York's second daughter – was created by Act of Parliament. It stretched from Oxford Road south as far as Leicester Fields, and from Hog Lane in the east to Colman Hedge Lane, which at first took the name So Ho. The land to the west of So Ho (present-day Wardour Street) was absorbed into the neighbouring parish of St James.

A plan for St Anne's church was commissioned, probably from Christopher Wren, who also designed the nearby church of St James in Piccadilly. Building started in the summer of 1677, with bricks made locally in a field called Knave's Acre (today's Brewer Street). But after fast progress at the beginning, work on the church came to a complete halt: four years after it had been commissioned, the site was shown on a map as an empty plot; and another four years later, government acts had to be passed in order to get the church finished. At this point, Wren's executive architect, William Talman, was appointed to oversee its completion.

St Anne's was eventually consecrated on 21 March 1686, by Bishop Compton. Even then it was far from finished. The tower lacked a spire (it did not get one until 1717, and even then one that did not last very long – it was replaced by the present spire in 1801), and a local lawyer called Sir John Bramston noted that 'all the pewes were nott sett, neither below nor in the galleries'. Still, Bramston added, the Bishop 'made noe scruple of consecrating it; yet he would be ascertained that all the workmen were payd or secured their monie and dues first, and to that end made perticular inquiries of the workmen'.

St Anne's was never an outstanding architectural success. It was a rather heavy and plain building, described in 1708 in Hatton's *A New View of London* as 'pleasant and pretty large, with an Arched Roof divided into Pannels, with Fretwork, and supported by about twelve Pillars of the Ionick Order, and the Galleries are elevated on those of the Tuscan Order'. Still, it was undoubtedly the most important building in the parish, and it quickly acquired a loyal congregation from among the fashionable people who were moving into the area.

Even before the consecration of St Anne's, something had happened that before long was to make the name of Soho infamous: in 1677 Charles II had granted the freehold of the Soho Fields to his favourite illegitimate son, the ill-fated James Scott, Duke of Monmouth.

Everything about Monmouth was romantic, even his conception. In 1648, during an eight-day visit to Holland, Charles II met and fell in love with James's mother, a Welsh-born woman called Lucy Walters. Charles, the most human and sympathetic of men, was said to have an 'inordinate love' for Lucy, a high-class courtesan who had taken to the streets in desperation after her father had abandoned her, her mother and her siblings in London. It was even rumoured that Charles had secretly married her.

Their son, James, was born in Rotterdam in April 1649, nine months after Charles and Lucy's brief – and obviously passionate – meeting. He was a beautiful boy, and, according to the memoirs of the Duke of York, the King 'took so great a liking to him, that he resolv'd publikly to own him and raise him in fortune and dignity'. At the Restoration, 11-year-old James Crofts – as he was called, after his guardian William Crofts, a Gentleman of the King's Bedchamber – was brought over from France and provided with splendid clothes, fine lodgings at the Charing Cross end of Colman Hedge Lane, and even a noble-born heiress for a fiancée – Anne Scott, the Countess of Buccleuch. In fact, James was made such a fuss of by his father that Samuel Pepys, who described him as 'the most skittish, leaping gallant that I ever saw' wrote in his diary that 'some doubt that, if the King should have no child by the Queen, which there is yet no appearance of, whether he would not be acknowledged for a lawful son', in which case, Pepys accurately prophesied, 'there will be a difference follow between the Duke of York and him; which God prevent!'

There were no limits to the honours showered on the boy by his doting father. Defying his advisers, Charles created James Earl of Doncaster and Duke of Monmouth on St Valentine's Day 1663, after which James was treated as fourth gentleman of the realm, taking precedence over everyone except the Duke of York and Prince Rupert. The 14-year-old boy's marriage to Anne Scott took place at Whitehall Palace; both the King and the long-suffering Queen attended the wedding feast. James, who adopted his wife's surname on his wedding day, was installed as a Knight of the Garter, and on his father's insistence was elected Chancellor of the University of Cambridge. He was given a huge income – but it was not enough to stop him getting into financial trouble: when he was 18 his 'Private Expenses and Cloaths' for nine months amounted to a phenomenal £8,996. 11s. 9d., and he was granted an advance of £18,000 to pay off his debts.

Far from becoming a spoiled brat, the young James grew into a sweet-natured young man with his father's charm – though not his intellect – and looks so dazzling that they inspired men and women alike. 'One could not know the Duke of Monmouth and refuse to praise him,' wrote a Frenchwoman, Madame D'Aulnoy, after James had been sent to Paris to be 'finished' under the care of his aunt, the Duchess of Orléans. Even the poet John Dryden, an early resident of Gerrard Street, who was not incapable of dipping his pen in acid when he felt like it (the epitaph he wrote for his wife read 'Here lies my wife: here let her lie! Now she's at rest, and so am I'), could only write of Monmouth that 'paradise seemed open in his face'. And poet and playright Aphra Benn wrote in 1684, at a time when James was very much out of favour, that

> Young Jemmy was a lad
> Of Royal Birth and Breeding,
> With every Beauty clad:
> And every grace exceeding;
> A face and shape so wondrous fine,
> So Charming ev'ry part;
> That every Lass upon the Green
> For Jemmy had a heart.

As well as enjoying grace and good looks, James was a natural humanitarian. Though he always fought bravely in battle – for instance, against the Dutch and against the Scottish rebels – when chided by his father for his lenient treatment of some Scottish prisoners, he is said to have remarked, 'I cannot kill men in cold blood, that is work only for a butcher.'

If this paragon had any faults, they were that he chose his advisers badly and that he was easily flattered – faults that were 'rather a proof that he had not the strongest of all minds than of any extraordinary weakness of character', as Charles James Fox wrote in the 18th century. And with no legitimate Protestant heir to the throne on the horizon, there were plenty of interested parties willing to use Monmouth to stop the future succession of the Catholic Duke of York, including powerful men, such as the Earl of Shaftesbury, who was later to play a large part in Monmouth's rebellion. After the Duke of York's unpopular second marriage in 1673 to Mary, the Duke of Modena's daughter, Shaftesbury pressed Charles II to acknowledge the legitimacy of his popular son. To Shaftesbury's surprise, the boy's doting father drew the line at this, declaring that he would rather see James hanged at Tyburn than see him succeed to the throne.

After the imaginary Popish Plot to overthrow the Protestant

monarchy in 1678, family relationships deteriorated on all sides. The following September found both uncle and nephew banished – the Duke of York to Scotland, and Monmouth to Holland, where he lodged with the English Ambassador. Shaftesbury persuaded Monmouth to come home without his father's permission in November, and the return to London of society's 30-year-old darling was heralded by the ringing of church bells, people crying in the streets and more than 60 celebratory bonfires lit between Fleet Street and Charing Cross. Everyone was delighted that he was back in England – everyone, that was, except the King, who refused to see him despite appeals by both his wife, the Queen, and his mistress, Nell Gwyn, on the lad's behalf.

After another abortive attempt at a reconciliation with his father in the summer of 1680, James started on the first of two famous journeys to the West Country to enlist support for his claim to the throne. It was at this time that he met and fell in love with 20-year-old Baroness Henrietta Wentworth. Their passion and deep love was mutual, and the two were to remain close friends and lovers for the rest of their brief lives. Through all the hard times to come, Henrietta was to resist pressure on her to give up James and marry someone else, choosing instead to defy convention as well as the law of the land. She stood by her lover through thick and thin, she hid him when he was being hunted, and she travelled and lived openly with him when he was banished. She and her mother even pawned their plate and jewellery to raise money for his military campaigns.

With his popularity with the King at rock-bottom level, and his mind anywhere but at home with his wife, the winter of 1680/1 was not an auspicious time for Monmouth to decide to buy a new house. Nevertheless, perhaps believing that his breach with the King could not last much longer, in February he leased a large plot of land on the south side of Soho Square from developer Richard Frith and his partners, and arranged for them to build him 'a fair Messuage' costing about £7,000, to be ready by the following Christmas.

Soho Square – or King's Square as it was first called, after its designer, Gregory King – was a plot in the north-east corner of the Soho Fields, just south of the Oxford Road. As yet, like much of the district, it was in embryonic form, but King – and developer Richard Frith, in whose office King worked – planned to make it the smartest place in the new parish, a square that would attract all the top nobility.

No expense was spared in its design. Each side-street had carefully planned views, and in the middle, separated from the street by wooden railings, was an attractive garden, with a path round the edge of four lawns, and trees planted at the corners of the grass. In the centre was Danish sculptor Caius Gabriel Cibber's statue of Charles II in full armour – the same statue that stands in the square today, still as debonair as ever, if rather the worse for wear. Now it stands on one of the pathways, behind an ugly concrete 'Superloo', but originally it topped a large stone fountain, the pedestal of which was carved with fruit, leaves, fish, symbolic statues of river-gods – representing the rivers Tyne, Humber, Severn and Thames – and a naked stone virgin with 'netts wrapped round her middle parts'. Four jets of water gushed out of jugs and into a large basin at the base – at least this was the general idea. In practice, the fountain was worked by a windmill at the end of Rathbone Place, directly to the north on the opposite side of Oxford Road, and unless the mill-sails were actually turning, no water came out of the jugs at all.

Monmouth House was a very large mansion, set well back from the square. Though the original design has been attributed to Wren, according to a contemporary letter its sole architect was 'Mr Ford, a joynor'. However, as James was slow to pay his builders, the mansion was slow in being built, and it was not fully completed until the early 18th century, when Thomas Archer (the architect of St John's, Smith Square) designed a new pedimented façade. 'There is nothing very shining in any part of this structure,' wrote Ralph of it in *A Critical Review of the Publick Buildings In and About London and Westminster*, published in 1734, 'but if the lower order could boast of beauties ever so exquisite, the upper is so Gothique and absurd that it would destroy them all.' Archer's Monmouth House has long since disappeared from Soho Square. But an echo of it remains in the pedimented façade of the Barclays Bank building which now occupies part of the same site.

The best description of the interior of Monmouth House was written in 1828 by J.T. Smith in his biography of the Soho-born sculptor Joseph Nollekens. Smith had visited Monmouth House with Nollekens during its demolition in 1773, and although Smith had only been a child of seven at the time, it obviously made quite an impression on him:

> There were eight rooms on the ground floor: the principal one was a dining-room towards the south, the carved and gilt panels of which had contained whole-length pictures. At the corners of the ornamented ceiling, which was of plaster, and over the chimneypiece, the Duke of Monmouth's arms were displayed.
>
> From a window, we descended into a paved yard, surrounded by a red brick wall with heavy stone copings which was, to the best of my recollection, full twenty-five feet in height. The staircase was of oak, the steps very low, and the landing places were tessellated with woods of light and dark colours . . .
>
> As we ascended, I remember Mr Nollekens noticing the busts of Seneca, Caracalla, Trajan, Adrian and several others, upon ornamented brackets. The principal room on the first floor, which had not been disturbed by the workmen, was lined with blue satin, superbly decorated with pheasants and other birds in gold. The chimneypiece was richly ornamented with fruit and foliage, similar to the carvings which surround the altar of St James's Church, Piccadilly, so beautifully executed by Grinling Gibbons. In the centre over this chimneypiece, within a wreath of oak leaves, there was a circular recess which evidently had been designed for the reception of a bust. The beads of the panels of the brown window shutters, which were very lofty, were gilt; and the piers between the windows, from stains upon the silk, had probably been filled with looking-glasses. The scaffolding, ladders, and numerous workmen, rendered it too dangerous for us to go higher, or see more of this most interesting house.

So much splendour, enjoyed by its owner so briefly. Over the next few years Monmouth was to spend only the odd night or week at his new house. For as it went up, so his popularity dropped, helped not only by his stubborn pride but by his 'supporters', who only ever succeeded in making trouble between him and the King.

One of these men was Lord Conway, the Secretary of State, who told the King that Monmouth had said he would rather die than submit to the Duke of York. Was this true or not? Charles II certainly believed it. Stung by what he saw as the continuing intransigence of his much-favoured son, he deprived James of his positions at Court, took down the Lely portrait of him that was hanging on the palace wall (it was later burned) and ordered his servants to have no dealings with him at all.

Equally hurt by his father's rejection of him, Monmouth embarked on another propaganda tour, this time to Cheshire. On his return he was arrested for disturbing the peace; he was subsequently granted bail and banished from Court. His and Shaftesbury's supposed involvement in the Rye House plot to assassinate both the King and the Duke of York led to Shaftesbury's flight to Amsterdam, where he died, and sent Monmouth into hiding at Henrietta's parents' country house, Toddington Manor.

On a secret visit to London in October 1683, Monmouth stayed in his new house in Soho Square, from where he wrote a letter to the King, begging his and the Duke of York's pardon.

> If I could have written to your Majesty sooner, with any safety to myself, I would have done it, to have told you that there is nothing has struck me so to the heart as to be put into a proclamation for an intention of murdering you, Sir, and the Duke. I do call God Almighty to witness, and I wish I may die this moment I am writing if ever it entered into my head, or I ever said the least thing to anybody that could make them think I could wish such a thing . . . What good can it do you, Sir, to take your own child's life away, that only erred, and *ventur'd his life to save yours?* And now, Sir, I do swear to you that from this time I never will displease you in anything . . . And for the Duke, that he may have a more firm confidence of the service I intend to do him, I do here declare to your Majesty, that I will never ask to see your face more if ever I do anything against him, which is the greatest curse I can lay upon myself. Monmouth.

Furious as he was with James, Charles could not stop loving him. He had known for months that James was in hiding at Toddington Manor, and yet he had done nothing about it. Now he granted his son a secret interview at Whitehall, and when Monmouth was recognized by a courtier as he was leaving, the King insisted that it could not have been his son as he was in Brussels. A few weeks later, when the prodigal son returned – not in sackcloth and ashes, but dressed up to the nines – to throw himself publicly and ceremoniously at his father's feet, Charles granted him a full pardon, restored him to Court and even sent him a gift of £6,000.

This second honeymoon period did not last long. Ironically, it was the publication of Monmouth's confession, in which he implicated his friends, that made Charles finally lose faith in him. By the early months of 1684 he had been banished again, this time to Antwerp, where Henrietta joined him. In the summer they travelled to Holland, where they stayed with the daughter and son-in-law of the Duke of York, Mary and William, the Princess and Prince of Orange. Having about as little sympathy with the Duke of York as Monmouth did, the royal couple made him very welcome. In fact, Mary was soon charmed by Monmouth, who taught her the latest English dances, flirted with her openly and, come winter, skated with her on the frozen canals.

In November 1684 Monmouth paid another clandestine visit to London, this time staying at the Wentworths' house in Stepney, for he dared not show his face at Monmouth House. A secret meeting with his father did much to restore their relationship. James returned to Holland full of hope, and waited patiently for a royal summons to return to England.

But the summons never arrived. Instead, on 16 February 1685 James received the news of his father's sudden death. Most hurtful of all to him was the fact that Charles had not even mentioned him on his death-bed. 'Oh, cruel fate!' he wrote in his diary.

With the accession of the Duke of York, Monmouth could no longer stay with his cousins. He and Henrietta were now virtual refugees. Often in disguise, they fled through France, while the anti-Papists in London did their best to coax them to return.

Eventually James succumbed. He set sail in May, and on 11 June arrived in Lyme, Dorsetshire, where he started to assemble forces under a standard on which blazed the words 'Pro Religione et Libertate'. Having been proclaimed King in the West Country, he took on the Royalist forces on Monday 6 July at Sedgemoor Heath. But the password he had chosen – 'So Ho' – failed to rouse his troops to victory in the pouring rain. He was overwhelmingly defeated. Demoralized and exhausted, he was captured some days later hiding in a thicket.

Like his father before him, James was capable of a genuine love of, and liking for, women. On the scaffold on Tower Hill, where he was executed on Wednesday 15 July, St Swithin's Day, he made a speech defending his lover: 'I have had a scandal raised upon me about a woman, a lady of virtue and honour. I will name her, the Lady Henrietta Wentworth. I declare that she is a very virtuous and godly woman. I have committed no sin with her; and that which hath passed betwixt us was very honest and innocent in the sight of God.' Having said this, he handed his servant his last possession – a toothpick case – and told him to 'give this to the person to whom you are to deliver the other things' – meaning Henrietta.

James faced his death with open eyes. It was a horribly bungled job. The axe, which he had insisted was not sharp enough, failed to sever his head after two blows, and it only fell with the fifth. Treating him as a martyr, the crowd stepped forward and dipped their handkerchiefs in his blood, so honouring the first inhabitant of Soho to come to a bad end.

Monmouth's decapitated body was unceremoniously buried beneath the communion table in the chapel of St Peter ad Vincula, on Tower Green. Henrietta, who was brought back to England by her family, could not face life without him. She quite literally pined away, became very ill, and died within nine months of his execution.

She was not the only one to suffer by James's downfall. The builders of Monmouth House, Frith and Thomas, were said to have been 'very great loosers [sic] by the misfortunes of the said Duke'. They had spent more than £4,000 on his mansion, and had been paid back less than half that amount. By the time James was executed the property had already been confiscated by the Crown. For a while it stood empty and half-finished and, as empty houses do, it started 'goeing into Decay'. Offered for sale in 1693, it was, surprisingly, bought by Monmouth's widow, the Duchess of Buccleuch. Still, it remained uninhabited until 1713, though between 1689 and 1694 one room was used as a chapel by a community of French Huguenots known as Le Quarré.

On the whole, the developers had done well out of the Monmouth affair, for the glamour of the Duke had attracted many titled and influential people to live in his square, which had consequently become the most fashionable address in town. By 1685 the ratepayers included five Ladies, four Baronets, two Peers and an Earl. In November 1690, John Evelyn wrote in his diary, 'I went to London with my family to winter at Soho, in the great Square.'

The classy inhabitants of 'the great Square' lived in large terraced houses of the sort that had become uniform in the City and Westminster since the Great Fire. Edward Howard, the second Earl of Carlisle, lived in a palatial mansion on the south corner of Sutton Street, with stables and coach-houses behind it backing on to Hog Lane. (Carlisle House, as it was known, was to remain in his family for nearly 70 years, after which it would become the most famous – at times infamous – entertainment venue in London. Of which more later.) His neighbour to the north was Thomas Belasyse, later the first Earl of Fauconberg, who lived at number 20 with his wife, Mary Cromwell, the Protector's daughter. In the early 1690s, Fauconberg's cousin Sir Henry Belasyse moved into a house just across the square, at the end of a lane then known as King's Square Court (present Carlisle Street).

Throughout the 1680s and 1690s, the demand for new houses in Soho soared, and builders and estate-owners rushed to profit from it. Landowning families such as the Pulteneys and the Salisburys sold off building leases on all the remaining vacant plots they possessed. The Leicester estate, which had been the subject of a series of bitter family lawsuits following the death of the second Earl in 1677, eventually passed to his son and heir Philip, formerly Lord Lisle. As soon as he got his hands on it, Philip sold off building leases on most of his father's precious garden to Richard Frith and his partners, who developed the land as part of Lisle Street and Leicester Street and also built a large mansion fronting on to the square called Ailesbury (later Savile) House.

Then, as if determined to make his father turn in his grave, the new Earl of Leicester gave permission for small one-storey shops and booths – and even a tavern – to be erected outside the front railings of Leicester House, which itself remained the property of the family.

On Saturdays he often entertained his new neighbour, the writer John Dryden, who in 1687 had moved from Covent Garden into a house on the south side of Gerrard Street, backing on to what remained of Leicester's garden. Gerrard Street, which occupied the site of the former Military Garden, had been built by Dr Nicholas Barbon, who had acquired a building lease on the Military Yard from Lord Gerrard in 1677. Gerrard Street was completed in 1685, by which time Barbon, the son of the famous anti-monarchist Praisegod Barbon (or Barebone), had already acquired the nearby estate belonging to Lord Newport, where he was developing houses and a large market.

Barbon and Richard Frith were also involved in building activities in other parts of London. How did they, and speculators like them, raise the money to build on such a large scale? The answer was dangerously simple, though it led to schemes of great financial complexity: they subcontracted out most of the work to other builders, bricklayers and carpenters, so spreading the risk of bankruptcy away from themselves and minimizing their own need for cash. Barbon in particular had a brilliant financial brain (Karl Marx, later a resident of Dean Street, even quoted his theories in the opening pages of *Das Kapital*). He was also a wily and manipulative 'undertaker' (as developers were then called), and although he never practised the medical skills he had learned in Utrecht, his crafty psychological stratagems obviously stood him in good stead, as can be seen from this breathtaking example, taken from the autobiography of the contemporary lawyer Roger North, of Barbon in action trying to buy up property from some landowners:

He appointed a meeting. They would certainly be early at the place, and confirm and hearten one another to stand it out, for the Doctor must come to their terms. So they would walk about and pass their time expecting the Doctor, and inquiring if he were come. At last word was brought that he was come. Then they began to get towards the long table (in a tavern dining-room for the most part), for the Doctor was come! Then he would make his entry, as fine and as richly dressed as a lord of the bedchamber on a birthday. And I must own I have often seen him so dressed, not knowing his design, and thought him a coxcomb for so doing. Then these hard-headed fellows that had prepared to give him all the affronts and opposition that their brutal way suggested, truly seeing such a brave man, pulled off their hats, and knew not what to think of it. And the Doctor, also being (forsooth) much of a gentleman, then with a mountebank speech to these gentlemen he proposed his terms, which, as I said, were ever plausible, and terminated in their interest. Perhaps they were, at this, all converted in a moment, or perhaps a sour clown or two did not understand his tricks, or would not trust him, or would take counsel, or some blundering opposition they gave; while the rest gaped and stared, he was all honey, and a real friend; which not doing he quarrelled, or bought off, as I said, and then at the next meeting some came over, and the rest followed. It mattered not a litigious knave or two, if any such did stand out, for the first thing he did was to pull down their houses about their ears, and build upon their ground, and stand it out at law till their hearts ached, and at last they would truckle and take any terms for peace and a quiet life.

Apart from with rather unscrupulous dealings like these, there were other ways in which developers such as Barbon cut costs. Houses, which were standardized into four classes, were, writes John Summerson in his book *Georgian London*, 'economically planned to the point of meanness, with coarse ornaments which repeated themselves over and over again'. Windows, staircases, banisters and all the fixtures and fittings were mass-produced. The standard of building was extremely low: houses constructed in the 1670s in the Pulteney-owned Windmill Field area of St James's parish were said in a survey of 1693 to be 'very weakly built', and it was doubted whether they would last the remaining 30 years of their lease.

Still, the developers of the Soho Fields – many of whom were small-time businessmen with little or no knowledge of building or town planning – co-operated with one another to a degree seldom experienced before or since. The roads were planned on a grid system, sometimes across three or four different property boundaries. Though the area west of Wardour Street grew up in a more haphazard manner, 19 acres in the northern part of St Anne's parish were laid out as a whole.

What had emerged from the jumbled fields and closes was an area with a cohesion of design and architectural style that was quite remarkable, given the piecemeal nature of its development. The streets and squares had a spacious and elegant feel quite unlike the rebuilt City, and it is not surprising that, during the next century, the richest, the most interesting and the most talented people in London decided to make Soho their home.

Refuge

To the English nobility the newly-built Soho provided a fashionable escape from the claustrophobic City. To its foreign inhabitants it was a refuge of a more basic kind.

French Huguenots were the first large foreign community to settle in Soho. But before their arrival in the early 1680s, there was an abortive attempt to establish a Greek community too.

Greek Christians had fled to Western Europe in the early 1670s to escape religious persecution by the Ottoman Turks. Some had settled in England, and in 1674 their leaders applied to Charles II for permission 'to Build a Church in any part of the City of London or Libertyes thereof'. Even though permission had been granted, the church was not actually built, for the community lacked both money and organizational flair, partly owing to the fact that many of the Anglo-Greeks were sailors 'serving on Board his Maties Fleete, & in Merchant Men', and were therefore out of the country for much of the time.

What they needed was a strong leader. In 1676, one turned up – Joseph Georgirenes, the former Archbishop of Samos, who had spent the previous five years in retreat in the Holy Grotto of the Apocalypse on the island of Patmos. Refreshed after this spell in retreat, Georgirenes arrived in England ready to organize the building and funding of the community church. Unfortunately, the result was a fiasco for everyone concerned.

After obtaining the Bishop of London's approval to go ahead with his scheme, Georgirenes set about choosing a site for a Greek church. Though most London Greeks lived in the City, his eye fell on the building plots of Soho. That was where Nicholas Barbon stepped in.

When he met Georgirenes, Barbon was on the point of developing Gerrard Street. Sensing the possibility of enticing a whole new group of inhabitants into his new housing development, he cannily offered 'to give me a piece of ground, and to build the Foundation at his own charge', according to Georgirenes's own account of the matter, published in 1682.

At first it seemed like an offer that Georgirenes could not refuse. But when the Bishop of London heard about Barbon's proposed gift, a struggle between God and Mammon ensued and, according to Georgirenes, Bishop Compton then made a counter-offer, promising 'to give me a piece of ground himself, and sent one Mr. Thrift with me, and marked out the ground'. The plot marked out by Thrift – alias developer Richard Frith – was the site on the east side of Hog Lane (currently Charing Cross Road), where St Martin's School of Art now stands. Georgirenes accepted the Bishop's 'gift' gratefully, and the building of the Greek church slowly went ahead, Georgirenes raising the necessary cash by asking for grants from the King and the Duke of York, and also, rather oddly, by selling mackerel pickled by a patented method brought over from Greece by one of his compatriots.

At first, everything seemed to go according to plan, and the church gradually took shape – albeit with substandard bricks. Then, in October 1678, a chapter of troubles began, when Georgirenes accused a Greek servant named Dominico Cratiana of running off with church funds. Cratiana was tried at Bristol, and Georgirenes lost his case. But while he was still imprisoned, Cratiana, perhaps trying to blacken Georgirenes's name, made counter-charges against him, implicating him in the Popish Plot. Eventually Cratiana was brought to London to be interrogated on this matter.

Meanwhile, a prominent nobleman named Sir Edmund Berry Godfrey had been murdered in London, and it was claimed by an informer that his corpse had been smuggled out of London in a sedan chair 'as far as the new Grecian Church in The Soho', where the sedan chair had been dumped and the corpse tied to the back of a horse and driven up to Primrose Hill. Hardly had this new bit of scandal died down, when Georgirenes put an advertisement in the *London Gazette* accusing another Greek priest, Joachim Ciciliano, of collecting funds in his name and 'Lewdly' spending them.

By 1681 Georgirenes had had more than enough of the Hog Lane chapel, which had seemed only to bring him bad luck. Claiming that the building was 'too remote from the abodes of most of the Grecians', who, it appears, had not followed him to Soho but had stayed 'chiefly in the furthermost parts of the City', he attempted to sell it. He had the church and land valued at £626, but the parish of St Martin's, claiming that they already owned the ground and that the Greeks had only a 'pretended Right' to the building, offered just £168 for it. Georgirenes was shocked. He insisted that he had never understood the leasehold nature of his tenancy, and that if he had, he would never have spent so much money on building the church. He also claimed he had found a buyer willing to purchase his lease for £230. When St Martin's parish upped their offer to only £200, he turned them down. At this point the vestry lost patience with him and simply took possession of the Hog Lane chapel, locking the priest and his congregation out.

That was the end of that. After Georgirenes and his tiny congregation had been unceremoniously ousted from their home in Hog Lane, alms-houses were built over the graveyard and the empty chapel was let to a congregation of French Huguenots who called it, confusingly L'Église des Grecs. This was the first of many French chapels that were to open up in Soho during the next decade.

The name Huguenot derives from the old Swiss-German word *eidgenosse*, meaning 'confederate', and, like the names Quaker and Methodist, it was first applied to a religious group – in this case, the French Protestants – as a derogatory term. Huguenot refugees had lived in London since the reign of Henry VIII; as far back as 1550, in conjunction with Dutch Protestants, the Walloons, they had established a church at Austin Friars in the City. Their Polish leader, Jean à Lasco, had been forced to flee the country during Mary Tudor's brief reign, but persecution on the Continent during the late 16th century – in particular the massacre on St Bartholomew's Day, 1572 – had driven an increasing number of Huguenots to seek sanctuary in Elizabethan England. However, their numbers remained small, and when the Protestants' champion, Henry IV of France and Navarre, signed the Edict of Nantes in 1598 guaranteeing the Protestants religious freedom, the stream of religious refugees pouring into England temporarily stopped.

It began again in earnest after Henry IV's assassination in 1610, when Louis XIII started a war of attrition against them. By the early 1640s, Huguenots were so numerous in London that they had two churches there – St Anthony's, in Threadneedle Street, and the Chapel of the Savoy, in the Strand, which was patronized by the richer citizens and was described by Samuel Pepys as a 'pretty place'. Pepys's wife was the daughter of a Huguenot family, and Pepys himself also attended services in the Threadneedle Street chapel. One Sunday in November 1662 he wrote in his diary, 'Dined alone with my wife with great content, my house being quite clean from top to bottom. In the afternoon I went to the French Church here in the City, and stood in the aisle all the sermon, with great delight, hearing a very admirable sermon from a very young man.'

France was losing out by the departure of its staunchly middle-class Protestants, who had constituted about 10 per cent of its population, a percentage made up mostly of aristocrats, skilled artisans and craftsmen. In fact, by 1669 so many Huguenots had left France that their emigration was stopped by edict. 'They are forbidden to quit their country', wrote Dean Drelincourt of Armagh, 'and yet, by their hard usage and persecution, in effect, not suffered to stay.' Little did Drelincourt realize that the persecution was about to get even worse: in 1681 Louis XIV instituted the dreaded *dragonnade*, billeting soldiers on Protestant families with the aim of terrorizing them into conversion. The stream of Protestant refugees suddenly became a flood.

Charles II was outraged. He protested strongly to Louis about the ill-treatment of the Huguenots, and in an order of Council stated that he held himself 'obliged in honour and Conscience to comfort and support all such afflicted Protestants who by reason of ye rigours and severitys, which are usd towards them upon ye account of their Religion shall be forced to quitt their Native Country, and shall desire to shelter themselves under his Matys Royall Protection for ye preservacon and free exercise of their Religion'. In addition, he offered them letters of denization and the right to practise their trades in England, and ordered that charity collections be taken for them throughout the country.

As if the *dragonnade* were not enough, in October 1685 Henry IV's Edict of Nantes – the Protestants' old charter of security – was revoked. Any Huguenot rights that still remained now vanished overnight. It was the final straw for the oppressed community. During the next few years an estimated 200,000 Protestants left France. Some 40,000-50,000 of these settled in England.

Like all refugees, they were but groups of individuals:

Suzanne Herbiron, button-maker, came from Paris three weeks ago. Peter Faisette officer of the French King's men of war turned out of his employment because he would not leave his religion and came hither three months ago. He hath no employment. Jean le Fanu, weaver, came from Roän three weeks ago with his wife. 10sh.

Their names — Olivier, Cazenove, Roget, Bosanquet, Plimsoll, Chaplin, Bouchard; their occupations — milliner, silk-weaver, silversmith, tapestry-maker; the numbers and ages of their children; and the gifts of money that were made to them; all these details were faithfully recorded in the church registers of the time. Some refugees were rich, and brought with them fine clothes, jewels, and even servants. Others arrived with nothing but the clothes on their backs and their precious skills. All of them were hard-working and frugal – it was Huguenots who first introduced into British kitchens that ever-so-English delicacy oxtail soup: until they came, the ox tails were thought to be useless for cooking and were simply thrown away.

A few Huguenots settled in the City. Most of them moved into the suburbs or to provincial towns where the practice of their trades was not restricted by the powers of the City of London livery companies. Huguenot silk-weavers, having congregated for a time in Canterbury, then moved to London and settled in the place they called the 'Hameau' on the east fringe of the City – Spitalfields, where in streets such as Fournier Street one can still see the glass-fronted attics they built to house their looms. Mirror-workers settled in Greenwich, clock-makers in Clerkenwell. A group of cloth-dyers and hat-makers moved out to what was then the village of Wandsworth. The goldsmiths, jewellers, tailors and tapestry-weavers settled predominantly in Soho. Initially they may well have been attracted to the area by L'Église des Grecs, in Hog Lane, or by the so-called Soho tapestry makers of the Great Wardrobe, who had a factory in the neighbouring parish of St Giles-in-the-Fields.

By 1693 there were 10 Huguenot chapels in Westminster, including five in Soho: L'Église des Grecs; Le Quarré, in Monmouth House; La Patente (named after James II's letters patent granting permission to establish more churches), in Berwick Street; Le Tabernacle, in Milk Alley (now Bourchier Street); and a small chapel later known as Le Petit Charenton, in a room in Newport Market.

It is to the Huguenots that Soho owes its tradition of fine craftsmanship and its cosmopolitan atmosphere. They arrived as the district was taking shape, and it is as if their talents, the scents of their herbs and spices and the sounds of their voices were woven into its character. Though they settled in quickly, they did not assimilate: they kept their own language, their own habits, their own cuisine, and their own, very Continental, way of life.

A survey of the new parish's population, conducted in 1711, showed that of Soho's 8,133 inhabitants, just under three-fifths were English. The remainder were French householders or French lodgers. In 1720, when writer John Strype compiled *A Survey of the Cities of London and Westminster*, he wrote of St Anne's parish that an 'Abundance of French People, many whereof are voluntary Exiles for their Religion, live in these Streets and Lanes, following honest Trades; and some Gentry of the same Nation'. And William Maitland, in *The History of London*, written nearly 20 years later, states that 'Many Parts of this Parish so greatly abound with French, that it is an easy Matter for a Stranger to imagine himself in France.' In fact, the atmosphere was so Continental that local business cards were frequently engraved in both English and French.

The English inhabitants of Soho's newly-built mansions provided the local Huguenot artisans with a ready-made market for their exquisite workmanship. And since it was a district of mixed housing, near the mansions of Soho Square and Golden Square were more ordinary areas, such as Compton Street and Newport Market, where, as Strype noted, the rents were cheap and trade was good.

There were a few bigots, of course, who objected to the King's support for this influx of foreigners. Daniel Defoe, a one-time resident of Broad (later Broadwick) Street, fought strongly against the 1694 bill to naturalize 'aliens', saying, 'Let us first kick the Bill out of the House, then the foreigners out of the Kingdom.' But attitudes like Defoe's were the exception – particularly among Sohoites, who have always taken pride in being London's most tolerant citizens. As the Government was quick to realize, the new immigrants did much to reduce the balance-of-trade deficit: it was no longer necessary to import luxury stockings, silks, linens, silver, gold and glassware from France, now that the people with the know-how to make them were living over here. The Huguenots could only benefit English society; as one contemporary writer put it, 'they confine themselves to their own business which they pursue with admirable address and skill to the great advantage, not only of themselves, but of the Nation in general'.

The Huguenot community in Soho was to produce 18th-century England's finest craftsmen: goldsmiths of the calibre of Paul Crespin, whose workshop on the corner of Greek Street and Compton Street produced goods for the King of Portugal and the Russian royal family; and of Augustin Courtauld, who in 1730 was commissioned above the heads of City craftsmen to make goods for London's Lord Mayor. They were also to be thanked for one of the best schools in 18th-century England – refugee Abraham Meure's boarding school, which by 1691 had opened at number 12 Greek Street, primarily for the education of French Protestants, but with a roll-call that soon included more than one future English Earl.

Ironically, a century later the Huguenots were followed to Soho by the people whose ancestors had once persecuted their own – French Roman Catholics in flight from the Revolution. In the 1850s they, in turn, were joined by French Liberals escaping the military rule of Napoleon III. In fact, Soho remained so French in atmosphere that, well into this century, it was known to outsiders as the Quartier Latin or the Quartier Français.

Persecution comes in many shapes and forms, and in whatever incarnation it appears – political, religious, social or sexual – Soho has always seemed to provide the persecuted with shelter and with the freedom to be themselves. Another, often less dramatic, but nevertheless deeply painful form of persecution is that of a child by a cruel or tyrannical parent. Its marks are sometimes physical, but even in its more subtle forms it can be no less harmful, and can leave emotional scars that are passed down through generations of the same family, as victims turn persecutors in their turn. It is a form of persecution to which no social rank is immune: in the first half of the 18th century, Leicester House was to serve as a refuge for the sons and heirs of two cruel royal fathers, George I and George II.

Lady Mary Wortley Montagu, who lived in Soho Square, would one day call George I 'an honest blockhead'. To his eldest son he was much worse. For, in spite of being an indiscriminate womanizer himself, he had divorced Sophia Dorothea, his wife of 12 years' standing, for her affair with Count Königsmark, and had forbidden her ever to see her two children again.

Soon after the affair was discovered, Königsmark had been murdered – probably at George's instigation. It was a fate that Sophia Dorothea might well have envied, for she was to give up not only her children, but her freedom too, remaining shut up in the Castle of Ahlden until she died in 1726, having been her husband's prisoner for 33 years.

On the death of Queen Anne on 1 August 1714, the Elector of Hanover succeeded to the British throne. He arrived in London two months later, with a retinue of 700 Germans in tow, including two mistresses, the Countesses von Platen and von der Schulenberg, and two Turkish valets. It was soon clear to his subjects that his interest in his new realm was confined to the amount of money he could extort from it. He never learned to speak English properly and so took little part in government, which he left to Sir Robert Walpole, with whom he conversed in broken Latin.

Once installed in St James's Palace, the new King lost no time in establishing a reputation as a gambler, a womanizer, a miser and a philistine. He was also openly intolerant of his eldest son, George, Prince of Wales, whom he publicly humiliated, kept permanently short of money and avoided talking to in company whenever he could.

His attitude to his handsome, intelligent daughter-in-law, Caroline of Anspach, was another matter. With no Queen to officiate at public functions, the King expected Caroline to act as first lady of the land – which she did, until the quarrel that forced her and her husband to leave St James's in November 1717.

The row blew up over who should be godfather to the couple's new baby, George William. The Prince of Wales wanted his uncle, the Duke of York, to have the honour, but the King insisted that it should go to the Duke of Newcastle, whom the Prince could not stand. Naturally, the King got his way, and the Duke of Newcastle was duly appointed godfather at a ceremony at St James's. Seething with frustration, at the end of the baptism ceremony the Prince insulted Newcastle. The King was furious. He wanted to throw his 34-year-old son in the Tower – locking Sophia Dorothea up had probably given him a taste for imprisoning his family – but was persuaded this would be bad for his image, and ended up locking him in his room instead. He then ordered the Prince and Princess of Wales to leave St James's Palace immediately, while insisting that the couple's three daughters, Anne, Amelia and Caroline, remain behind in his care. On his orders the new baby boy was taken to Kensington Palace; tragically he died on the way there.

No wonder the Prince of Wales hated his father, when he had deprived him first of his mother and then even of his own family. Now, finally, the break had come – and none too soon for the young couple. After taking temporary refuge with Lord Grantham in Albemarle Street, Mayfair, they began to look around for a house of their own.

It was not surprising that their eyes alighted on Soho, for by now it was well established, along with Mayfair, as one of the smartest two districts in town. The seal on Soho's success was set when, at the end of December 1717, it was announced that the Prince and Princess of Wales were to lease Leicester House, and that its neighbour, Ailesbury House (later known as Savile House) was to be retained for their attendants.

The Sidneys' grand house in Leicester Fields was still one of the largest in London. By now it was the property of the sixth Earl of Leicester, and it had been rented out for the last 15 or so years. In the first weeks of January it was quickly prepared for its royal tenants, who moved in at the end of the month. It was to remain their home for 10 years.

Not long after the move, St Anne's church was informed that the Prince had 'discovered an Inclination to come to this Church'. Lady Williamson, one of the congregation, was asked to give up her pew in favour of the royals, and a carpenter was commissioned to alter the pew and make it fit for blue-blooded worship. The Prince and Princess soon became regulars at the church, and the children born to them in later years were all baptised in its font.

Infuriated by the Prince and Princess's show of independence, George I declared that anyone who had anything to do with them would be banned from Court. Life in St James's Palace was extremely dull anyway, and Leicester House soon became a centre of political and social opposition. 'The elder Whig politicians,' Walpole explains, 'became ministers to the King. The most promising of the young lords and gentlemen of that party, and the prettiest and liveliest of the young ladies, formed a new

Court of the Prince and Princess of Wales. The apartment of the bed-chamber-woman in waiting became the fashionable evening rendezvous of the most distinguished wits and beauties.'

The most outstanding 'wit' at Leicester House was the Waleses' new neighbour, Sir Isaac Newton, who had moved to Soho from Chelsea in 1711, and now lived at number 35 St Martin's Street, a small street on the south side of Leicester Fields. Although he was cared for by three male and three female servants, Newton lived quite frugally, devoting his time to revising his *Principia* and to observing the sky from a small glass observatory which he had constructed on the roof.

When he was not working, Newton frequently strolled across Leicester Fields and spent the evening in conversation with Princess Caroline. The Prince's attractions, however, such as they were, were waning rapidly. He was becoming as crass, pompous, mean and bad-tempered as his father – and just as much of a womanizer: the 'beauties' of whom Walpole had written soon got fed up with fending him off. By the time George I died on 12 June 1727, the novelty of the alternative social scene at Leicester House had completely worn off, and its salons were as deserted as those of St James's Palace.

The Prince and Princess of Wales were summering at Richmond when the King died. They immediately returned to Leicester House where, the following day, 43-year-old George was proclaimed King at the gateway, and soon afterwards held the first council of his reign at the house. The courtiers who had deserted him now crawled out of every corner. 'The square was thronged with multitudes of the meaner sort, and resounded with huzzas and acclamations,' Lord Hervey wrote, 'whilst every room in the house was filled with people of higher rank, crowding to kiss hands, and to make the earliest and warmest professions of zeal for the new King's service.' For the next four days, 'Leicester House, which used to be a desert, was thronged from morning to night, like the 'Change at noon.'

The King and Queen gave up their Soho home that Christmas in order to move back to St James's Palace, where Caroline and Sir Robert Walpole conferred over political policy, leaving the King free to chase women and to travel to Hanover, both of which he did regularly. For a while the mansion in Leicester Fields was occupied again by its owners, the Sidney family. Then, in 1742, the whole sordid royal father/son drama was replayed in the same salons in scenes of uncanny similarity – only this time with George II in the role of the cruel father and Prince Frederick Louis in that of his heir.

Poor Fred. His sister Amelia hated him. His father said of him, 'My Dear Son, my first-born, is the greatest Ass, and the greatest Liar, and the greatest *Canaille,* and the greatest Beast in the whole world, and I heartily wish he was out of it.' According to his mother he was a 'nauseous little beast, and he cares for nobody but his nauseous little self'.

Who could blame him, when it had been clear right from the start that his parents did not care for him at all? Though they adored their daughters, they had abandoned Fred when he was only seven years old when they left Hanover for England, and did not even summon him over for his father's coronation 14 years later. He came anyway, much to their annoyance, arriving unannounced at St James's in a hackney coach. He was 22 and, not unnaturally, terrified of the remote figures his parents had become.

Once here, he was cold-shouldered by the King, who kept him short of money – like father, like son – and stopped him marrying the woman he had secretly chosen (it would have been the first marriage between a Lady Diana Spencer and a Prince of Wales). His attempts to curry favour with the English were met with suspicion and contempt in the palace: when he earned the love of Londoners by helping to put out a fire in the Inner Temple, Queen Caroline remarked, 'My God, popularity always makes me sick, but Fred's makes me vomit.'

Why did his family hate him so much? Was he really so obnoxious? The common people liked him well enough; but, as the hard-done-by son of an unpopular monarch, he became – like his father before him – a natural focus for political opposition, a fact that cannot have endeared him to the King and Queen, who not so long ago had been in the same position themselves. Horace Walpole wrote of Fred that his 'best quality was generosity, his worst insincerity and indifference to truth', and talked of his indiscriminating passion for women – a trait he seemed to have inherited from his grandfather. That he got into debt is no surprise, when his parsimonious parents paid him a bare quarter of the £100,000 allowed him by the civil list, and when his taste in women was wide-ranging and sometimes expensive, embracing women as diverse as an apothecary's daughter in Kingston and a prima donna at the Opera House, and including Vanella Fane, 'a Maid of Honour who was willing to cease to be so – at the first opportunity', as Horace Walpole described her, whom Fred set up in a house in Soho Square.

Even after his marriage to 17-year-old Princess Augusta of Saxe-Gotha (the wedding was a quiet affair, in order to save money), Fred was kept on such a short financial rein that he could not afford a house of his own. Overcome with rage, he ventured on an act of open rebellion: he kept Augusta's pregnancy a secret for as long as he could, then removed her from the Court, which was staying at Hampton, on the very night she went into labour, taking her all the way to London to have the baby instead. Lady Archibald Hamilton, one of Fred's mistresses, travelled up from the country to St James's Palace with the couple, and it was probably she who supervised the birth. Miss Cannon, midwife, was called in at the last minute, and the baby – 'a little Rat of a Girl' – was born between two borrowed tablecloths, because no bed linen had been prepared.

The King and Queen were furious with Fred – Caroline particularly so, as it was rumoured that Fred and Augusta had feared she would poison the baby, and had manoeuvred the last-minute flight from Hampton simply in order to prevent her being present at the birth. Just as they themselves had been thrown out of the palace 20 years before, the King and Queen now gave Fred and Augusta notice to quit as soon as possible, and forbade the Court to have anything to do with them.

After stints at Kew Palace, at Carlton House (which Fred had acquired several years earlier) and at the Duke of Norfolk's mansion in Mayfair, Fred took a lease on Leicester House. He moved in during the winter of 1742/3 after alterations had been made to the building, probably under the direction of his architect, William Kent. Once again, Soho's largest mansion became the centre for political opposition, attracting men such as Chesterfield, Marlborough and Lord Carteret.

It also became the first – and only – real home that poor Fred ever knew. Here he entertained his many foreign and English friends with sumptuous meals and lavish masques and plays, which were performed by visiting professional actors and sometimes by Fred's children, on whom he lavished all the affection he himself had never had. He also used the spacious rooms to indulge his love of the fine arts, commissioning works by living artists and collecting old master paintings.

But Fred was not fated to enjoy himself for long. In the early spring of 1751, he developed pleurisy after catching a chill in his garden at Kew. After a few days of suffering, on 20 March he appeared to rally: as Bubb Doddington, the future Lord Melcombe wrote, 'for half-an-hour before he was very cheerful, asked to see some friends, eat [sic] some bread and butter and drank coffee'. But later that same day an abscess in his chest burst and he died in a matter of moments – according to one report, while his French dancing master, Desnoyers, played the violin at his bedside.

Leicester House was plunged into mourning, with the walls of the state rooms, the curtains and the mirror-frames covered in black cloth. Even the lantern-frames were painted black. In the outside world Fred's death was taken more lightly; as his hatchment was put up outside the front gate, Walpole overheard two workmen talking: 'He has left a great many small children,' said one. 'Ay,' replied the other. 'And what is worse they belong to our parish!'

Three weeks later Fred's corpse was secretly taken in the middle of the night to the House of Lords. The following evening he was buried at Westminster Abbey 'without either anthem or organ'. The sadness of his life is summed up in this poem, attributed to Walpole:

> Here lies Fred,
> Who was alive and is dead:
> Had it been his father,
> I had much rather;
> Had it been his brother,
> Still better than another;
> Had it been his sister,
> No one would have missed her;
> Had it been the whole generation,
> Still better for the nation:
> But since 'tis only Fred,
> Who was alive and is dead –
> There's no more to be said.

Leicester House was not to give up its connection with royalty just yet. It was arranged between the King and his widowed daughter-in-law that she should stay on there with her youngest children, and that her two eldest sons, the Duke of York and 13-year-old George, the new Prince of Wales, should remain next door at Savile House.

By the time of Fred's death, Soho's reputation as the home of the titled classes had faded, and most of the aristocrats who had leased houses there during the late 17th and early 18th centuries had already moved on to Mayfair. They left quickly: of the 80-odd titled English living in Soho in the 1690s, only 20 remained by the early 1740s.

Soho's unpaved roads – for instance, Great Marlborough Street, which had once been described as surpassing 'anything that is called a street in the magnificence of its buildings and gardens' – were now considered too narrow and mean for the top nobs, and mansions that only a decade before had been 'inhabited all by a prime quality', were now felt to be small and cramped in comparison to the spacious mansions that were going up in Grosvenor Square and Berkeley Square – addresses that were also nearer Hyde Park, which had superseded St James's Park as the fashionable morning and evening rendezvous spot.

'Within the memory of many now living,' wrote Henry Fielding in 1752, 'the circle of the People of Fascination included the whole parish of Covent Garden and a great part of St-Giles-in-the-Fields; but here the enemy broke in and the circle was presently contracted to Leicester Fields and Golden Square. Hence the People of Fashion again retreated before the foe to Hanover Square; whence they were once more driven to Grosvenor Square and even beyond it, and that with so much precipitation, that had they not been stopped by the walls of Hyde Park, it is more than probable they would by this time have arrived at Kensington.'

With so many new developments going up to the north and the west, those with a financial interest in Soho realized that something drastic would have to be done if the area was not to decline any further. So when the relatively short building leases obtained by the original developers came to an end, longer ones were granted by the ground landlords, and many of the houses mass-produced by Barbon, Frith and undertakers like them were rebuilt in a more substantial manner. In addition, a special Act of Parliament was passed 'for the better paving and lighting of the parish of St Anne', stone roads were laid, and the protective posts that had, inadequately, separated pedestrians from carriages were replaced by raised pavements.

Still, the streets anywhere in London were far from clean or evenly laid. Walking was treacherous enough by day. At night it was necessary to pay torch-bearing linkmen to light a way through the puddles, the mud, the holes in the road and the muck-heaps. Anyone who could afford to travelled in hired or private sedan chairs – which also prevented the rich from being pelted with mud or robbed by the starving poor, the highwaymen, and the thousands of gin-drinkers who hung about the streets. In 1751, magistrate Henry Fielding estimated that about 100,000 people in the metropolis were addicted to gin – which worked out at about one-fifth of the total population.

But Soho was not to decline so far – for the time being. Though it was not as expensive as Mayfair, it was still one of London's smartest districts, and consequently the mansions vacated by the _haut monde_ did not stand empty for long. They were perfect bases for the foreign ambassadors and envoys who felt more at home in Soho's continental atmosphere than they did in other parts of town. The Swedish envoy had taken a house in Leicester Square as early as 1693, and had been followed into Soho by the Sicilians, the Portuguese, the Russians and the French, to name but a few. The mansions of Soho Square were particularly suited to large foreign legations: the Venetian Ambassador occupied several houses in Soho Square (numbers 31/2, 2 and 12) between 1744 and 1791; the Spanish delegation moved into number 7 in the late 1740s; the King of Naples's envoy installed himself in Carlisle House in 1754, and the Russians took over Fauconberg House at about the same time. Monmouth House was leased by the French Ambassador, the Comte de Guerchy, in 1763, and by a Russian minister three years later.

The diplomatic privileges enjoyed by foreign legations allowed them to do what was forbidden to the English – to take part in Roman Catholic Mass. Consequently many ambassadors built their own Catholic chapels in or near their premises. For instance, the Portuguese Ambassador, who moved into numbers 23 and 24

Golden Square in 1724, installed a small chapel in the outbuildings between his house and neighbouring Warwick Street. English
Catholics, deprived of hearing Mass elsewhere, secretly attended
this chapel, which they reached through a narrow passage on the
east side of Warwick Street.

After the Bavarians took over the Portuguese Embassy in the late
1740s, this chapel seems to have been used almost exclusively by
English Catholics, and although the ecclesiastic authorities turned
a blind eye to it, the chapel became a focal point of the anti-Papist
Gordon Riots of 1780, when it was practically burned to the ground.
Its late 18th-century replacement – the compact red-brick church
of Our Lady of the Assumption and St Gregory – still stands in
Warwick Street, a small, almost forgotten monument to those less
tolerant religious times.

Wealthy businessmen and politicians also snapped up large Soho
houses when they became vacant, and by 1733 Soho boasted 27
resident Members of Parliament. One man who was both MP
and businessman was Richard Beckford, a wealthy planter from
the West Indies, who was not in himself a particularly interesting
person but made a lasting impression on Soho by bequeathing it
his beautiful house, which today remains Soho's finest building,
number 1 Greek Street.

Richard Beckford was born and brought up in Jamaica, where
his father, Peter, was a wealthy planter and the Speaker of the
Assembly. When Richard grew up, he followed his father into the
family business and into Jamaican politics. However, in the late
months of 1753 he announced his resignation from the Assembly,
on the grounds that he had decided to emigrate to England, 'for
the establishment of his health'.

Richard's brother, William, was already living in London, where
he had been sent to Westminster School as a boarder at the age
of 14. William had not returned to Jamaica after his education.
Instead, he had decided on a career in English politics, and had
become an alderman for Billingsgate ward in the City of London.
In 1751 he had moved into number 22, Soho Square, from where
he ran political campaigns – both on his own account and on behalf
of his brother: for by the time Richard arrived in London during
the early summer of 1754, William had secured him a seat in the
House of Commons as an MP for Bristol.

It is not known whether Richard stayed with his brother when he arrived in London. But he certainly took to Soho, for within a few weeks he had started negotiating to lease a house on the south-east corner of Soho Square, only a stone's throw away from William's.

Number 1 Greek Street, a four-storeyed grey-brick mansion, had been built in the 1740s to replace an earlier building on the site. The house had been empty for some years, and had not yet been completed, for it was the custom at the time to leave the interior decoration to the future lessee. Richard, who intended to live in a style appropriate to a wealthy plantation-owner, commissioned elaborately carved door-frames, doors and fireplaces for his new mansion, as well as some remarkable rococo plasterwork, which was executed, it is believed, *in situ* by the same Italian craftsmen who had worked on nearby Monmouth House.

Beautiful as his house was, Richard did not stay there very long. Not surprisingly, the English climate was not as good for his health as he had hoped, and he and his mistress left for France towards the end of 1755, less than a year after he had arrived in England. The French air did not do much for him either: he died in Lyon the following January.

His house lives on, almost untouched by time, its interior still one of the finest remaining examples of the rococo style popular in the mid-18th century. It is complete in many details – including the solid front door, still fastened at night with its original bolts and heavy iron chain. The double-height hall, which has a cantilevered stone staircase with mahogany handrails, and richly stuccoed wall-panels, leads to three magnificently decorated rooms. A tribute to Soho's glorious past, the house is opened twice weekly to the public. But for all that it is no museum-piece, being still very much a working home. In 1862, number 1 Greek Street was bought by the House of Charity, a private charity set up around the corner in Rose (today Manette) Street to provide a temporary home for destitute men, women and children. A chapel was added at the back of Richard Beckford's house, but otherwise few changes were made to it. Since World War II, the House of Charity has been known as the House of St-Barnabas-in-Soho, and, at the time of writing, offers a semi-permanent home to 39 women.

Though Richard Beckford's stay in Soho was so short-lived, his elder brother William lived in Soho Square for a total of 19 years.

His house, number 22, was in no way as grand as his brother's – but then it was only a *pied-à-terre*, for he was also the owner of Fonthill Abbey, a huge country mansion in Wiltshire which he filled with treasures and curiosities shipped over from the West Indies. It was at Fonthill Abbey that William's son, William Beckford the Younger, the fastest novelist in the business (he claimed to have written *Vathek* in 'three days and two nights of hard labour'), was born in 1759.

During the time he lived at number 22, Alderman Beckford twice became Lord Mayor of the City of London. He was a brave man who was never afraid of standing by his principles or sticking his neck out in defence of liberty – even if it meant causing trouble for himself. When John Wilkes, the controversial MP for Middlesex, was expelled from the Commons in 1769 and then denied his seat after being re-elected by his constituency, Lord Mayor Beckford became one of Wilkes's staunchest supporters. Cries of 'Wilkes for Liberty' resounded through London's streets after the House of Commons supported the election to Parliament of Wilkes's opponent Luttrell, who had polled less than 300 votes in the election, compared to Wilkes's 11,000. Beckford was as furious as the mob, and decorated number 22 Soho Square with a huge, three-foot high banner, embroidered with the word LIBERTY in white letters. This could have got him into terrible trouble, but few people saw the banner. As Horace Walpole pointed out, 'Luckily the evening was very wet, and not a mouse stirred.'

The outspoken Lord Mayor was not content merely to make a splash with a banner. Soon afterwards he obtained an audience with George III, before whom he made a famous speech supporting Wilkes's right to take up his seat in the House of Commons.

We are determined to abide by those rights and liberties which our forefathers bravely vindicated at the ever memorable Revolution [he said to the furious King], and which their sons will ever resolutely defend. We therefore now renew at the feet of the throne our claims to the indispensable rights of the subjects – a full, free and unmutilated Parliament, legally chosen in all its members – a right which this House of Parliament have manifestly violated, depriving at their will and pleasure, the county of Middlesex of one of its legal representatives, and arbitrarily nominating, as a knight of the shire, a person not elected by a majority of the freeholders.

The speech made Beckford more than a local hero. But the strain of it also broke his health, and he died of a chill four weeks later.

Prominent as Alderman Beckford was in political society, it was not to be him, or his brother Richard, or even Arthur Onslow, the Speaker of the House of Commons who lived at number 20, who made sure that the Square and its environs stayed on the social map. That job was left to the new occupant of Carlisle House, the mansion standing at the south corner of Sutton Street between Beckford's and Onslow's houses. During the 1760s, the salons of this house were to become the most notorious and famous in London – and the woman who ran them was to prove one of the most extraordinary, colourful and resourceful individuals that Soho has ever seen.

——— 3 ———

A Woman's Place

She was, perhaps, the quintessential Soho character: inventive, talented, clever, wildly extravagant and at the same time completely hopeless at saving money. She combined these qualities with a streak of ruthlessness which did not stop short of selling her own son. She surrounded herself with a mystique of drama, and she cunningly manipulated the people around her in order to get what she wanted. Yet she redeemed her faults with her energy, her indomitable spirit, and her ability to laugh at her own lack of scruples. In short, she was a survivor, who time after time came bouncing back when circumstances would have crushed anyone of a lesser mettle. In the words of the Chevalier de Seingalt – better known as Casanova – who was her lover, the father of her daughter and the man who probably understood her better than anyone else, she was 'an adventuress in the widest acceptation of the term'.

Her name was Theresa Cornelys – or that was what she called herself when she arrived in Soho in 1760, for during her many-faceted career she was also known as Madame de Trenti and La Pompeati. However, none of these was her real name, for when she was born in Venice in 1723 she was named Theresa Imer after her father, an actor of Austrian descent. Little is known of her childhood – only that she showed great potential as a singer and actress, both on and off stage, if Casanova's account of her is to be believed.

He later wrote in his memoirs that she had an 'exquisite voice' and was an 'excellent musician', but that 'her fortune was not altogether owing to her talent, her charms had done more for her than anything else'. These 'charms' seem to have shown themselves early on in life: according to Casanova, who met her in Venice when she was 17 years old, she was 'pretty, whimsical, and a regular cocotte'. Urged on by her mother, she had already captivated a rich and elderly senator named Malipiero, who eventually took her to live with him in his palazzo, where he kept her for 10 years.

During this time Theresa Imer married – presumably for respectability – a young dancer called Pompeati, by whom she had a son.
In later years Pompeati was to commit an extremely grisly suicide
in Vienna: it was said that he cut open his stomach with a razor,
and 'died tearing at his entrails'.

In her late twenties Theresa Imer had become frustrated with life
as a kept woman, and, leaving her protector, Malipiero, in Venice,
she set out with Pompeati to carve herself a career as an actress. A new
lover in Germany – the Margrave of Bayreuth – held her attention
for a short while before she moved on northwards, this time without
her husband. In Brussels, so she later told Casanova, she captivated
Prince Charles of Lorraine, 'who obtained for her the direction of
all the theatres in the Austrian Low Countries' – demanding work
which she did for some time.

But things did not continue to go well for her, and by 1753 she was
back in Venice, this time in reduced circumstances, sharing simple
lodgings with her eight-year-old son. Here Casanova met her again,
at the house of Madame Manzoni, and remarked that 'her fortune
would have been established on a firmer basis than mine if she had
followed a prudent line of conduct. She unfortunately indulged
in numerous caprices . . .' One of these was to invite Casanova
to breakfast the following morning, where he 'found her in bed
with her son, who, thanks to the principles in which he had been
educated, got up and left the room as soon as he saw me seated
near his mother's bed. I spent three hours with her, and I recollect
that the last was delightful'.

'The consequence of that pleasant hour' Casanova discovered in
Amsterdam five years later, when he saw Theresa Imer, again by
chance, at a concert. She was now the lover of a rich Dutchman
called Cornelis de Rigerboos, and had established a reputation as a
singer 'of great repute'. Casanova's companion at the concert told
him that the mysterious Madame de Trenti, as she was currently
calling herself, 'is said to have lovers in every town, but instead of
enriching her they make her poorer. She always wears black, not
only because she is a widow, but also on account of a great grief
she is reported to have gone through.'

After her performance that night – for which she received 'tu-
multuous applause', she turned up at Casanova's lodgings hand in
hand with her beautiful daughter, a four-year-old called Sophie,

who bore a striking resemblance to Casanova himself. 'I of course rose to greet her, when all at once she fell fainting on the sofa,' Casanova reported, adding with some scepticism, 'though whether the fainting fit was real or assumed I cannot say.' The dramatics over, she recovered enough to eat a large supper and to stay up talking about herself until dawn. When told that Sophie was indeed his child, Casanova offered to take her off Theresa's hands, but in a rare show of motherly love she refused outright to part with the child, declaring that she adored Sophie and would die if separated from her. Instead, she suggested that Casanova should take charge of her 12-year-old son, whose manners he had praised five years earlier. Casanova recorded the conversation that followed this offer of her son in a deadpan, but nevertheless shocked, fashion:

'Where is he?'
'He is boarding or rather in pawn, at Rotterdam.'
'What do you mean by in pawn?'
'I mean that he will not be returned to me until I pay the person who has got him all my debts.'

One has to hand it to this incorrigible woman. Not only did she talk Casanova into redeeming the boy at a cost of 80 florins and looking after his education for the time being, but she also persuaded him to give her 100 ducats so that she and Sophie might follow her new lover, John Freeman, to London. From what little we know of Freeman, it seems that he was a more convincing actor than she was, for though he was employed as a musician, he had persuaded her that he was a clergyman who would help her to make her fortune if she accompanied him to England.

In October 1759, Theresa, Sophie and John Freeman arrived in London – Theresa using the name Mrs Cornelys, which she seems to have adapted from the Christian name of her Dutch lover Rigerboos, and Freeman going by the name John Fermor. Theresa had sung in London once before – on 7 January 1746, in a performance of Gluck's *La Caduta de' Giganti* – and with Fermor's help she now tried to relaunch her career at the Little Theatre in the Haymarket.

The concerts were a flop, and she was forced to take stock of her situation. She was 37 years old, past her operatic prime, a single parent with a small daughter to support. On top of this, the 'charms' that Casanova had enthused about were on the wane. If she was to conquer London society, as she clearly intended, she would have to use means other than purely physical ones.

Then she and Fermor had a brainchild: that 'a Concert and Assembly furnished out in an elegant Manner and carried on by Subscription in some commodious house for that purpose would probably meet with Encouragement and be a profitable undertaking'. With the help of influential and wealthy friends, Theresa Cornelys now set about finding premises for this venture, and in the early spring of 1760 she decided on Carlisle House in Soho Square.

Confusingly, there were now two Carlisle Houses in the vicinity of the square. The original Carlisle House, built in the square by the Howard family, stood on the corner of Sutton Street. Seven years before Mrs Cornelys appeared on the scene, the Howard family had sold their lease on the house to two upholsterers from Greek Street, who had used the outbuildings backing on to Hog Lane as workshops, and had leased the mansion out to a series of diplomats including the King of Naples's envoy, who had lived there for four years, and who had converted part of the side-buildings in Sutton Street into a Roman Catholic chapel.

The second Carlisle House was situated just off the square, at the end of King's Square Court (now Carlisle Street). Built in the 1680s, it had originally been occupied by a cousin of the Fauconbergs, and had in 1718 been inherited by the estranged wife of the third Earl of Carlisle from her mother, the Dowager Duchess of Essex. Its name, Carlisle House, seems to have originated at about this date.

It was the mansion in Soho Square that Theresa leased that April. As soon as she was in possession of it, her prodigious organizational skills and her talent for self-promotion came into play, and she set about preparing her premises – and the public – for a series of novel entertainments she had planned. Her next-door neighbours, Alderman Beckford and Speaker Onslow, could not have suspected what was about to hit the relatively sedate square when, a few months later, a line of carriages and sedan chairs pulled up outside Carlisle House and disgorged crowds of smartly dressed 'subscribers' to the first of Mrs Cornelys's 'Society' evenings.

In these two words lay genius, and the secret of Mrs Cornelys's success. She seems to have realized, way back in the 18th century, what it took the advertising industry a couple of hundred years more to find out – that by appealing to people's snobbishness and appearing to limit the goods on offer, she would enormously increase the demand for what she was selling. The people she entertained were not merely customers – they were members of an exclusive private 'Society' that only the most interesting, fashionable and wealthy people could join. Entrance to her Assemblies was by pre-paid ticket only – no money was taken at the door, which was consequently surrounded by scores of hopeful would-be entrants, like many fashionable night-clubs today.

The Society's first two evenings of music and card-playing were a great success, and as the word spread among the *haut monde*, Mrs Cornelys started an advertising campaign to drum up even more interest. Her next meetings were announced in *The Public Advertiser*: 'The Nobility and Gentry, Subscribers to the Society in Soho Square, are acquainted that the Third Meeting is on Thursday next, and the fourth on the 15th of January, 1761, to begin at seven o'clock.' Word-of-mouth reports of the evenings in Soho Square were encouraged, too, especially through the all-important servants' grapevine: Theresa acknowledged their contribution to her success in 1763 by holding a special ball 'to the upper servants of persons of fashion, as a token of the sense she had of obligation to the nobility and gentry, for their generous subscriptions to her assembly'. Within a few months of the first opening, the sedate twice-monthly meetings of the Society had turned into wild masquerades and balls, and the goings on at the Assembly Rooms in Soho Square became the talk of the town. When it was clear that she had a runaway success on her hands, Theresa, like many a small entrepreneur, sensibly decided to use her profits to expand.

There was nothing small, however, about her ideas for refurbishing Carlisle House. The old outbuildings in Sutton Street, used as a Catholic chapel by the King of Naples's envoy only a few years earlier, were demolished to make way for a two-storeyed building designed by Jacob Leroux of Dean Street. Though externally plain, the new building contained a vast, ornate concert room on the first floor with an apse at the far end, huge sash windows and a rococo ceiling. Below was a banqueting room capable of seating 400 people at the same table. Fixtures and fittings – large mirrors, chandeliers and furniture 'in an Elegant and Grand Manner' – were hired from the builder, Samuel Norman, who was partly paid with 1,400 subscription tickets to future assemblies. Theresa raised the cash she needed with the help of one of her racy society friends – the Honourable Mrs Elizabeth Chudleigh, who was soon to become a Duchess by a bigamous marriage to the Duke of Kingston. Mrs Chudleigh later caused quite a stir by appearing at a Carlisle House masque in the guise of the mythical Greek character, Iphigenia, clad in a long topless gown.

Once Mrs Cornelys had premises whose size and grandeur matched her ideas, there was no stopping her. The evening entertainments at Carlisle House escalated from ordinary balls and masques into full-scale 'drums'. A drum was, in 18th-century parlance, 'a riotous assembly of fashionable people of both sexes at a private house; not unaptly styled a drum, from the noise and emptiness of the entertainment'. Large drums were known as drum-majors, routs, tempests, hurricanes and squeezers. Mrs Cornelys's drums definitely fell into the last two categories, as witnessed by Fanny Burney, who attended one in 1770:

> The magnificence of the rooms, splendour of the illuminations and embellishments, and the brilliant appearance of the company exceeded anything I ever saw before [she reported in her diary on 20 April]. The apartments were so crowded we scarce had room to move, which was quite disagreeable, nevertheless the flight of apartments both upstairs and on the ground floor seemed endless . . . The Rooms were so full and so hot that nobody attempted to dance . . . I must own this evening's entertainment more disappointed my expectations than any I ever spent, for I had imagined it would have been the most charming in the world.

To Mrs Cornelys, problems such as overcrowding were simply challenges to be overcome. Her advertisements soon offered 'tea below stairs and ventilators above' and promised that 'complaints of excessive heat will be obviated without subjecting the Subscribers to the least danger of catching cold'. As for the crowds of onlookers that gathered outside in the square, she had ways of turning even these to her advantage: 'To Prevent Confusion, the Nobility and Gentry are humbly requested to order their own Chairs at the Door in Sutton-street, and the Hackney Chairs to that in Soho-square,' she announced in one advertisement, 'and to be positive in their Commands, that the Coachman let them down and take them up (as on former Seasons) with the Horses' heads towards Greek-street.'

Mrs Cornelys elevated her role as hostess to a fine art. There was always something special, planned or unplanned, to see and hear at one of her evenings. One night it was the French inventor and musical instrument maker Joseph Merlin, who crashed into a valuable mirror while careering through the apartments on the roller skates he had invented (characteristically, *la patronne* demanded £500 as compensation for the breakage). Sometimes subscribers could listen to a concert conducted by foreign musicians of the calibre of Johann Christian Bach and Karl Abel. And on one occasion the house was transformed for a *fête champêtre*, with pine trees transplanted into the concert room, and Gothic arches hung with 'an incredible number of lamps of variegated colours'. 'The Bridge-Room', we are told, was, on this occasion, 'converted into an elegant garden, the sides were full of shrubs and odiferous flowers, at the extremity was a kind of arbour filled with greenhouse plants and pots of flowers, and in the centre was an elegant pavilion hung with festoons of silk; on the top (to which the company ascended by a temporary staircase) was spread a table for a dozen persons, in the middle of which was a fountain of water, and a reservoir, with gold and silver fish swimming about in it.'

Festivities like these were expensive, to say the least, and financial backing by Mrs Elizabeth Chudleigh and her cronies was not sufficient to stop Mrs Cornelys frequently getting into debt. No matter that she could gross upwards of £1,200 in a single night, as fast as she raked the money in it slipped through her fingers. Her lifestyle was more than extravagant: she kept two secretaries, 33 servants, and six horses. Fed up with trying to keep tabs on them all, she soon decided that what she needed was a man to watch over her interests.

The person she chose for this unenviable position was her son, *le petit Aranda*, as he was now called, and in 1763 she duly wrote to Casanova, asking him to bring the boy over from Paris, where he was still being educated at the Chevalier's expense. When the travellers arrived in London, Casanova followed the instructions

Theresa had sent him, and brought the boy straight to Soho Square. But to his indignation there was no heartfelt greeting for either lover or son: instead, Theresa sent down a servant 'in grand livery' to take them to lodgings nearby, run by 'a fat woman named *Rancour*' who informed them that Theresa would not be able to see them until 10 o'clock that night.

Casanova was furious at Theresa's rudeness, but did his best to control his anger. Matters were not improved when she eventually arrived in a sedan chair, well after 10 o'clock, and did not greet him with 'those caresses which I had a right to expect'. By now the son she had not seen for six years was asleep on the sofa, and Theresa and Casanova went arm-in-arm to dine . . .

> into another room which I had not seen. The table was laid for four, and I was curious enough to enquire who was the fourth person.
>
> 'It was to have been my daughter, but I left her behind, as when I told her that you and her brother had arrived she asked me if you were well.'
>
> 'And have you punished her for doing so?'
>
> 'Certainly, for in my opinion she ought to have asked for her brother first and then for you.'

When Aranda woke up, Theresa explained what she wanted him to do for her. 'I give twelve balls and twelve suppers to the nobility, and the same number to the middle classes in the year. I have often as many as six hundred guests at two guineas a head. The expenses are enormous, and alone as I am I must be robbed, for I can't be in two places at once. Now that you are here you can keep everything under lock and key, keep the books, pay and receive accounts and see that everyone is properly attended to at the assemblies; in fine, you will perform the duties of the master.'

The exhausted boy soon went to bed, and Theresa, in her inimitable style, spent the rest of the evening talking about herself. 'In the three hours for which we talked together,' Casanova wrote in an aggrieved tone, 'this woman did not once ask me how I was, whether I was comfortable, how long I intended to stay in London, or whether I had made much money. In short, she made no enquiries whatever about me, only saying with a smile, but not heedlessly, – "I never have a penny to spare."'

Two things are clear from Theresa's high-handed behaviour that day: first, her head had been turned by her phenomenal success in England; and secondly, she was as hopeless a mother as she was at managing money. She was indifferent to her son, and she stifled her daughter so much that the girl became physically ill, and had to be placed – at Casanova's expense, of course – in a boarding school at Harwich. Always Theresa's most outspoken critic, Casanova had warned her years ago that 'if she had intended to make actors of her children she had succeeded to admiration; but if she wished them to become useful members of society her system had failed lamentably, as they were in a fair way to become monsters of deceit.' In future years the son Theresa neglected did his best to support her. But Sophie, who she doted on, disowned her mother completely. Casanova's prediction that she would become a monster of deceit apparently came true, for John Taylor, a journalist who knew Sophie well, said in later years that she was 'an artful hypocrit' [sic].

Still, not every woman can be a perfect mother. It was enough that Theresa Cornelys was the perfect hostess. Casanova, who attended one of the Carlisle House assemblies about a fortnight after he had arrived, gave this marvellous, evocative description of the evening:

> The ball lasted all night without ceasing, as the company ate by relays, and at all times and hours; the waste and prodigality were worthy of a prince's palace. I made the acquaintance of all the nobility, and the Royal Family, for they were all there, with the exception of the king and queen, and the Prince of Wales. Madame Cornelis must have received more than twelve hundred guineas, but the outlay was enormous, without any control or safeguard against the thefts, which must have been perpetrated on all sides. She tried to introduce her son to everybody, but the poor lad looked like a victim, and did nothing but make profound bows. I pitied him from my heart.

Despite the many lawsuits and claims against her – Mrs Cornelys seldom dared to leave the house during Casanova's visit, in case she was arrested – tickets to the twice-monthly assemblies remained the hottest in town throughout the 1760s, and were even thought fit gifts for foreign dignitaries. 'Persons of distinction', including foreign and English royalty, ambassadors and noblemen, came. Macaronies (as dandies were then called) clamoured to get hold of the limited number of engraved invitations. Intellectuals such as Horace Walpole not only deigned to put in an appearance, they thoroughly enjoyed themselves, as we can see from Walpole's letter to Lord Hertford on 25 January 1764: 'The ball last night, at Carlisle House, Soho, was most magnificent: one hundred and fifty men subscribed, at five guineas each, and had each three tickets. All the beauties in town were there, that is, of rank, for there was no bad company. The Duke of Cumberland was there too; and the Hereditary Prince so pleased, and in such spirits, that he stayed till five in the morning.'

The opening in February 1765 of a rival establishment – William Almack's in King Street, St James's – left Mrs Cornelys undaunted. According to Walpole she simply 'enlarged her vast room, and hung it with blue satin, and another with yellow satin; but Almack's room, which is to be ninety feet long, proposes to swallow up both hers'. That summer she advertised a complete refurbishment of her premises which 'will this year alone, amount to little less than 2000*l*. and that, when finished, it will be, by far, the most magnificent place of public entertainment in Europe'. Next, she announced the addition of 'the most curious, singular, and superb ceiling to one of the rooms that was ever executed or even thought of', and soon after this she started to redecorate two rooms in the popular Oriental style – a project which cost her around £5,000. Known as the China or Chinese Rooms, these were linked to the main house by a Chinese bridge, which was probably designed by the cabinet-maker Thomas Chippendale, who also made the furniture. Chippendale, whose workshop was in the neighbouring parish of St Martin-in-the-Fields, was never paid in full; when Theresa went bankrupt in 1772 he was one of her main creditors.

For the present, however, her success was undiminished and, if anything, her assemblies became even more crowded, riotous and lavish than before. On a Saturday night in September 1768, at a ball given at Carlisle House in honour of the King of Denmark's visit to England, more than 2,000 wax candles were burned, and tea was served from specially imported Dresden china. On 27 February 1770, right in the middle of the Wilkes affair, Horace Walpole wrote a letter to Sir Horace Mann describing a fancy-dress ball at which one woman, a Miss Monckton, appeared as an Indian Sultana wearing £30,000 worth of jewellery:

> Our Civil war has been lulled to sleep by a subscription masquerade, for which the House of Commons literally adjourned yesterday. Instead of Fairfaxes and Cromwells, we have had a crowd of Henrys the Eighth, Wolseys, Vandykes, and Harlequins; and because Wilkes was not mask enough, we had a man dressed like him, with a visor, in imitation of his squint, and a cap of liberty on a pole. In short, sixteen or eighteen young lords have given the town a masquerade; and politics, for the last fortnight, were forced to give way to habit makers. The ball was last night at Soho; and, if possible, was more magnificent than the King of Denmark's. The bishops opposed: he of London formally remonstrated to the King, who did not approve it, but could not help him. The consequence was, that four divine vessels belonging to the holy fathers, *alias* their wives, were at this masquerade. Monkey again! A fair widow, who once bore my whole name, and now bears half of it, was there, with one of those whom the newspapers call *great personages* – he dressed like Edward the Fourth, she like Elizabeth Woodville, in grey and pearls, with a black veil. . . The mob was beyond all belief: they held flambeaux to the windows of every coach, and demanded to have the masks pulled off and put on at their pleasure, but with extreme good humour and civility. I was with my Lady Hertford and two of her daughters, in their coach: the mob took me for Lord Hertford, and huzzaed and blessed me! One fellow cried out, 'Are you for Wilkes?' another said, 'Damn you, you fool, what has Wilkes to do with a masquerade?'

With success like this, why did Theresa eventually go bankrupt? To begin with, she was not without her enemies. Her advertisements, overloaded with superlatives as they were, came in for some heavy criticism, like this sarcastic and anonymous letter printed in *The Public Advertiser* in the summer of 1770: 'Sir, – You are desired to inform the public that Mrs. Cornelys's great shew box [sic], which was exhibited on Monday the 13th inst., to the Grown Children of Fashion about this Town, is larger by several square feet that those usually carried about the street, for the Diversion of School-boys and pretty Misses. The figures were large as life, and made to move and look so like Nature,

that they might have been almost mistaken for rational creatures.'

The moral minority, such as it was, disapproved strongly of
some of the licentious goings-on at the assemblies and at a grand
masque the following February 'Colonel L-tt-ll', a mysterious killjoy,
appeared as a corpse in a shroud, complete with a coffin bearing this
warning verse:

> Mortals attend This pale, unseemly spectre,
> Three months ago was plump and stout as Hector.
> Cornelys', Almacks, and the Coterie,
> Caus'd, in the bloom of life, the change you see,
> Oh shun harmonic rout and midnight revel,
> Or you and I shall soon be on a level.

February 1771 was not a good month for Mrs Cornelys. *The
Universal Magazine* claimed that 'a certain Lady not far from
Soho' was being prosecuted because she 'does keep and maintain
a common disorderly house, and did permit and suffer divers
loose, idle, and disorderly persons, as well men as women, to
be, and remain, during the whole night, rioting, and otherwise
misbehaving themselves'. Then she was fined £50 by the courts
for hosting two unlicensed operas in January, a fact which did not
stop her staging a third as soon as she could arrange it, insisting
that this 'Harmonic Meeting' was not for private gain but to raise
money to give coals to the poor, and for 'the benefit of commerce'.
'I concluded she would open a bawdy house next for the interests of
the Foundling Hospital,' wrote Walpole, who reported this latest bit
of Soho scandal in a letter to Sir Horace Mann 'and I was not quite
mistaken, for they say, one of her maids, gained by Mr Hobart*,
affirms that she could not undergo the fatigue of making the beds
so often. At last Mr Hobart informed against her, and the bench
of justices, less soothable by music than Orpheus's beasts, have
pronounced against her. Her Opera is quashed.'

Theresa could always pay fines. But the threat of competition was

---

* Mr Hobart was the manager of the King's Theatre in the Haymarket, an official
opera venue, so he had strong reasons for wanting to put a stop to Mrs Cornelys's
entertainments.

harder to handle. The opening of Almack's had spurred her on to new heights of success, but the dent it made in her business was insignificant compared to that made by the Pantheon. This huge suite of rooms, between Oxford Street and Great Marlborough Street, had been in the planning stages for years, and at one point Mrs Cornelys had negotiated with the landowner, Philip Elias Turst, to run it. But the negotiations had broken down, and Margaretta Ellice, a former employee at Soho Square, had eventually been chosen as a shareholder instead.

The building of the Pantheon, which began in the summer of 1769, took two-and-a-half years to complete, and cost an estimated £37,000. It was designed by architect James Wyatt, and constructed by his brother, Samuel. Both were living in Newport Street, Soho, at the house of their brother John, a surgeon.

When the doors of the Pantheon were thrown open to the public on Monday, 27 January 1772, the full magnificence of its card-rooms, vast tea- and dining-room, and huge classical rotunda with a coffered dome and colonnades, galleries and statues was revealed. 'There were present upwards of seventeen hundred of the first people of this kingdom,' reported *The Gazetteer and New Daily Advertiser*, 'among whom were all the Foreign Ambassadors, the Lord Chancellor, Lord North, Lord Mansfield, Lord and Lady Clive, and eight dukes and duchesses. A foreign Nobleman observed, that it brought to his mind the enchanted Palaces described in the French Romances, which are said to have been raised by the potent wand of some Fairy; and that, indeed, so much were his senses captivated he could scarcely persuade himself but that he trod on fairy ground.'

Though Fanny Burney thought that the Pantheon was more awe-inspiring than conducive to having a good time, Gibbon declared that 'In point of Ennui and Magnificence, the *Pantheon* is the wonder of the XVIII Century and the British Empire.' Even Horace Walpole, who visited the building during its construction, admitted that 'It amazed me myself. Imagine Balbec in all its glory! The pillars are of artificial *giallo antico*. The ceilings, even of the passages, are of the most beautiful stuccos in the best taste of grotesque. The ceilings of the ball-rooms and the panels painted like Raphael's *loggias* in the Vatican. A dome like the Pantheon, glazed . . .' When it burned down in a fire 20 years later Dr

Burney, Fanny's father, eulogized it as 'the most elegant structure in Europe, if not on the Globe'.

Theresa Cornelys's fall was as swift as her rise had been. Nine months after the Pantheon opened, she was bankrupt and in gaol, and her house in Soho Square, 'together with all the rich and elegant Furniture, Decorations, China, etc. thereunto belonging, too well known and universally admired for their Aptness and Taste to require here any Publick and extraordinary Description thereof', was up for auction.

But she was not to be beaten so easily. After a spell in the King's Bench prison, she went to Southampton, where she kept a hotel. Then she reappeared on the London scene in June 1775, when she masterminded a Venetian regatta on the Thames – the first of its kind to be held in London – and the refreshments and management of a fête at Ranelagh. And on 11 December that year, the *London Chronicle* announced that 'Mrs Cornelys seems to be coming into play again. She is once more got into Carlisle House, and is to superintend the masquerade next Wednesday.'

She remained there on and off for several years, probably managing assemblies for the new owners. During this time she tried hard to attract back her old customers with 'superb decorations' and 'illuminations after a new taste', but by now the fickle followers of fashion had deserted her, and her evenings no longer attracted the top people that they once had. Fanny Burney, that 'worshipper of rank', as Leigh Hunt called her, denied ever having been to Carlisle House, when asked to accompany Dr Shepherd there.

Still, Theresa struggled on, even though on one occasion in July 1777, 'there were not however above Fifty Persons in the Rooms till Twelve, and the whole Company did not exceed Three Hundred, many of whom were in their modern Cloaths, with Masks, and some without'.

Theresa's connections with Soho ended the next year, and Carlisle House passed to new owners who attempted to keep the assemblies going without her. When it became clear that the Pantheon had them beaten, they turned Carlisle House into 'an Academy of Sciences and Belles Lettres', with a private library and tuition for foreigners in the 'language, constitution and customs of England'. Mrs Cornelys's Wednesday night masquerades were replaced by meetings of a so-called 'School of Eloquence', consisting of debates on cultural subjects such as 'Whether the art of oratory be or be not of any utility and importance' or 'Is Pride in the Class of the Virtues, or of the Vices?', and political subjects such as 'Whether it will be most conducive to the general good of the Community that the East India Company should be dissolved, or their Charter renewed'.

On Sundays, the rooms were opened up for private receptions or sometimes for evening 'promenades', where, according to the *Journal and Letters* of American tourist Samuel Curwen, 'The employment of the company is simply walking through the rooms; being allowed tea, coffee, chocolate, lemonade, orgeat, negus, milk, etc; admission by ticket, cost, three shillings; dress, decent, full not required; some in boots; one carelessly in spurs happening to catch a lady's flounce, he was obliged to apologise and take them off. The ladies were rigged out in gaudy attire, attended by bucks, bloods and macaronies, though it is also resorted to by persons of irreproachable character.'

These promenades, so dismal-sounding in comparison with the routs and masquerades of previous years, were surprisingly popular for a time, perhaps with more ordinary people who had missed out on seeing Carlisle House during Mrs Cornelys's heyday. On Curwen's visit in November 1780, the house was so thronged with gawpers that 'it was full two hours before I could procure a dish of tea . . . and when served, it was in a slovenly manner on a dirty tea-stand'. He concluded 'I never saw a place of public resort where the company was treated with so little respect by servants.'

Had Mrs Cornelys been dead, she would have been turning in her grave. As it was, she had temporarily slipped into obscurity. But she was to attempt yet another come-back. At the age of 72, she turned up a few miles away in the village of Knightsbridge, where she had taken a house called The Grove, which, with the aid of a few coloured mirrors, she fixed up as a rural equivalent of Carlisle House. In these rather tawdry premises she set herself up as a 'Purveyor of Asses' Milk' – a substance which was to 18th-century health-fanatics what live yogurt is to today's – and advertised fashionable breakfast assemblies and 'a superior style of female archery' in the landscaped gardens.

No one went there. Before long her creditors forced her into the Fleet Prison. As her friend, the actress Becky Wells, recalled in her autobiography *The Life of Mrs Sumbel, late Wells,* 'when Mrs Cornelys was stepping into the carriage to go to prison, she struck her breast against a door, which caused her the most shocking cancer.' She was all alone in the world. Her son was dead. The daughter whom she had adored wanted nothing whatsoever to do with her. Her spirit broke at last, and she died in gaol on 19 August 1797. Becky Wells, who was at her deathbed, reported that she had 'found her sitting up in bed with a large crucifix exclaiming in a voice that denoted the most dreadful horror, "the devil is dragging me down", which she kept constantly repeating, and expired in the most shocking agonies.' It was a pathetic end for a courageous woman who had presided over Soho Square's most glorious days.

As for Carlisle House, it was pulled down in 1791, having been empty for some years, and it was replaced by two more modest mansions. Mrs Cornelys's new building at the back, however, survived to be turned into a Roman Catholic chapel, which was principally used by the poor Irish families who had begun to move into Soho and St Giles.

Exactly 100 years later, the chapel and the house on the corner of Sutton Street were demolished to make way for a brand new Italianate church, the present St Patrick's, which was designed by architect John Kelly. Workmen demolishing the old chapel must have been slightly bewildered when they unearthed this small engraved copper plaque:

> Not vain but grateful In Honour of the Society And my first Protectress Ye Honble Mrs. Elizabeth Chudleigh Is Laid the First Stone of this edifice June 19, 1761 by me Teresa Cornelys.

Right from the start, there had been something about Soho Square which had attracted highly intelligent women. One of its very first residents had been Oliver Cromwell's daughter, Mary, who, with her husband Thomas Belasyse, later the first Earl of Fauconberg, moved into number 20 in 1683, and stayed until her death 30 years later. According to her neighbour, Gilbert Burnet, the Bishop of Salisbury, another square resident, Mary was 'a wise and worthy woman' who 'would have been more likely to hold the post [of Protector] after her father's death than either of her brothers'.

This was a compliment indeed, coming as it did from an arch male-chauvinist like Burnet. For though he married many times (according to Macaulay he specialized in picking 'amorous and opulent widows'), the Bishop had so little respect for the opposite sex that he even tried to persuade Princess Mary of Orange that she should renounce all power in favour of her husband when she succeeded to the English throne, in order to 'lay the foundation of a perfect union between them'.

It was a man's world, and Burnet intended to keep it that way. Still, he admitted that it was said of Oliver Cromwell's children that 'those that wore breeches deserved petticoats better, but if those in petticoats had been in breeches, they would have held faster.' Had Burnet still been around in Mrs Cornelys's day, he would no doubt have been scandalized to witness one French diplomat swim against the tide of public opinion and voluntarily renounce breeches for a life in petticoats, at the same time making sure his name became part of the English language.

The word 'Eonism', first coined by Havelock Ellis, is defined by the *Concise Oxford Dictionary* as 'Transvestism, especially by a man.' But was the Chevalier d'Eon a man who liked dressing up as a woman or a woman who had spent most of her life living as a man?

Christened Charles-Geneviève-Louis-Auguste-André-Timothée d'Eon de Beaumont when he was born in Burgundy, d'Eon was certainly brought up as a boy. After a studious childhood, he became a captain in the dragoons, going on to work as a spy in the service of Louis XV. In the 1750s Louis sent him to the court of the Russian Empress Elizabeth, where he lived so extravagantly – disguised, according to rumour, as a woman – that his expenses added up to some 10,000 livres. His long battle to get this money was to cause a sense of grievance in him against the French government that would form the core of several quarrels with them in later years.

D'Eon first came to London in 1762, to take up a position as secretary to the Duc de Nivernais, who had been appointed as a peace negotiator after the recent Anglo-French war. A small, delicate-featured man with smooth skin, a high voice and sharp blue eyes, d'Eon was a virtuoso swordsman and a brave fighter in battle. He was also extremely touchy and intransigent. As one contemporary wrote of him, 'The shades of his character were most inflexible tenacity of disposition, and a great degree of pride and self-opinion; general distrust and suspicion of others, and violence of temper which could brook no opposition.'

All these difficult traits were kept well-hidden at first, as he settled down to become a diligent worker in the French legation's Mayfair premises. 'D'Eon is at work from morning to night,' Nivernais wrote to the Duc de Praslin, the French Foreign Minister. 'I cannot sufficiently extol his zeal, his vigilance, his activity . . . He is very active, very discreet, never exhibiting curiosity or officiousness; never giving cause for mistrust or acting defiantly, *quod est inveniendum*, because here the majority of men are like the most unmanageable of horses.' In fact, he made himself so indispensable that when Nivernais was recalled to France, d'Eon was appointed Minister Plenipotentiary and left in charge of affairs in England until a new ambassador arrived. As a member of King Louis's secret service – for which he continued to work – d'Eon was trusted with many important secret documents during this time, including a highly confidential plan to invade England after the declaration of peace.

When the new ambassador was appointed, d'Eon was unpleasantly surprised. For he was the Comte de Guerchy, with whom d'Eon had fallen out during a campaign in the Rhineland many years before. The Duc de Broglie, under whom d'Eon had fought in the Rhineland, and who was now head of the French secret service, wrote to d'Eon on 17 May 1763, warning him about de Guerchy: 'I need not speak to you of the new Ambassador with whom you have to do, for it appears to me that you have already formed a pretty correct estimate of his character. I will only add that he is the most astute man I know, and at the same time the most mistrustful; you therefore cannot be too much upon your guard against his suspicious and uneasy disposition.'

Friction between d'Eon and de Guerchy started the moment the new ambassador arrived. Monmouth House had been rented as an embassy, but d'Eon refused to move in there when his new boss did. Instead he continued to lodge in his old rooms in Mayfair, and only put in the odd appearance in Soho Square – usually when de Guerchy was out. The two men quickly became extremely antagonistic towards each other, and in the late autumn of 1763 d'Eon was involved in a very public quarrel with one of de Guerchy's employees, a French adventurer called Peter de Vergy.

At the same time, he became suspicious of everyone and everything which had anything to do with his boss – and with some things that had nothing to do with him at all. For instance, a locksmith came one day to oil the door of his rooms, and d'Eon was convinced that he saw him take a wax impression of the key – presumably to give to de Guerchy. When two of de Guerchy's servants took lodgings in the same house, d'Eon was convinced that they had come there to spy on him. They probably had: their arrival was followed by strange noises in the chimney in the early hours of the morning, which the men claimed not to have heard. D'Eon insisted that de Guerchy had hired a chimney sweep to make the noises, and that he had ordered his men to deny hearing them, in order to get d'Eon certified as a lunatic. To get away from de Guerchy and his lackeys, d'Eon decided to seek sanctuary in Soho, so, in the autumn of 1763, he moved to number 38 Brewer Street, where his cousin and fellow member of the secret service, the Marquis de la Rozière, lodged at the house of a Belgian wine merchant, Monsieur Joseph Lautem.

On Friday, 28 October – a night when de Guerchy was dining with Lord Sandwich – d'Eon made a rare evening visit to Monmouth House. It was to be a memorable occasion for both Frenchmen, for afterwards d'Eon publicly accused the ambassador of trying to poison him.

'After the meal I began to feel unwell and very drowsy,' d'Eon wrote to King Louis soon afterwards. 'On leaving the house, the use of a sedan-chair at the door was offered me, but I refused, preferring to walk home, where, in spite of myself, I fell sound asleep in my armchair.' He eventually went to bed, where he suffered from terrible burning pains in his stomach, and fell into such a deep sleep that he did not wake until midday. From his descriptions it might appear that what d'Eon was suffering from was too much to eat and drink – but he had other ideas. 'I have since discovered,' his letter continued, 'that M. de Guerchy, who has a physician in his house, caused opium to be put into my wine, in the belief that I should fall into a deep sleep after dinner, when I would have been placed in a chair, and instead of being taken to my own home, carried to the Thames, where it appears there was a boat in readiness to take me away.'

This story was not, as it turned out, a paranoid delusion on d'Eon's part, though at first de Guerchy claimed that it was. But then his former henchman, de Vergy, suddenly switched sides, and admitted that he himself had indeed been involved in a plot to drug and kidnap d'Eon that night and drown him in the Thames. The scandal reverberated around London for weeks, to the ambassador's acute embarrassment.

News of the goings-on between the former Minister Plenipotentiary and the new ambassador was quick to reach France, where ministers began to realize that, because of the secret information in d'Eon's possession – not least the plan for a possible French invasion of England – he could easily turn from being a mere nuisance into a dangerous threat. By the time d'Eon wrote from Brewer Street to the French King complaining about the attempt on his life, there were more plans afoot to kidnap him – this time by Praslin, the French Foreign Minister, who had been trying unsuccessfully to get the Chevalier extradited from the Court of St James.

When he got wind of these new plans to kidnap him, d'Eon reacted in an extraordinary way: he turned his lodgings into a fortress manned by troops drawn from his old dragoon regiment. Armed with pistols and sabres, the dragoons kept guard out in Brewer Street, while d'Eon stayed up in his rooms, a hot poker at his fingertips. That was not the worst of it: he mined his study and bedroom, and even the staircase, and threatened to blow up the whole house – and himself with it – if he was attacked.

To de Guerchy it was a declaration of war. Taking up the gauntlet, he publicly announced that d'Eon had been dismissed from his post, and was no longer to be received at Court. He then hired some journalists to write a scurrilous pamphlet claiming that d'Eon was a crazy hermaphrodite – an outlandish claim which rested on d'Eon's apparent lack of interest in sex. In retaliation, d'Eon published a small collection of his confidential correspondence about his fight with de Guerchy, an action which scandalized the whole of society and alienated his former friends, who were not at all pleased to see their private letters to him in print.

D'Eon was becoming desperate. By now he had lost his job and most of his friends, and had run out of money. In a last-ditch attempt to blackmail the French government into settling his long-standing claims over his Russian expenses, he threatened to sell the most secret papers in his possession – including the invasion plan – to the English, an action which might well have resulted in a full-scale war. He also challenged de Guerchy to a duel, an offer which de Guerchy ridiculed.

And so it went on, with accusations and counter-accusations flying across the Channel and between Brewer Street and Soho Square. By now, even the French King realized that d'Eon was 'mad and perhaps dangerous, but there is nothing to be done with the mad except shut them up'. This Louis did by settling a pension of 12,000 livres on him, and appointing him the new and less taxing job of sending home reports on the English political scene.

His pride and his purse both assuaged, d'Eon settled down for the time being, throwing himself into the literary and social life of London. One of his favourite haunts at this time was Carlisle House in King's Square Court, which in 1763 had been bought by yet another of the colourful foreigners who had come to live in Soho: Domenico Angelo Malevolti Tremamondo.

Domenico Angelo, as he was known for short, was a highly skilled Italian swordsman and riding-instructor who had come to London in the early 1750s. His first appointment had been as a riding and fencing master to the young George III, then Prince of Wales, who was at the time living in Savile House, Leicester Square.

Realizing the advantages of staying in a thriving area like Soho, Angelo had purchased the lease of Carlisle House, and announced in *The Public Advertiser* that he intended 'to build a Riding House and Stables upon the large square of the Ground behind it, by Subscription, upon the following terms:- Each Subscriber, upon Payment of Ten Guineas, to be entitled to learn Riding for Two Years, at a Guinea per month of twelve lessons, and to have Two Horses broke without any Expense, further than the Keep of the Horses, if they chuse to keep them in Mr. Angelo's Stables.'

His school of arms and riding at Carlisle House was immensely popular, and the income from it – coupled with fees of 100 guineas for boarders – made Angelo a wealthy man. This allowed him to indulge his love of entertaining, and to gather round his table the cream of London's artistic and literary intelligentsia: musicians Bach and Abel, fresh from their concerts at the other Carlisle House in Soho Square; the Venetian landscape painter Canaletto, who had been enticed to England by promises of work, and lodged in Silver (today Beak) Street between 1749 and 1751; Sir Joshua Reynolds, who had lived in Soho since 1753; Thomas Rowlandson, who had been educated round the corner at the Soho Academy; actors Thomas Sheridan, who lodged briefly in Frith Street, and David Garrick, a resident of nearby Covent Garden; and even the controversial politician John Wilkes. According to Henry Angelo, Domenico's son, who published his *Reminiscences* in 1830, Wilkes, Sheridan and d'Eon were often seated together at his father's table. And Henry remembered one notable occasion when, in the company of the Chevalier and Omai the Otaheitan (a Tahitian who had been brought to London by Soho Square-based scientist Sir Joseph Banks) 'and all three mounted *en cavalier*, with cocked hats, long-tailed horses, and *demie-queue* saddles, we pranced up Oxford-road, to the delight of a number of lookers-on'.

Unlike many of d'Eon's friends, Domenico had not dropped him during his quarrels with de Guerchy, but instead had let him take refuge at the school, where he had given fencing lessons in return for food. D'Eon, Henry Angelo wrote, 'was rather inclined to corpulency', for he was a 'great eater, and *à-la-Français*, I have often observed that he partook of every dish, even if he sent away his plate directly after'.

Was it this tendency to plumpness that made people suddenly begin to question the sex of the beardless, hot-tempered little Frenchman? Or was it the visit to London, in 1769, by Princess Dashkoff, who had known d'Eon at the Russian Court, and who may well have seen him there in his disguise as a woman? Rumours about him seemed to coincide with her visit, for soon afterwards the Chevalier's high-pitched voice, his rounded shape, and his lack of interest in finding himself a wife were being interpreted as signs that he was not, in fact, a man, but a woman who had lived all her life as one.

D'Eon, it turned out, was in no hurry to scotch the rumours. In fact he seemed to enjoy his new notoriety – even to encourage it. 'It is not my fault if I exist such as nature formed me,' he wrote ambiguously to his old friend de Broglie. 'Perfectly or imperfectly formed, I have ever, heart and soul, faithfully served the King, in politics as in war.'

Casanova, who met the Chevalier at the French Embassy in Soho Square, wrote emphatically in later years that he was 'a handsome woman . . . In spite of her manly ways I soon recognised her as a woman; her voice was not that of a *castrato* and her shape was too rounded to be a man's.' If anyone should have been able to tell a man from a woman, it was surely Casanova.

However, the great lover was writing with hindsight. At the time, speculation was rife and London society became obsessed with the true nature of d'Eon's sex. City insurance companies were becoming overloaded with gambling policies on the subject. Soon so much money was at stake that d'Eon was plied with bribes of up to £1,000 a time to literally reveal himself. When he left for France seven years later these policies had been underwritten to the tune of an incredible £120,000.

In letters to the furious French government, to whom the whole business was a further unnecessary embarrassment, d'Eon at first insisted that he was a man. Then, in a sudden volte-face, he confessed that he was really a woman after all. Relieved to have the whole affair over at long last, the French government, represented by Caron de Beaumarchais, agreed that he could return to France, as a woman, without being prosecuted by the authorities over his past behaviour. His future in petticoats was sealed.

His first public London appearance as a woman was on 6 August 1777, when 'Mademoiselle' d'Eon stepped out of number 38 Brewer Street dressed 'in an elegant sack', as one contemporary journal put it, 'her head-dress adorned with diamonds, and bedecked in all the other elegant paraphernalia of her sex'. A week later, as City underwriters were being forced to pay out their dividends, d'Eon left for France. But the crowd gathering in Brewer Street to have a last look at the enigmatic figure were in for a disappointment: for when 'she' walked out of the house and climbed into the waiting post-chaise-and-four, 'she' was not wearing a dress, but her old red and green dragoon uniform complete with the cross of St Louis.

Back in France, it seemed that d'Eon had no intention of living as a woman, even if he was one. However, the French King and government had other ideas, and an order was issued from Versailles on 19 August commanding the 'Chevalière' to 'lay aside the uniform of a dragoon, which he has been in the habit of wearing, and resume the garments of her sex'. A trousseau was duly prepared for him, at the expense of Marie-Antoinette. This did not please d'Eon at all: he wrote to a friend that 'being invested with the character of a female, [I] am forced, in spite of myself, to adopt the vocations and virtues incumbent thereon'. Getting used to wearing women's clothes was extremely hard: 'In the seclusion of my apartment I am forcing myself to become accustomed to my melancholy fate,' he wrote in one letter, 'I am trying to walk in pointed shoes with high heels, but have nearly broken my neck more than once; it has happened that, instead of making a courtesy [sic], I have taken off my wig and three-tiered head-dress, taking them for my hat or my helmet.'

Though a farcical picture, it is also a pathetic one. And La Chevalière was not to become any easier with her female persona in future years. She nearly always signed herself as a man, and, perhaps as a sign of mourning for her former self, 'always dressed in black silk', as Henry Angelo recorded, 'and looked like a woman worn out with age and care'. There were, however, some female habits that d'Eon refused to adopt, for Angelo noted that 'when he dined at our house, though dressed as a woman, when the ladies retired he remained to enjoy the glass and conversation.'

He soon discovered that there were distinct disadvantages in being a woman – one of which was not being able to rejoin the army. 'I must represent to you most humbly and most firmly,' he wrote to the Comte de Maurepas in 1785, 'that the year of my female novitiate having expired, it is impossible for me to continue a profession of that sex. The expenses are beyond my means, and my income is too limited . . . This very sedentary life is completely ruining the elasticity of my body and mind.'

So the 'Chevalière' returned to England, this time for good. Back in her lodgings in Brewer Street, now middle-aged, she scraped together a living by playing chess matches and putting on public fencing displays – either at Angelo's, or in partnership with a famous actress and fencer called Mrs Bateman, who lived on the corner of Carlisle Street and Soho Square. On one occasion, when the Chevalière was nearly 60 years old, she performed an assault at arms with Monsieur de Saint-George at Carlton House in front of the Prince of Wales. A newspaper report stated that 'Mademoiselle d'Eon . . . though encumbered, as she humorously declared herself, with three petticoats, that suited her sex much better than her spirit, not only parried skilfully in all the thrusts of her powerful antagonist, but even touched him by what is termed a *coup de temps*, which all his dexterity could not ward off.'

The French Revolution put an end to d'Eon's pension, and at the same time the small property she had inherited from her family became forfeit to the state. So when, on 26 August 1796, at the age of 67, she was wounded in the armpit during a fencing display at Southampton, she had no income to fall back on. For a time she lived by pawning her diamonds; then, when the money ran out she could not pay her rent, and was evicted from the Brewer Street lodgings she had occupied, as both man and woman, for a total of 33 years. But help was at hand – a Frenchwoman named Mrs Mary Cole took pity on the wounded fencer and brought her to her house in Lambeth, where she nursed her for 11 years. It was a quiet existence, far removed from the violent and exciting days of d'Eon's youth. 'My life,' she wrote, 'is spent in eating, drinking, and sleeping, praying, writing, and at work with Mrs Cole, repairing linen, gowns and head-dresses.'

D'Eon died at 10 p.m. on 21 May 1810, aged 81. During her last years she had been bedridden. Incredibly, she had kept the secret of her sex up to the last. But the truth was not to be buried with the corpse. For when Mrs Cole and the doctor laid the Chevalière out, they were horrified to discover that the old lady was not what she had seemed. Mr T. Copeland, a surgeon who lived in Golden Square, was brought in to perform a post-mortem. 'I hereby certify that I have inspected and dissected the body of the Chevalier d'Eon,' he wrote, 'in the presence of Mr Adair, M. Wilson and Le Père Elysée and have found the male organs in every respect perfectly formed.'

While d'Eon was cramming his feet into crippling high heels in Brewer Street, the most famous woman painter in 18th-century England was rumoured to be struggling into men's breeches in Golden Square, in order to get access to life classes at the newly founded Royal Academy of Art.

'Die Seelen Mahlerin', they dubbed Angelica Kauffman in Germany – the Paintress of Souls. She was born in Switzerland in 1741. When she was 16 years old her mother died, and she began travelling and working with her father, who was a professional artist. But Angelica's skills soon left his far behind, and while they were in Italy, her portraits and copies of the masters attracted the attention of English tourists doing the Grand Tour, including the painter Nathaniel Dance, who developed 'a passionate love' for her.

It is not hard to understand why, for Angelica Kauffman's prodigious talent was coupled with charming manners and striking looks. Count Bernsdorff, the Danish Prime Minister, described her as having 'a most peculiar and most womanly dignity which inspires the utmost respect . . . by no means a beauty, nevertheless *extremely* attractive . . . the features are noble, the expression sweet; it would be impossible to pass such a face without looking at it, and having looked, you must admire, and there are moments when she is absolutely beautiful.'

Enticed by promises of work, the excited 25-year-old artist set off alone for London in the early summer of 1766. From the moment she arrived at Lady Wentworth's house in Charles Street, Mayfair, she caused a sensation. Within weeks she and her paintings were all the rage. The most notable artists in town – including Sir Joshua Reynolds – came to pay homage to her and stayed to become her friends. Commissions fell into her lap. Boswell tells of Johnson sitting for his portrait to Reynold's 'sister', even though Johnson thought 'public practice of any art . . . and staring in men's faces, is very indelicate in a female'.

Angelica Kauffman was fêted everywhere and by everyone. Garrick honoured her when she visited Drury Lane. Poems were dedicated to her, including this one in *The Public Advertiser*:

> While Fair Angelica, with matchless grace,
> Paints Conway's lovely form and Stanhope's face,
> Our hearts to beauty willing hommage pay,
> We praise, admire, and gaze our souls away.

Within 12 months of her arrival, Kauffman had become the most popular portrait painter in London, with the sole exception of Reynolds. She was even patronized by the royals – George III's eldest sister, Princess Augusta of Brunswick, commissioned a portrait from her early in the year. With her paintings so much in demand, she could afford to charge top prices, and was soon asking up to 20 guineas a head. Before long she had earned enough money to hire two servants of her own and to rent a large house in Soho, which was at the time fast becoming the most popular place in London for artists to live and exhibit their work.

Golden Square, built nearly 80 years earlier, was still one of Soho's smartest areas. It was 'a very handsome open place' as John Strype had described it in his *A Survey of the Cities of London and Westminster* (1720), 'railed round and gravelled within, having very good houses inhabited by gentry on all sides'. Angelica's occupancy of number 16 now brought it an added popularity, for day and night the street in front of her house was jammed with carriages bringing admirers and sitters to her studio.

Kauffman was elated by her phenomenal success. 'No other painter has ever received such an honour!' she wrote ecstatically to her father when Princess Augusta returned to Golden Square, bringing her mother and the Princess of Wales with her. When, in the summer of 1767, Angelica brought her father over to London to live with her, her life could not have been better. She was young, beautiful, talented, popular and now rich and successful. But, as in most Soho stories, she was not to have an easy future: that very autumn, love was to rear a very ugly head.

So far, Soho had not proved a particularly happy place for marriages. For proof of that, one need only think of Dryden's epitaph for his wife. In life, when Mrs Dryden had complained that her husband paid so little attention to her that she wished she was a book, he had replied, 'Pray, my dear, if you ever do become a book let it be an almanack, for then I shall change you every year.' Bishop Gilbert Burnet had not been an exemplary husband either. He deserted his first wife – a 'peevish and bitter' woman, as he called her – when she was on her deathbed, and married his second wife when the first Mrs Burnet was barely cold in her grave. This is not to suggest that all the blame for bad relationships between the sexes lay with the men: when Alexander Pope declared his passionate love for Lady Mary Wortley Montagu, the famous letter-writer who lived at number 10 Soho Square during the 1740s, she burst into such a peal of derisive laughter that he became her deadly enemy from that moment on.

Still, Sohoites were not without their passionate love affairs: the Irish actress Peg Woofington, who lived at number 78 Dean Street, was involved in a scandalous *ménage à trois* with actors David Garrick and Charles Macklin. And the district had already seen several famous elopements. Way back in the late 1660s, it had been reported that 'Lady Ann Knollys, daughter of the Earl of Banbury, is missing from her grandmother's, the Countess of Portland, at Newport House, having it is believed been conveyed thence by a young gentleman of Dorsetshire named Fry.' It is hoped that the marriage was a happy one, because for marrying Fry without her grandmother's consent, Lady Ann later lost her right to inherit the entire Newport estate. More recently Jane Thornhill, the daughter of painter Sir James, had estranged herself from her father by running off with his erstwhile apprentice, William Hogarth, probably from the Thornhills' house at 75 Dean Street. The Hogarths later settled in Leicester Square, but at the time of the elopement William was just starting out as an engraver, and Sir James considered the marriage beneath his daughter. At first he refused to see the couple. Later, favourably impressed by some of his son-in-law's work, and realizing that he was suitable husband material after all, father, apprentice and daughter were reunited.

But few Soho marriages, either before or since, have been as disastrous as Angelica Kauffman's. It was to leave deep emotional scars on her, ruin her financially – and, but for her own well-deserved popularity, would have ruined her reputation as well.

The quiet, handsome foreigner to whom Miss Kauffman lost her heart in the autumn of 1767 introduced himself as Count Frederick de Horn, and she had no reason to disbelieve him. In a series of conversations – always held in private – he told her about his distinguished military career and his aristocratic and wealthy Swedish family. He also confided to her that he was, like herself, a Roman Catholic, and this shared secret drew them closer together.

Within a few weeks of their first meeting, Frederick proposed to Angelica, and said that they should marry very soon – in fact, as soon as a large amount of money he was expecting from his family arrived. When it did, he promised, he would formally ask Angelica's father for her hand in marriage. Until then, they should keep their betrothal a complete secret.

A few days later, Frederick turned up at Golden Square in a terrible state. When Angelica asked him what was wrong, he confessed that he had been implicated in a conspiracy against the King of Sweden, and that he was in imminent danger of being extradited to face a trial that would probably end with his death.

He could see no way of saving himself – except one: if Angelica married him straight away the English royal family, with whom she had become a favourite, might intercede on his behalf. He was not forcing her to marry him now, he insisted, the choice was entirely hers. 'But you must decide secretly, and at once,' he told her. 'Either we marry immediately, or I am lost forever.'

It was blatant emotional blackmail. And Angelica fell for it. The two of them slipped out of the house to a nearby Roman Catholic chapel – very possibly the one belonging to the Portuguese Embassy behind Golden Square – where they were married. Later, they were to have a more public Anglican ceremony at St James's church, Piccadilly. But for the first few weeks Frederick insisted that their marriage should be kept secret, even from his new father-in-law, until his funds arrived.

Day after day passed, and still no money came from Frederick's relatives. Anxious though she was to tell her father that she was married, Angelica faithfully held to her promise of secrecy. Then, after three weeks, during which she had supported her new husband to the tune of a great deal of money that she could ill afford, the charming quiet foreigner she had married suddenly changed into a domineering tyrant who announced that, since he was her husband, *he* would manage all her financial affairs from now on.

Meanwhile, Kauffman Senior was becoming extremely suspicious of the stranger who had been hanging around his daughter's studio. When Frederick admitted to him that he and Angelica were married, and that in future he intended to take charge of her hard-earned cash, the poor man was horrified. He asked Horn for some sort of security pledge, but none arrived, and Horn refused to discuss the matter any further.

By this time Kauffman was more than a little anxious for his daughter, and he and some of his friends started to make enquiries of their own concerning the identity of the so-called Count. When Frederick found out, he threw Kauffman's friends out of the house, and, turning on Angelica, furiously forbade her ever to see her father again. Then he packed his own bags and ordered Angelica to pack hers too: they were both leaving London for good, he told her. She had no choice in the matter. She was his wife, and as such she must do whatever he said.

Distraught, Angelica fled to her father. Now the bevy of influential friends whom Horn had once claimed would intervene to stop his extradition, united against him. Enquiries were made abroad about him, and a letter was written challenging him to defend his high-handed behaviour. Horn's unconvincing reply finally convinced Angelica of the awful truth – she had been taken in by a pack of lies, and married an out-and-out con-man.

Yet what could she do about it when, by law, she was bound to obey him, and all her property was legally his? With moral support from her father, Angelica confronted Frederick and told him that she refused to live with him until the matter of his identity was cleared up. Whereupon Frederick flew off the handle, and, after a series of terrible rages, seized his hat and stormed out into Golden Square with the parting words, 'You will see who I am, you will regret your insolent behaviour!'

Horn's dramatic departure was followed by a visit from his lawyer, who demanded that Angelica join her husband immediately so that he could resume his financial and marital rights over her. If she would not obey him, the lawyer said, Frederick demanded a formal separation from her – and a lump-sum payment of £500.

One might have thought it was worth the money to get rid of Frederick. But since he had already spent a large chunk of her savings, Angelica refused to pay him off, and told the lawyer he would have to take legal action if he wanted money. Before the matter came to court, however, her friends' enquiries on the Continent turned up news about her husband's identity: he was not Count Frederick de Horn, but a former valet in the real Count Frederick's service. He was, in fact, a con-man, known by different names in The Hague, Hamburg and Breslau. On top of that he was already married.

At last 'Horn' was running scared. But he was not to give up his bigamous rights over Angelica's property without a final struggle. In February 1768 he agreed to relinquish his claims over her in an out-of-court settlement of £300. Relieved to be rid of him at last, Angelica threw herself back into her work, in an attempt to restore her depleted bank balance. And she resumed the name Kauffman, which thence forward she would never give up, even when she married for a second, and happier, time.

4

Artists and Artisans

'I have visited many painters,' Angelica Kauffman had written to her father when she first arrived in London, 'but Mr Reynolds is the finest of them all, a very great master.'

Miss Kauffman and Sir Joshua, the two most famous portrait painters in London, soon became such close friends that marriage between them was even rumoured to be on the cards, and Angelica's few enemies claimed that she had jilted love-lorn Nathaniel Dance in the hope of marrying the more successful painter.

Generous, endlessly good-natured, kind and wealthy, Sir Joshua Reynolds was, in his friend Dr Johnson's words, 'the man with whom, if you should quarrel, you will find the most difficult ever to abuse'. Without doubt he was the most eligible bachelor in London's artistic circle, and gossips were constantly linking his name with one lady or another. Fanny Burney was also said to have been after him, but she ended up by marrying a penniless French general called D'Arblay, so giving her new surname to what had once been Soho's Portland Street.

With as many as seven sitters a day, booked in and out of his studio with the precision of doctors' patients, Reynolds did not have time for a wife, even if he had wanted one. Ever since he had arrived in Soho from Plymouth in 1753, first lodging in St Martin's Lane and later taking a large house near Newport Market in Great Newport Street, his career had gone from strength to strength. By 1760, his position required an even grander home, and he had moved to number 47 Leicester Fields, where he was to stay for the rest of his life.

Though a sizeable house on the west side of the square, number 47 was not nearly big enough for Reynolds's professional needs, and he was 'obliged to be at the further expense of 1500*l*. for a detached gallery, painting rooms, and such other conveniences as his extensive concerns required'. The heart of this network of reception and work areas was the studio itself, a modest octagonal room measuring about 20 feet by 16 feet, with one single small window raised nine feet up on one wall.

Reynolds's habits were not as low-key as his studio would have one believe. Parked outside the house was his magnificent coach, which had gilded wheels and wooden panels carved to represent the four seasons. His role as a host was legendary. His sister, who kept house for him, was in charge of a dining table at which there were frequently so many last-minute guests that there were not enough plates, cutlery or food to go round, and those who did not shout for their meal might well end up with nothing to eat. Dinner parties were held in the ground floor front room of the Leicester Fields house, and notables present might include Dr Samuel Johnson and James Boswell, Hannah More, David Garrick, Oliver Goldsmith, Angelica Kauffman and Fanny Burney – whose novel, *Evelina, or a Young Lady's Entrance into the World*, had absorbed Reynolds so much that he had refused to put it down even during mealtimes, and had apparently had to be spoon-fed by his sister while turning the pages.

When Fanny first dined at Reynolds's house, she felt quite intimidated by the exalted company, but she soon relaxed, for Reynolds always took great care to put his guests at their ease. Indeed, quarrels between members of the literati were often patched up at his house. Reynolds suffered – or rather enjoyed – a convenient deafness, and if the conversation began to bore him he would simply lower his ear-trumpet, smile benignly, and let the others get on with it.

There was another brilliant artist who lived in Leicester Fields – or Square, as the area was now becoming known: William Hogarth, who lived at number 30 from 1733 until his death in 1764, four years after Reynolds moved in across the square. Brought up in Smithfield, near the City – and in the grim confines of the Fleet Prison, where his father was imprisoned for debt, as a young boy Hogarth was apprenticed to a goldsmith, Ellis Gamble, who lived just south of Leicester Fields, in Blue Cross Street (currently Orange Street). In 1720, after serving his apprenticeship, he set up as an independent engraver, working from a room, or rooms, 'at ye Golden Ball ye Corner of Cranbone Alley little Newport Street', close to where his two sisters kept a small linen-draper's shop.

The cocky Cockney painter was the antithesis of his charming neighbour, Reynolds. Barely five feet tall, he had piercing eyes and a dent in his bulbous forehead caused by a childhood accident. He dressed plainly – he never wore wigs or fancy hats – and spoke with unfashionable frankness. Yet he was an outspoken and highly intelligent man with an original, lively mind, and a good sense of humour – all of which enabled him, at the age of 31, to sweep off her feet a good-looking 19-year-old bride – Jane, the daughter of Sir James Thornhill. In 1733, four years after their elopement, the couple moved from their lodgings in Covent Garden to number 30 Leicester Fields. It was here, at the sign of the 'Golden Head' – a gilded likeness of Van Dyck which Hogarth carved out of cork and hung outside his door – that the Hogarths lived for the next 31 years, and where the artist produced his most famous works.

Portrait-painting was, as Hogarth said himself, 'the chief branch of the art by which a painter can procure himself a tolerable livelihood and the only one by which a lover of money can get a fortune'. However, despite the financial rewards, he himself had no intention of becoming a 'phizmonger', as he called the fashionable portrait painters who, like Sir Godfrey Kneller, sketched in the outlines of their sitters, and left it to a factory of 'drapery men' to fill in the rest. Hogarth was ambitious for something more than money – he wanted to show people, and life, as they really were.

Then, as now, London was a city of vivid contrasts: of elegance and squalor, excess and starvation, wealth and poverty; and the bustling taverns and streets of the City, Covent Garden and the West End became Hogarth's direct inspiration, and the backdrop to many of his satirical engravings and paintings. *Gin Lane* is set against the spire of St George's, Bloomsbury; *Morning* – one of a series called *The Four Times of Day* – in Covent Garden's Piazza. But though many of his Leicester Fields neighbours appeared as characters in his engravings, only one of his prints provides us with a glimpse of 18th-century Soho: the 1738 engraving *Noon*, which shows a group of well-dressed parishioners emerging from l'Église des Grecs, the French church in Hog Lane.

In 1757, the controversial artist was appointed serjeant-painter to the King. Seven years later, on 25 October 1764, he died in his house in Leicester Square. His coffin was carried from there to St Nicolas's church in what was then the fishing village of Chiswick, where he and Jane had had a country villa since 1749.

Hogarth had always been strongly opposed to the foundation of a Royal Academy of art, which he saw as benefiting no one but a few salaried professors. It was not until 1768, four years after his death, that the Royal Academy was eventually founded, and its president was none other than Sir Joshua Reynolds, who had been persuaded to take the job after a two-hour conversation in his studio with Benjamin West – the artist who, incidentally, painted the reredos of Soho's parish church.

The foundation of the Royal Academy was the culmination of a great flowering of the arts in England. Long gone was the philistinism of the days of George I. As Reynolds said in his opening address to the Academy, 'There are at this time a greater number of excellent artists than were ever known before at one period in this nation.'

He might well have said, 'in Soho', for during the latter half of the 18th century and the early years of the 19th century, the area was, quite simply, the centre of artistic life. Never can there have there been so many skilled craftsmen, painters and sculptors working in one place at one time. The skills brought to England by the Huguenots in the late 17th century now showed themselves in hundreds of workshops – by the middle of the century almost every street had its master clockmaker, jeweller, toymaker or goldsmith. Some of the finest tapestries of the day – 'Soho tapestries' as they are still known – were woven in the Dean Street area, many in the popular Chinoiserie and Arabesque styles.

Reynolds, Hogarth and Kauffman were but three of the fine artists working in Soho. A glance at the rate books throws up literally hundreds more names of painters and sculptors who were either living or showing their work there. Some were English-born; others were visiting foreigners who, like Canaletto, had been lured over to London with promises of patronage by the gentry.

Johann Zoffany lived on the corner of Soho Square and Frith Street, and later in Great Newport Street. The painter Joseph Francis Nollekens lived at 29 Dean Street, where his miserly son, Joseph, the sculptor, was born in 1737. Cipriani lodged for a time in Whitcomb Street (as the southern tip of Wardour Street was called). Sculptor John Flaxman lived in 27 Poland Street and after the marriage which, according to Reynolds, would leave him 'ruined for an artist' he moved to a 'modest mansion' in Wardour Street.

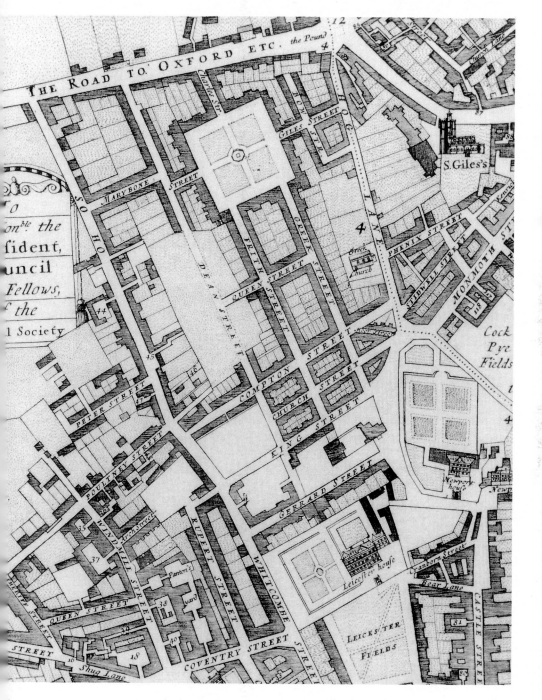

Detail of William Morgan's map of 1681-2.

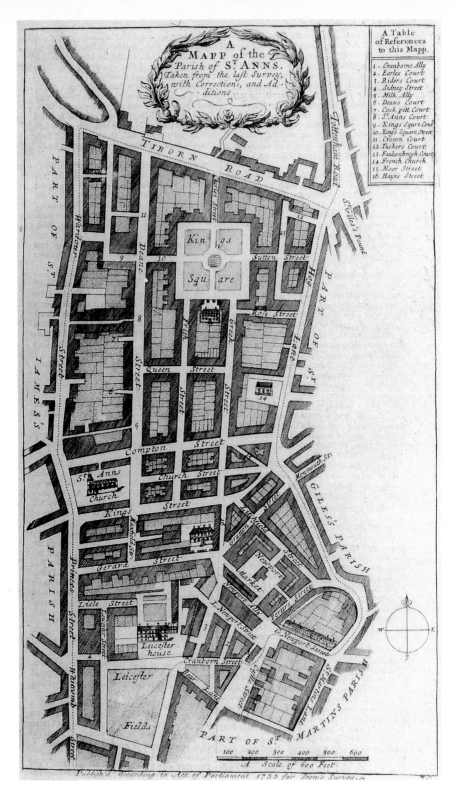

Blome's map of the Parish of St Anne, c.1690.

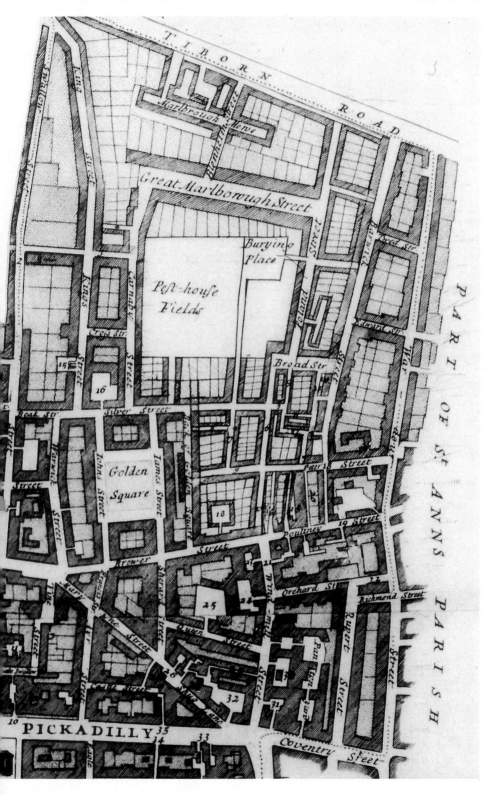

Detail of Blome's map of the Parish of St James, c.1720.

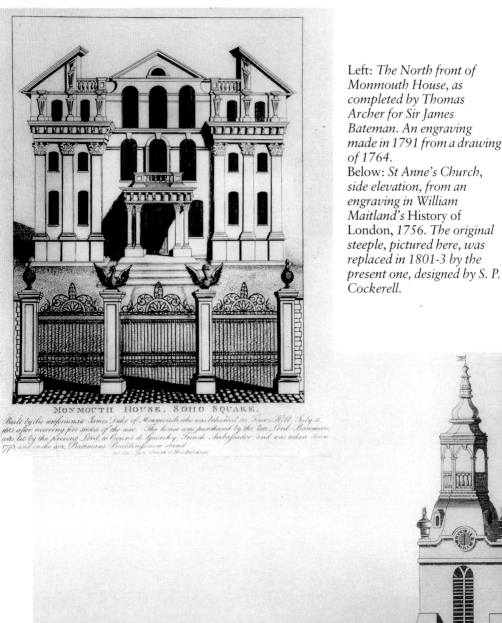

MONMOUTH HOUSE, SOHO SQUARE.

Built by the unfortunate James Duke of Monmouth who was beheaded on Tower Hill, July 15. 1685 after receiving five strokes of the axe. The house was purchased by the late Lord Bateman was let by the present Lord, to Count de Guerchy, French Ambassador, and was taken down 1773, and in the site, Bateman's Buildings now stand.

Pub: Jan. 1. 1791 by J. Smith, G.Moor Buildings.

Left: *The North front of Monmouth House, as completed by Thomas Archer for Sir James Bateman. An engraving made in 1791 from a drawing of 1764.*
Below: *St Anne's Church, side elevation, from an engraving in William Maitland's* History of London, *1756. The original steeple, pictured here, was replaced in 1801-3 by the present one, designed by S. P. Cockerell.*

'Noon', an engraving made in 1738 by William Hogarth, depicting a group of
parishioners leaving the French (originally the Greek) Church in Hog Lane.
Even in those days, Soho inns boasted 'Good Eating'. In the background is
the steeple of the church of St Giles-in-the-Fields.

Soho or King's Square in 1754 (from an earlier engraving c.1727), looking north. The windmill at the top of Rathbone Place pumped water to the base of Charles II's statue. On the east side of the square, on the south corner with Sutton Street, is the house that later became Mrs Cornelys's Assembly Rooms.

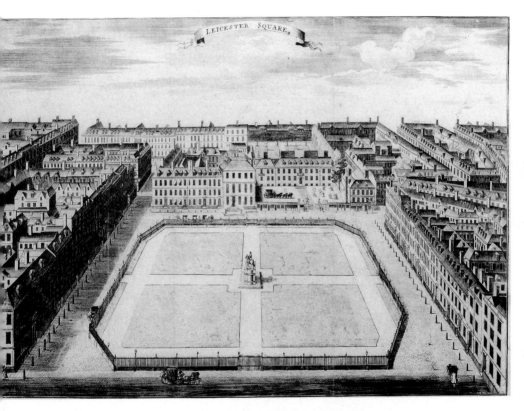

Leicester Square in the mid-18th century, looking north. Leicester House, home of the Prince of Wales, is set back from the street and guarded by soldiers. To its left, with steps leading up to the door, is Savile (also called Ailesbury) House.

The Chevalier d'Eon.
Right: *As an old woman, in a sketch by Condé, c.1793-4.*
Below: *In a contemporary cartoon.*

MADEMOISELLE de BEAUMONT, or the
CHEVALIER D'EON.
Female Minister Plenipo. Capt. of Dragoons &c. &c.

Revelry at Carlisle House, Soho Square, in the 1760s. The bare-breasted woman is Mrs Elizabeth Chudleigh, the bigamous Duchess of Kingston and one of Theresa Cornelys's patrons. She is pictured here at a masquerade, clad as Iphigenia, the legendary Greek heroine.

A masquerade at Mrs Cornelys's Assembly Rooms, Carlisle House, in the latter half of the 18th century. The engraving was accompanied by a satirical poem, which began:

> '*Here, may the Wand'ring Eye with pleasure See*
> *Both Knaves and Fools in borrow'd shapes agree;*
> *Here Lords and Ladies wave their wonted pride,*
> *And walk with Jilts and Bullies, side by side.*'

The Pantheon, Oxford Street, shown here during a display of Mr Lunardi's Balloon in 1784. Built in 1769-72 to the designs of architect James Wyatt, the Pantheon put Theresa Cornelys out of business in a matter of months.

'The Unpleasant Rencontre', designed and etched by D. T. Egerton in 1825. A client of the brothel known as Hooper's Hotel, in Soho Square, is surprised by his wife and her servant as he leaves by a discreet side-door on to Sutton Street.

THE UNPLEASANT RENCONTRE

Design'd & Etch'd by D. T. Egerton.

Some Ladies are so fastidious, that should they stumble on their Lord and master elect as he is stealing out of the Temple of Venus, they might cease to treat him with their former cordiality and perhaps talk of postponing the happy day; this bore encreases in proportion to the Lady's weighty recommendations, and as far as you have succeeded in keeping at bay a host of daily visitors by the prospect of shortly being united to an Heiress.

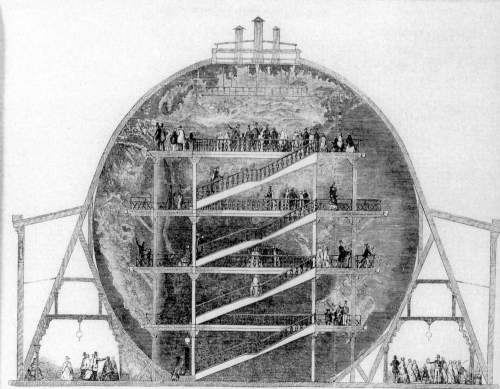

MR. WYLD'S MODEL OF THE EARTH.—SECTIONAL VIEW.—(SEE NEXT PAGE.)

ASCOT RACE PLATE.

THE three Cups, or groups, contended for in the past week, at Ascot, are fine specimens of modelling and construction, and will support the reputation of their respective artists.

The principal prize, the EMPEROR OF RUSSIA'S VASE, is modelled by Mr. Cotterill, and manufactured by Messrs. Garrard, goldsmiths to the

Crown, Haymarket. It is a shell-shaped cistern, or wine-cooler, supported on scrolls, which rest on a base of ebony ; the surmounting group being a sledge attacked by wolves. The composition is remarkably fine, and the execution alike meritorious.

The QUEEN'S GOLD CUP is by the same artist and manufacturers. It is a group of travellers in the desert, at their place of repose for the evening, a camel and its driver, and a Turkish horseman, whose Arab steed is displaying his characteristic antipathy to the camel.

The ROYAL HUNT CUP, the third prize, is from a design of Mr. Brown, manufactured at the establishment of Messrs. Hunt and Roskell (successors to Storr and Mortimer), New Bond-street, goldsmiths and silversmiths to her Majesty. It is a cup of the Italian school, and surmounted with a Highland deer-stalker and his dog : the vase is rated with oak, and bears a group of stags ; and at the foot are a bloodhound, staghound, and greyhound. The whole is cleverly modelled and ably executed in silver.

Opposite: *Wyld's Monster Globe, Leicester Square: an exterior view and, below it, a cross-section from* The Illustrated London News, *1851.*
Above: *Berwick Street market in 1926.*

The corner of Old Compton Street and Dean Street on 11 May 1941, showing the damage inflicted by a 1,000-kilogram high-explosive bomb which dropped in the small hours of that morning, during the last big raid of the Blitz. Four people were killed in the blast, and St Anne's Church, which had been partially destroyed in a raid eight months earlier, was damaged still further.

Canaletto lodged in Silver (currently Beak) Street, at the house of a cabinet-maker called Mr Wiggan, where he invited his patrons to come and see his *View of St James's Park*. Painters Thomas Rowlandson and J.M.W. Turner were both educated at the Soho Academy in Soho Square. Rowlandson later exhibited his work from number 4 Church (currently Romilly) Street.

These are but a handful of artists' names, selected from hundreds which crowd the rate books. If they were all to be honoured, nearly every house from Greek Street to Glasshouse Street would boast its own Blue Plaque.

Of all the artists, both foreign and British, who moved in and out of Soho during the late 18th century, a baby who was to prove by far the greatest genius was born above a shop in Broad (currently Broadwick) Street on 28 November 1757. The third in a family of five children, he would spend all but a few years of his early life within a stone's throw of his birthplace, and he would pluck his inspiration as much from the turbulent streets and times he lived in as from his infinitely imaginative and fertile mind.

William Blake and his family were very much local people. His mother, Catherine Harmitage, had lived at 28 Broad Street, a house on the corner of Carnaby Market, since at least 1748. The man she married, James Blake, was from Rotherhithe, but at the time of his marriage he, too, was living in Soho, with his brother John, at number 5 Glasshouse Street.

Here Catherine joined him after their wedding. After the birth of their first son, James, the couple moved back to the Harmitage family home in Broad Street, where James Blake Senior set up his hosiery business. Two more births followed at two-yearly intervals: another boy, who, it appears, died in infancy, and William, in 1757.

Despite his father's dissenting views, William was baptized in the local church, St James's, Piccadilly, as were his brothers and, later, his sister. Almost as soon as he could talk, his parents realized that they had a 'problem child' on their hands. For, unlike his prosaic older sibling, William was so sensitive – to things like the lowing of the cattle in Carnaby market's slaughterhouses, and the half-buried corpses in the nearby graveyard – that he was even excused the brutalizing influence of going to school.

Instead, he became a solitary wanderer who was allowed to spend his time exactly as he wanted to, and to educate himself. He read whatever he felt like reading – contemporary writers such as Rowley and Chatterton, as well as Shakespeare and the Elizabethans. He walked all over the metropolis: through Soho's network of houses, stables and craftsmen's and artists' studios into Covent Garden, Whitehall and the City, and across London or Westminster bridges into the countryside south of the Thames. It was there, on Peckham Rye, in fact, that he had his first mystical vision – of a tree filled with angels. He was about nine years old at the time. When he told his parents what he had seen, his father, not surprisingly, accused him of telling lies, and threatened to thrash him – an incident which has been used to cast the poor man as some glowering tyrant instead of the indulgent parent that he really was. In the end, Catherine Blake intervened on her son's behalf, and William was not punished at all.

Other visions followed – including angelic figures wandering through a group of hay-makers, and, more disturbingly, God's face pressed against the window of the Broad Street house. By the time that his younger brother Robert was born, it was clear that 10-year-old William was a child of extraordinary gifts, both visionary and artistic. Though he did not have a lot of money to spare, James Blake enrolled William at Mr Henry Pars's drawing school in the Strand, where for the next four years he learned to sketch from 'plaster casts after the antique'. At the same time, he became a regular visitor to the local artists' studios, sale-rooms and auction houses where, presumably with more financial help from his father, he began to purchase a small portfolio of prints.

What were the Blakes to do with their outspoken, unruly, mystical child? One thing was clear: he was not going to go into the family hosiery business. His future obviously lay in becoming some kind of artist. Ever indulgent, they offered to have him trained as a painter in a local studio, but the painter in question wanted so much money to take him on that William declined on the grounds that he did not want his brothers and sister to suffer on his behalf. In the end it was decided that he should be apprenticed to an engraver, and his father introduced William to a suitable craftsman, a man named William Wynne Ryland.

Blake's first meeting with his prospective employer sparked off the first of his prophetic visions: afterwards, he told his father that 'it looks as if he will live to be hanged'. Twelve years later, Ryland earned himself a place in posterity by being the last man to be hanged at Tyburn. His crime was forging bills of exchange on the East India Company – an engraving skill that might have come in useful in Blake's poorer days.

Eventually William was apprenticed to a well-known topographical and antiquarian engraver called James Basire, with whom he lived and worked for the next seven years in Great Queen Street, Lincoln's Inn Fields. Blake did not always get on with his fellow apprentices, and to get him out of their way Basire sent him to sketch in Westminster Abbey, where Blake absorbed a love of Gothic architecture and had another important vision: of the aisles and galleries filled with monks, priests and censer-bearers, while the roof shook to the sound of imaginary organ music, chanting and chorale.

Having visions was not without its disadvantages. 'I am not ashamed, afraid, or averse to tell you, what Ought to be Told,' he would write to his friend Thomas Butts in 1802, 'that I am under the direction of Messengers from Heaven, Daily & Nightly; but the nature of such things is not, as some suppose, without trouble or care. Temptations are on the right hand & left; behind, the sea of time & space roars & follows swiftly; he who keeps not right onward is lost, & if our footsteps slide in clay, how can we do otherwise than fear & tremble?'

When he left Basire, 21-year-old Blake set up in business as a journeyman engraver, at the same time enrolling himself as a student at the Royal Academy schools, where he studied drawing under the Keeper, George Michael Moser. It was here that he fell out with the art establishment for the first time, as he later noted: 'I was once looking over the Prints from Rafael and Michael Angelo in the Library of the Royal Academy Moser came to me & said You should not Study these old Hard Stiff & Dry Unfinished Works of Art. Stay a little & I will shew you what you shuld Study He then went & took down Le Bruns & Rubens's Galleries How I did secretly rage. I also spoke my Mind . . . I said to Moser, These things that you call Finished are not Even Begun how can they then, be Finished? The Man who does not know The Beginning, never can know the End of Art.'

Blake also crossed swords with the Royal Academy's president, Sir Joshua Reynolds, after calling on him in his studio in Leicester Fields with a small portfolio of work. Reynolds made the mistake of suggesting certain improvements in Blake's style, and Blake never forgave him.

Though it was already clear that, in his work at least, Blake was a loner intent on going his own way, he was not immune to the pleasures of city life. He had made good friends among Soho's artistic circle: with painter and illustrator Thomas Stothard, who lived in a street adjoining Newport Market; with sculptor John Flaxman, who lived round the corner in Poland Street and was working in Josiah Wedgwood's Greek Street showrooms to earn money; with Henry Fuseli, who lodged in Cranbourn Street and later in Broad Street; and with two future patrons, the Reverend A.S. Mathew and his intellectual wife Harriet, in whose house in Rathbone Place, just north of Oxford Street, Blake was, according to writer J.T. Smith, 'listened to by the company with profound silence, and allowed by most of the visitors to possess original and extraordinary merit'.

Despite these friendships, Blake was nothing short of a revolutionary in his attitude to the art world. The Royal Academy's contempt for his chosen profession – engraving – was to alienate him from it. What mattered most to him was content. He had little time for the mannerism of decorative and portrait art. 'The Enquiry in England is not whether a man has Talents & Genius,' he would one day write in answer to Reynolds's *Discourses* to the Royal Academy, 'but whether he is Passive & Polite & a Virtuous Ass & obedient to Noblemen's Opinions in Art & Science. If he is, he is a Good Man. If Not, he must be Starved. Liberality! we want not Liberality. We want a fair Price & Proportionate Value & a General Demand for Art.'

Blake's work was as much inspired by politics as by his visions. He mixed in radical circles, and was friendly with so-called 'seditious' publishers. Over the years, his circle of friends included radicals such as Tom Paine, William Godwin and Mary Wollstonecraft. However, he always kept himself apart from political movements – for instance, though he hated slavery, he never actually joined the anti-slavery movement.

The years of his youth were particularly turbulent times in England. Revolution in America, a shortage of corn, the unpopularity of the King, and the revolutionary changes in industrial production and village life had all led to an explosive situation which culminated in the Gordon Riots of June 1780. The catalyst to the riots was Lord George Gordon's petition to repeal the Roman Catholic Relief Act, which had liberalized the laws against members of the Roman Catholic church. The riots themselves affected Blake and Soho in a way neither place nor person ever forgot.

On 2 June 1780, the day that the Whig Suffrage Bill – another unpopular measure – was going through Parliament, a crowd of 60,000 of Lord Gordon's supporters assembled at St George's Fields and marched on Westminster. That night they descended on Soho, where they ransacked the Roman Catholic chapels belonging to the foreign legations; among others, the chapel in Glasshouse Street belonging to the Portuguese Ambassador was set on fire and almost destroyed.

After a night on the razzle, the rioters turned their anger on houses belonging to magistrates, clergymen and even the Lord Chief Justice Lord Mansfield, whose London home was burned to the ground. A party of armed rioters even set off to destroy Mansfield's country home, Kenwood House near Highgate, but fortunately they never arrived: when they stopped to work up some courage at the nearby Spaniards inn, the inn-keeper managed to get them drunk, and while they were quietly sleeping he sent for help. When they came to, the hung-over rioters were all arrested.

Back in Soho, 'a large mob of riotous persons' descended on Savile House in Leicester Fields on 5 June. The mansion where George III had been brought up was currently the home of Sir George Savile, who had introduced the Roman Catholic Relief Bill into Parliament two years before. According to *The London Evening Post* the mob broke in, 'gutted the best part of the furniture, which they piled up in the street, and set fire to'. Twenty-four hours later they were back, 'intoxicated with the wines and spirituous liquors they had plundered', and attacked what was left of the house.

Meanwhile, on the 6th, Blake himself had been caught up in the most dramatic scene of mob rule London has ever witnessed. Along with the poet George Crabbe, he was swept up in the front ranks of a huge crowd which surged along Holborn towards Newgate Prison, where the roof was torn off, the building was set fire to and hundreds of prisoners were released.

On the 7th, the rioters went too far – they turned their attention on the Mansion House and that holy of holies, the Bank of England.

At last, armed troops were called out, and the riots were quelled, though not without bloodshed. More than 300 rioters were killed, and hundreds more were wounded. Many of those arrested were tried in the Turk's Head tavern in Gerrard Street, which during the riots had become the impromptu headquarters of the local magistrates.

Soon Blake was occupied by more mundane matters than revolution, when he became involved with 'a lively little girl' called Polly Wood. Unfortunately for Blake, her intentions were not nearly as serious as his. When they were taking a stroll round the neighbourhood one day, he accused her of making eyes at another man, and she replied brusquely, 'Are you a fool?'

This no-nonsense brush-off may indeed have cured Blake of jealousy, as he later claimed, but it also sent his sensitive soul into a sharp decline. He became ill, and was sent to recuperate to Kew, in Richmond, where he lodged with a market gardener by the name of Boutcher or Boucher. Boutcher and his wife had a very pretty brown-haired daughter called Catherine, to whom Blake related the lamentable saga of his rejection by Polly Wood. She was apparently so distressed by the story of unrequited love that Blake suddenly said, 'Do you pity me?' She answered, 'Yes indeed I do.' 'Then I love you,' Blake said. And that was that – the beginning and end of a 12-word, whirlwind courtship. The couple were married a year later, by which time Blake had made enough money to keep Miss Boutcher in the – luckily – simple style to which she was accustomed, in lodgings in Green Street, off Leicester Fields.

Blake's 'beloved Kate', as he called her, was well-suited to her husband. They shared a love of walking in the country, and a propensity to visions: the very first time Kate saw William she nearly fainted, so she later told her friends, recognizing him for the husband he would later become. She had considerable artistic talent, too, and once he had taught her to read, write and draw, she worked closely with him at all times – in fact, it was said that their drawings were indistinguishable. She was so dedicated to him that she wore herself out – 'I never saw a woman so changed,' said one friend after not seeing her for seven years.

When his father died in July 1784, two years after the marriage, Blake moved back to Broad Street, this time to number 27, where he opened a print shop with his friend and erstwhile fellow-apprentice, James Parker. The Blake family were prospering. In fact, they were taking over the neighbourhood. William's elder brother James had remained next door at number 28, the old family home, where he ran the hosiery business. Another brother, John, had moved across the road to number 29, where he had opened a bakery. When young Robert, William's favourite brother, joined him as an apprentice, the circle was complete – the whole family were employed in three different professions in three houses in the same street.

A print shop was 'a rare bird' in London, as Blake said himself, and the firm of Parker & Blake did not do very well. A year after they had moved into Broad Street, William and Kate gave up their rooms above the shop, which Parker kept on, and moved round the corner to number 28 Poland Street, where they took lodgings in a narrow house which backed on to a timber yard. Its main advantage seems to have been that it was near the King's Arms pub, which was the haunt of artists and the birthplace of the revived Druid movement which was to inspire Blake in later years.

'Always be ready to speak your mind, and a base man will avoid you,' wrote Blake in *The Marriage of Heaven and Hell*, which he published in 1790. However, his belief in free speech did not seem to extend to his wife. When she quarrelled with his brother Robert one day, William flew off the handle and ordered her to 'Kneel down and beg Robert's pardon directly, or you never see my face again.' She objected, but did as she was asked, getting down on her knees and saying, 'Robert, I beg your pardon, I am in the wrong.' At which Robert accused her of lying, and insisted that he had been wrong all the time.

Gallant Robert was too good to live. At the age of 19 he became fatally ill. For a fortnight William nursed him day and night, not once going to bed himself. When Robert eventually died, William claimed he saw his spirit rise through the ceiling 'clapping its hands for joy'. The whole experience so exhausted him that he immediately fell asleep for three days and three nights.

Robert often reappeared to Blake in visions, in one of which he told Blake the details of a technical process – relief etching – with which he could reproduce his poems and designs. The next day, Kate went out shopping with their last half-crown and bought the finest materials she could. They cost her a total of 1s.

10d. – an investment that paid off throughout the rest of their lives.

After a short flirtation with the Swedenborgian church, Blake became disillusioned with Soho life and moved south of the river to Lambeth, where he prospered for the first time. Ten years later he moved even further out – to a thatched cottage in Felpham, Sussex, of which he wrote to Flaxman, 'No other-formed house can ever please me so well.' But though he found Felpham more 'spiritual' than London, living in the country had its drawbacks, and three years later he returned to his brother James's house in Broad Street, taking rooms soon afterwards in South Molton Street, on the edge of Mayfair.

Financially, leaving Lambeth was a great mistake for Blake. But money had never been a high priority with him. He despised the capitalist society in which he lived, a society in which, as he wrote, 'Christian Charity is held out as a Motive to encourage a Blockhead, & he is Counted the Greatest genius who can sell a Good-for-Nothing Commodity for a Great Price.' A revolutionary, visionary, poet and painter, he was above all a man of genius – something that was recognized, though not rewarded, in his own lifetime.

From South Molton Street, he and Kate moved to a two-roomed first-floor tenement in Fountain Court, just off the Strand, where from one of the windows the Blakes could just catch a glimpse of the Thames, which shone, so William said, 'like a bar of gold'. Though small and poorly furnished, the rooms were neat and clean, and became a meeting place for their friends and admirers. 'There was a strange expansion and sensation of freedom in those two rooms very seldom felt elsewhere,' one of them later told Blake's biographer Gilchrist.

Blake was not a materialist. As he wrote in 1820, for him 'The Whole Business of Man is the Arts.' Five years later, he expanded this in a conversation to Henry Crabb Robinson, which Robinson later recorded, in his *Reminiscences*, published in 1852.

He spoke with Seeming complacency of himself – Said he 'acted by command' [-] The Spirits said to him 'Blake be an artist & nothing else. In this there is felicity.' His eye glistend while he spoke of the joy of devoting himself solely to divine art – [']Art is inspiration[.]

When Michael Angelo or Raphael or Mr Flaxman does any of his fine things he does them in the spirit[.'] Bl said ['] shd be sorry if I had any earthly fame for whatever natural glory a man has is so much detracted from his spiritual glory[.] I wish to do nothing for profit. I wish to live for art – I want nothing what[ever.] I am quite happy[.']

William Blake died as remarkably as he had lived, as his friend of 40 years' standing, J.T. Smith, recorded. On 12 August 1827, 'he composed and uttered songs to his Maker so sweetly to the ear of his Catherine, that when she stood to hear him, he, looking upon her most affectionately, said, "My beloved, they are not mine – no – they are not mine." He expired at six in the evening,' Smith concluded, 'with the most cheerful serenity.' He was buried in the nonconformists' cemetery at Bunhill Fields.

As Blake had probably found out by the time he left for Lambeth, Soho is not an ideal place for a writer to work. For life in Soho is meant to be lived to the full, not recorded for the benefit of posterity. Apart from the myriad distractions of living in a place where so much is going on, and where the temptations to leave one's desk are so great, it is simply too noisy a place to get down to the solitary business of writing.

There had never been peace and quiet in Soho since the days when the back window of Dryden's house overlooked the silent orchards in the Earl of Leicester's garden. As James Boswell discovered on 1 April 1775, when he tried to sleep off a hangover in his Gerrard Street lodgings ('at Mr Goodwin's, a tailor . . . a very neat first floor at sixteen shillings'), it was impossible to have a lie-in in Soho, for, like it or not, one was woken by the sound of street-sellers shouting their wares, the clatter of carriages on cobblestones, or the steady beat of hammer on anvil which rang out from scores of Huguenot metal workshops.

Still, Soho – and in particular, its restaurants, taverns and bars – has been a magnet to the literati since Johnson and Reynolds started their literary club at the Turk's Head tavern, number 9 Gerrard Street.

The idea for The Club, as it was simply known, came to the two men while they were sitting at Reynolds's Leicester Fields fireside in 1764. The Club met weekly at seven o'clock on Monday nights, and the members sat up talking till the early hours of the morning. The original members included Oliver Goldsmith and statesman and philosopher Edmund Burke, who grew to like Gerrard Street so much that he later came to live there. David Garrick, Sir Joseph Banks and James Boswell also all eventually joined the élite membership. After the Turk's Head was closed down in 1783, The Club moved to new premises at Prince's, in Sackville Street.

The lodgings which Edmund Burke took at number 37, just down the road from the Turk's Head, were overlooked by those of J.T. Smith, who lodged on the opposite side of Gerrard Street. 'Many a time when I had no inclination to go to bed at the dawn of day,' Smith recollected in *A Book for a Rainy Day*, 'I have looked down from my window to see whether the author of the "Sublime and Beautiful" had left his drawing-room, where I had seen that great orator during many a night after he had left the House of Commons, seated at a table covered with papers, attended by an amenuensis who sat opposite to him.'

Four years after The Club was founded, 12-year-old Fanny Burney penned the first entry in her diary from her family's home at number 50 Poland Street. 'Addressed to a Certain Miss Nobody,' the opening page set out Fanny's aims: 'To have some account of my thoughts, manners, acquaintance and actions, when the hour arrives in which time is more nimble than memory, is the reason which induces me to keep a Journal. A Journal in which I must confess my *every* thought, must open my whole heart!'

Despite the fact that her mother died while the family were living there, Fanny adored number 50, which she called 'this ever dear house, in charming London'. Walking down Poland Street on 4 November 1771 – exactly a year she had moved to Queen's Square, Bloomsbury – she remembered it as 'a place I cannot but love, from remembring [sic] the happiness I have known there'.

Fanny's second Soho home was Sir Isaac Newton's former house, in St Martin's Street, on the south side of Leicester Square. In 1774, when she moved in, Fanny snobbishly wrote in her diary that it was 'an odious street – but well situated, and nearly in the centre of the town; and the house is a large and good one. It was built by Sir Isaac Newton! and, when he constructed it, it stood in Leicester *Fields*, not *Square*, that he might have his observatory unannoyed by neighbouring houses, and his observatory is my favourite sitting place, where I can retire to read or write any of my private fancies or vagaries.'

One of these 'vagaries' was *Evelina*, the epistolary novel that shot Fanny into the limelight. When it was first published in 1778 it was claimed that its author was only 17 years old. However, since Fanny was born in King's Lynn, Norfolk, on 13 June 1752, she must have been at least 22 before she had written a word of it.

The poet Percy Bysshe Shelley was 19 years old when he drifted into Soho in the spring of 1811, shortly after he and his friend Thomas Jefferson Hogg had been sent down from Oxford University – Shelley for writing a pamphlet called *The Necessity of Atheism*, and Hogg for supporting him. Like the Burneys, Shelley stayed in Poland Street, to which he was initially attracted by its name: according to Hogg, it 'reminded him of Thaddeus of Warsaw and freedom', and Shelley swore he would stay there even if it meant sleeping on a doorstep. The Thaddeus referred to was presumably Thaddeus Kosciusko, the Polish patriot, who had lodged in the Sablonnier Hotel, Leicester Square, in May 1797.

Hogg had been following his friend in and out of London lodging-houses for hours, for Shelley was extremely fussy about where he stayed: even an unfortunate noise in the street could put him off a place. So Hogg was extremely relieved to see a notice in the window of a house on the corner of Noel Street, advertising rooms to rent. Even now 'Shelley took some objection to the exterior of the house,' Hogg noted with some alarm, 'but we went in, and this time auspiciously.'

Hogg continued, in his biography of the poet, *The Life of Percy Bysshe Shelley*:

There was a back sitting-room on the first floor, somewhat dark, but quiet, yet quietness was not the principal attraction. The walls of the room had lately been covered with trellised paper; in those days it was not common. There were trellises, vine-leaves with their tendrils, and huge clusters of grapes, green and purple, all represented in lively colours. This was delightful; he went close up to the wall and touched it: 'We must stay here; stay for ever!' There was some debate about a second bedroom, and the authorities were consulted below; he was quite uneasy, and eyed the cheerful paper wistfully during the consultation. We might have another bedroom; it was upstairs. That room, of course, was to be mine. Shelley had the bedroom opening out of the sitting-room; this also was overspread with the trellised paper. He touched the wall and admired it.

'Do grapes really grow in that manner anywhere?'

'Yes, I believe they do!'

'We will go and see them then, soon; we will go together!'

'Then we shall not stay here for ever!'

As it turned out, Shelley tired of the wallpaper very quickly, and 'forever' only lasted a few weeks. While they were there, he penned a truculent, not to say obnoxious, letter to his father, who was obviously anxious to know what his son was going to do with himself in the future.

My dear Father, As you do me the honour of requesting to hear the determination of my mind, as the basis of your future actions, I feel it my duty, although it gives me pain to wound 'the sense of duty to your own character, to that of your family, and feelings as a Christian', decidedly to refuse my assent to both the proposals in your letter, and to affirm that similar refusals will always be the fate of similar requests. With many thanks for your great kindness – I remain, your affectionate, dutiful son, Percy B. Shelley.

Hogg wrote a wonderful description of his friend charging excitedly around the Soho streets: 'When he felt hungry, he would dash into the first baker's shop, buy a loaf, and rush out again, bearing it under his arm, and he strode onwards in his rapid course, breaking off pieces of bread and swallowing them.' Shelley made this chewed-up dough into a sort of makeshift bread pudding by buying 'common pudding raisins' which he bought loose from a local grocery shop, stuffed into his pockets, and threw into his mouth at the same time as the bread.

William Hazlitt's stay in Soho was not very much longer than Shelley's. He moved into number 6 Frith Street early in 1830, and died a few months later, on 18 September, aged 52. He was buried in St Anne's churchyard. The cause of his death was some kind of gastric disease, caused either by cholera or by drinking too much tea, which Hazlitt was addicted to.

While he was in the house, Hazlitt wrote a number of essays, including one prophetically titled *The Sick Chamber*. His visitors described with amazement how he would carry on writing in their presence, 'with wonderful ease and facility of pen, going on as if writing an ordinary letter. His usual manuscript was clear and unblotted, indicating great readiness and sureness in writing, as though requiring no erasures or interlining.'

However, this natural writer was not to be envied in any way. His life was full of professional and personal disappointments, and he was prone to terrible bouts of depression. His friends could hardly believe that his very last words were, 'Well, I've had a happy life,' especially since only a few months previously he had written, 'My public and private hopes have been left in ruins or remain only to mock me.' Would he be cheered up to know that his name lives on in Frith Street, where his former digs have been turned into a luxury hotel called Hazlitt's?

A distraction that Soho writers have always faced is music – be it from harpsichords, violins, pianos, barrel-organs, saxophones, ghetto-blasters or the tuneless songs of the blind drunk. From the earliest times, some of the finest musical instrument makers in London had premises in the area – which also had its fair share of concert rooms. The Turk's Head tavern in Gerrard Street, known, in an earlier incarnation, as the Romer tavern, was one of the area's earliest music venues. It was visited in 1710 by visiting tourist, Z.C. von Uffenbach, who recorded that 'the host, a Frenchman called Binet, holds a weekly concert', which took place in 'a large room with a small apartment adjoining it where there hung a great quantity of choice musical instruments'.

George Frederick Handel, Court Composer to George II, lived in Brook Street, Mayfair, but many of his late oratorios were played 'at the Great House in Thrift-street, Soho, (late the Venetian Ambassador's)'. The Great Room, as it was also known, backed on to Dean Street, occupying part of the site where the West End Great Synagogue now stands, and it may well have been converted from the Venetian Ambassador's chapel. It was certainly as draughty as a church, for in 1751, about a year after it had opened, advertisements were assuring the public that 'the Room will be disposed in the most convenient and elegant Manner for the Reception of the Company, and kept in proper Warmth by the Help of a German Stove, to prevent them from catching Cold'.

Another famous musical venue was Hickford's Rooms in Brewer Street, which was *the* main concert hall in London during the mid-18th century. It was here that the first public London performance by 'the greatest wonder of which Europe or the world can boast' was due to take place on 17 May 1764. This concert was put off until 22 May, probably because of the wonder's ill-health. For once the advertisements had not overstated their case – the star was none other than Wolfgang Amadeus Mozart, then only eight years old.

The Mozart family – Wolfgang, his parents and his sister, who was a musical genius herself – had arrived in London three weeks earlier, and had taken rooms in Cecil Court, just off St Martin's Lane, at the house of a haircutter called Mr Cousin. 'In London, everyone seems to me to be in fancy dress,' Mozart Senior wrote home doubtfully after venturing out into the West End for the first time.

His tone changed as soon as he realized just how much money he could make. A performance put on for George III and Queen Charlotte at St James's Palace on 27 April – during which Wolfgang was petted on the Queen's knee – was rewarded by a double payment of 24 guineas. 'If this happens every three or four weeks, we can put up with it!' Leopold Mozart remarked gleefully.

After yet another cancellation, the Mozart family's first public concert eventually took place on 5 June, the day after the King's birthday, and, as Leopold reported afterwards, 'not only all the ambassadors, but the principal families in England attended it and everyone was delighted'. Leopold had made a fortune out of the event: 'I have had another shock,' he wrote to a friend in Salzburg, 'that is, the shock of taking in one hundred guineas in three hours. Fortunately it is now over.' Since the hire of the hall and musicians had only cost him 20 guineas, he had made a huge profit of nearly £80.

By late September, after a short stint away from the West End, the money-making musical circus was back, this time in Frith Street, where the Mozarts took rooms at number 20, the house of a staymaker named Williamson. It is to be hoped that Williamson and his neighbours appreciated good music, for here Mozart composed several works, including duets for him to play with his sister, and here, the following spring, the public were invited to put their talents to the test.

> Mr Mozart [began the announcement that appeared in May], the father of the celebrated young musical Family, who have so justly raised the Admiration of the greatest Musicians of Europe, proposes to give the Public an Opportunity of hearing these young Prodigies perform both in public and private, by giving on the 13th of this month a Concert, which will be chiefly conducted by his son, a boy of Eight years of Age, with all the overtures of his own composition. Tickets may be had at 5s. each of Mr. Mozart, at Mr Williamson's in Thrift Street, Soho, where Ladies and Gentlemen will find the Family at home every day in the week from 12 till 2 o'clock, and have an opportunity of putting his talents to a more particular proof by giving him anything to play at sight, or any Music without a Bass which he will write upon the spot without recurring to his harpsichord.

One of the harpsichords played by the pint-sized genius at the concert on 13 May was a special one made for the King of Prussia by a local musical instrument maker, Burckhardt Tschudi, who had premises in Meard Street. Tschudi apparently 'rejoiced that his extraordinary instrument be played for the first time by the most extraordinary performer in the world'.

The French inventor and violin-maker Joseph Merlin – he who had broken a £500 mirror at one of Theresa Cornelys's assemblies – may possibly have tuned the boy wonder's piano while the family were lodging in Frith Street, or even provided him with a violin. Merlin, who was in the employment of the Spanish Embassy in Soho Square, had invented a violin of his own, which he used to play while racing around the legation's headquarters on his roller skates. Merlin eventually opened a shop on Oxford Street where all his inventions were on sale. These included a piano that converted into a work-table, a wheelchair for gout-sufferers, and a Heath Robinson-esque 'tea-table, where the housewife can open and close the cock of the tea-urn with her feet and rotate the table-disk to pour out the cups and thus send tea and sugar the round'.

The proximity of Soho to Covent Garden and the West End theatres made the cheap rooms and hotels of early 19th-century

Golden Square ideal *pieds-à-terre* for foreign musicians who came to London looking for work – a situation which Charles Dickens evocatively described in *Nicholas Nickleby*:

> Two or three violins and a wind instrument from the Opera band reside within its precincts. Its boarding-houses are musical, and the notes of pianos and harps float in the evening time round the head of the mournful statue, the guardian genius of a little wilderness of shrubs, in the centre of the square. On a summer's night, windows are thrown open, and groups of swarthy mustachioed men are seen by the passer-by, lounging at the casements and smoking fearfully. Sounds of gruff voices practising vocal music invade the evening's silence; and the fumes of choice tobacco scent the air. There, snuff and cigars, and German pipes and flutes, and violins, and violincellos divide the supremacy between them. It is the region of song and smoke. Street bands are on their mettle in Golden Square; and itinerant glee-singers quaver involuntarily as they raise their voices within its boundaries.

Visiting musicians and composers from overseas also congregated in Soho. Franz Liszt lodged in Great Marlborough Street in 1840, and he liked it so much that he returned to the same house the following year. And in August 1839, the same year as *Nicholas Nickleby* was published, Richard Wagner and his wife found cheap lodgings with a sea-captain's wife in Old Compton Street. They arrived in London with the score of *The Flying Dutchman*, which Wagner was then working on, and their 'very large' dog, Robber. Unlike his owners, however, Robber was not impressed with Old Compton Street, and as soon as the Wagners stepped inside the lodging-house he made off on his own towards Oxford Street. Consequently, the couple's first hours in Soho were spent with their noses pressed against the window, anxiously awaiting their best friend's return. Eventually 'we joyfully recognised Robber', Wagner later wrote, 'strolling unconcernedly towards the house from a side street'.

But life was not all lost dogs, libretti and literature in Soho. During their stay in Old Compton Street, the Wagners were so poor that they could barely afford to eat. They were not alone in their poverty. As the 18th century drew to a close, it was becoming clear that the area was radically changing – and changing for the worse.

The rich had long since deserted Soho for Mayfair. In the last three decades of the century all its grandest buildings had disappeared. Gerard House in Gerrard Street was split up into two sections. Monmouth House, which had become a school, was demolished in 1773. Both Leicester House and Mrs Cornelys's Temple of Festivities were pulled down in 1791.

Slowly but surely, the infrastructure of Soho was crumbling. The large family estates once belonging to the Leicester, Portland, Pulteney, Newport and Pitt families were broken up in the 1780s, when the freeholds of individual houses were sold off to scores of private landlords. By the late 1790s, even the artistic world had had enough of Soho, and was drifting north to Fitzrovia or west to Marylebone.

Realizing that there was no chance of enticing so-called desirable residents back, the new owners let their properties fall into decay, or subdivided them into cheap tenement rooms. Though the number of houses stayed constant, the population of the area soared.

5

Downhill All the Way

There had always been poverty in Soho. Few of its foreign residents had arrived with money in their pockets. Like all immigrants before and since, they had to work extremely hard for their success. And though some had achieved it, beyond their wildest expectations – Domenico Angelo, Angelica Kauffman, Leopold Mozart, to name but three – others had found it hard, or impossible, to make ends meet.

The King of Corsica was one such penniless foreigner – though his stay in Soho was a very short one. Born Theodore Anthony Neuhoff, he had spent his youth travelling round Europe – first as a page in the service of the Duchess of Orléans, later as an adventurer. At one point he even sold his wife's jewels in order to pay off his debts.

He ended up in Genoa, at a time when the republic was at war with the island of Corsica. Fired by sympathy for the Corsican prisoners of war he met there, he determined to become their saviour, and set sail for their island with a cargo of 4,000 muskets to help them fight off the Genoese. The islanders were so impressed by his grand arrival that they invited him to become their King, an offer which he naturally accepted. He was duly crowned with a garland of laurel and oak leaves.

After a short reign, the Corsicans lost confidence in him, and he was forced to leave the island under a cloud. He eventually came to London, where he soon got into debt and ended up in the King's Bench Prison. He managed to get himself freed only by registering 'his kingdom of Corsica for the use of his creditors'. Horace Walpole told the story of what happened next in a letter to Sir Horace Mann: 'As soon as Theodore was at liberty he took a chair and went to the Portuguese minister, but did not find him at home; not having sixpence to pay, he prevailed on the chairman to carry him to a tailor he knew in Soho, whom he prevailed upon to harbour him, but he fell sick the next day, and died in three more.'

Theodore died on 11 December 1756, and the kind tailor, who lived in Chapel Street, was now landed with his corpse. Luckily, an oilman from Compton Street called John Wright volunteered to pay for the 'King's' burial, and a grand tombstone was erected at Walpole's expense, bearing the following inscription penned by Walpole himself.

> The grave, great teacher, to a level brings
> Heroes and beggars, galley-slaves and kings.
> But Theodore this moral learn'd e'er dead;
> Fate pour'd its lesson on his living head,
> Bestow'd a kingdom, and denied him bread.

The threat of bankruptcy haunted ordinary people. The penalties were incredibly harsh, ranging from death by hanging to transportation to the colonies and unlimited imprisonment. Still, to make money one had to spend it first, and in doing so one ran a serious risk of getting into debt, as Mrs Cornelys had found out to her cost. For, despite the popularity of her assemblies, the contents of Carlisle House had been seized several times under distress warrants – even in 1762 and 1763, two of her most successful years. Her aura of wealth had in fact been a façade. As Casanova had reported, she 'who seemed to be living so luxuriously . . . was in reality poverty-stricken' and Sunday was 'the only day on which Madame Cornelys could go abroad without fear of the bailiff'.

Still, in the 18th century Soho had for the most part been a thriving area of prosperous people, and what poverty there was had been limited and somewhat picturesque. Standards had been kept up, even by the penniless but enterprising *trompe l'oeil* artist Capitsoldi, who, because he could not afford to buy any furniture for his Warwick Street lodgings, 'proceeded to paint chairs, pictures and window curtains on the walls of his sitting room . . . so admirably executed that, with an actual table and a couple of real chairs, he was able to entertain on occasion a friend in an apartment that appeared adequately furnished'.

By the time philosopher Thomas De Quincey arrived in London in 1802, the cast of Soho's poverty had changed and the area was well on the way to becoming what the Reverend Cardwell, vicar of St Anne's, would one day call 'a prolific place for suicides'.

A gifted child from a comfortably-off family, Thomas De Quincey was from birth 'an intellectual creature: and intellectual in the highest sense my pursuits and pleasures have been, even from my schoolboy days', as he wrote of himself. He was a brilliant scholar, who by the age of 15 'not only composed Greek verses in lyric metres, but could converse in Greek fluently and without embarrassment'. Yet he suffered from what he called a 'chronic passion of anxiety' coupled with a rebellious temperament which drove him away from respectability and towards the hidden underbelly of life. By the age of 17 he had had enough of his grammar school in Manchester, and after quarrelling with one of his guardians, who demanded 'unconditional submission' from him, he did what many thousands of teenagers before and since have done: he ran away and dropped out.

His first stop was Wales. Then, when he had spent most of the allowance his mother had given him, he came to London, a city which, then as now, exerted a gravitational pull on the young and disaffected. Here he ended up practically penniless and almost starving, at the offices of an attorney and money-lender known sometimes as Mr Brown and at other times as Mr Brunell, whose premises were on the east corner of Greek Street and Soho Square.

> The house [De Quincey wrote in his *Confessions of an English Opium Eater*] was not in itself, supposing that its face had been washed now and then, at all disrespectable. But it wore an unhappy countenance of gloom and unsocial fretfulness, due in reality to the long neglect of painting, cleansing, and in some instances of repairing . . . the deep silence that invested the house, not only from the absence of all visitors, but also of the common household functionaries, bakers, butchers, beer-carriers, sufficiently accounted for the desolation, by suggesting an excuse not strictly true – viz., that it might be tenantless.

Through Brown's office, De Quincey applied for the loan of a small sum of money, and while he waited for it to arrive he eked out a meagre existence while lodging in a nearby boarding house. A couple of months later he was penniless. Rather than let the boy sleep out in the cold streets, Brown gave him permission to stay in the empty rooms above the office.

The building which De Quincey entered at dusk that first evening evokes a vivid picture of a Soho house at a poignant turning point in the area's history:

Unoccupied, I call it, for there was no household or establishment in it; nor any furniture, indeed, except a table, and a few chairs. But I found, on taking possession of my new quarters, that the house already contained one single inmate, a poor, friendless child, apparently ten years old; but she seemed hunger bitten; and sufferings of that sort often make children look older than they are. From this forlorn child I learned, that she had slept and lived there alone for some time before I came: and great joy the poor creature expressed, when she found that I was, in future, to be her companion through the hours of darkness. The house was large; and, from the want of furniture, the noise of the rats made a prodigious echoing on the spacious staircase and hall; and, amidst the real fleshly ills of cold, and, I fear, hunger, the forsaken child had found leisure to suffer still more (it appeared) from the self-created one of ghosts. I promised her protection against all ghosts whatsoever! but alas! I could offer her no other assistance. We lay upon the floor, with a bundle of cursed law papers for a pillow: but with no other covering than a sort of large horseman's cloak . . . The poor child crept close to me for warmth, and for security against her ghostly enemies. When I was not more than usually ill, I took her in my arms, so that, in general, she was tolerably warm, and often slept when I could not.

If it had not been for Brown's love of classical literature, De Quincey would probably have starved to death during the following weeks. As it was, Brown, though 'one of those anomalous practitioners in lower departments of the law' who himself lived 'in constant fear of bailiffs', loved intelligent company, and De Quincey kept himself alive by walking in on Brown while he was breakfasting downstairs, chatting to him 'and, with an air of as much indifference as I could assume, took up such fragments as he had left'.

By day, De Quincey wandered the streets of the West End, weak, sleepless and almost delirious through lack of food. When he was too exhausted to keep moving, he would sit for a while in some doorway, before being moved on by the watchmen whose business it was to keep up the tone of the neighbourhood. It was at this time that he got to know some of the scores of prostitutes who had already begun to frequent Soho and the parish of St Giles. In these 'sisters in calamity' he found what he felt was missing from the more prosperous echelons of society: 'humanity, disinterested generosity, courage that would not falter in defence of the helpless, and fidelity that would have scorned to take bribes for betraying'.

Among these 'female peripatetics', as De Quincey called them, was one who grew special to him – a destitute, timid and friendless 15-year-old girl whom he called his 'noble-minded Ann'. Night after night they wandered the cold, inhospitable streets of the West End together. Then, De Quincey reported,

> One night when we were pacing slowly along Oxford-street, and after a day in which I had felt more than usually ill and faint, I requested her to turn off with me into Soho-square: thither we went; and we sat down on the steps of a house, which, to this hour, I never pass without a pang of grief, and an inner act of hommage to the spirit of that unhappy girl, in memory of the noble action which she there performed. Suddenly, as we sat, I grew much worse: I had been leaning my head against her bosom; and all at once I sank from her arms and fell backwards on the steps. From the sensations I then had, I felt an inner conviction of the liveliest kind that without some powerful and reviving stimulus, I should either have died on the spot – or should at least have sunk to a point of exhaustion from which all re-ascent under my friendless circumstances would soon have become hopeless. Then it was, at this crisis of my fate, that my poor orphan companion – who had herself met with little but injuries in this world – stretched out a saving hand to me. Uttering a cry of terror, but without a moment's delay, she ran off into Oxford-street, and in less time than could be imagined, returned to me with a glass of port wine and spices, that acted upon my empty stomach, (which at that time would have rejected all solid food) with an instantaneous power of restoration: and for this glass the generous girl without a murmur paid out of her own humble purse at a time – be it remembered! – when she had scarcely the wherewithal to purchase the bare necessaries of life, and when she could have no reason to expect that I should ever be able to reimburse her.

Prostitutes were well-known in Soho. One of its earliest residents had been 'a lewd woman' named Anna Clerke, who in 1641 was bound over to keep the peace after 'threteninge to burne the houses at So:ho'. Anna's presence was followed by that of high-class courtesans like Elizabeth Price, a resident of Frith Street, described as 'a Player and mistress to several persons', and Elizabeth Flint, 'generally slut and drunkard; occasionally whore and thief', who had lived in 'genteel lodgings' in Meard Street in the 1750s, along with her spinnet and a servant-boy 'that walked before her chair'.

Attitudes towards prostitution in the 17th and 18th centuries were not governed by the hypocrisy which was to become endemic in Victorian society. Mistresses were openly acknowledged, and prostitutes could operate freely where they chose to. It was even said in the 18th century that 'their business is so far from being considered as unlawful, that the list of those who are in any way eminent in this profession is publicly cried about the streets: the list, which is very numerous, points out their places of abode, and gives . . . the several qualifications for which they are remarkable. A new one is published every year, and sold under the piazza of Covent garden, with the title of *The New Atlantis*.'

The licentious goings-on at Carlisle House were legendary. And, by the late 1770s, its neighbour, the old Spanish Embassy, had become a notorious high-class brothel, known both as The White House or Hooper's Hotel, after its proprietor, Thomas Hooper. The wealthy and noble-born Londoners who frequented Hooper's included 'Old Q', the Duke of Queensberry, and George, Prince of Wales. Clients entered the building discreetly through a side door in Sutton Street, and each room inside was named and decorated in a different style. There was a Silver, a Gold and a Bronze room, each inlaid with mirrors in appropriate colours; a Painted Chamber; a Grotto; and a Skeleton Room, where a mechanical skeleton leaped out of a closet. Since the brothel later got a mention in a book called *The Mysteries of Flagellation*, it seems that all sorts of sexual tastes were catered for in these theme rooms. The mind boggles as to what went on in The Coal Hole.

By the time De Quincey befriended Ann, the fun and games had gone out of commercial sex. Prostitution was no longer a respected profession by which women could earn money and position, but a matter of dire necessity for thousands of destitute young girls and women with no other means of support. Over the weeks he knew her, De Quincey discovered that his 'youthful benefactrice' had been forced into her way of life, having lost what little property she had to a 'brutal ruffian'. Her desperate story of victimization was by no means atypical. There was no one she could turn to for help. 'The stream of London charity,' De Quincey reflected, 'flows in a channel which, though deep and mighty, is yet noiseless and underground; not obvious or readily accessible to poor houseless wanderers: and it cannot be denied that the outside air and frame-work of London society is harsh, cruel and repulsive.'

The Industrial Revolution and the Napoleonic Wars had brought a huge drift of country people to the metropolis. Cut off from their rural roots, and untrained in the traditional skills of London's craftsmen, they managed in the inhospitable capital as best they could, which was not very well. The local parish poorhouses could not cope with them. Poverty and prostitution became inseparable problems, which each London parish did its best to get rid of by moving them out of its parish boundary – when St George's, Bloomsbury, and St Giles-in-the-Fields clubbed together to buy the lease of 76 Dean Street, in the year 1800, in order to house children from their workhouses there, the parishioners of St Anne's objected, pointing out that the house might become 'a common receptacle for your promiscuous poor'.

The increasingly stark division between posh Mayfair and poor Soho was recognized by architect John Nash in his plans for a new road to link Marylebone Park with Carlton House, the Prince Regent's home. Nash saw Regent Street as providing 'a complete separation between the Streets occupied by the Nobility and Gentry, and the narrower Streets and meaner houses occupied by mechanics and the trading part of the community'. Regent Street was to cut cleanly through the parish of St James, roughly following the line of the ancient trackway now called Swallow Street and once called Shugge Lane. 'My purpose,' Nash later wrote, 'was that the new street should cross the eastern entrance to all the streets occupied by the higher classes and to leave out to the east all the bad streets, and as a sailor would express himself, to hug all the avenues that went to good streets.'

At the south end of the new thoroughfare was to be a curved colonnaded walkway called The Quadrant, designed by Nash to be a fashionable shopping centre where 'those who have nothing to do but walk about and amuse themselves may do so every day in the week, instead of being frequently confined many days together in their Houses by rain . . . The Balustrades over the Colonnades will form Balconies to the Lodging-rooms over the Shops, from which the occupiers of the Lodgings can see and converse with those passing in the carriages underneath, and which will add to the gaiety of the scene, and induce single men, and others who only visit Town occasionally, to give a preference to such Lodgings.' As it was, the covered walkways were popular with neither the shopkeepers, who complained that their premises were dark, nor the customers: The Quadrant, Leigh Hunt wrote in 1861 in his *Saunter Through the West End*, 'except in very hot weather, looked dull, narrow, and heavy. The "sweep" so much boasted of, is not sufficiently long or wide to produce the impression which it was intended to make.' And he added, completely missing Nash's original point, 'Piazzas . . . are not fit for this country . . . The use of them in the south is to screen people from the sun: but here we have not enough sun to render them necessary on that account.'

Though Nash may not have made the street an overwhelming architectural success, the creation of Regent Street and a circus at Piccadilly gave Soho a definite and important boundary in the west, so helping it to keep its village atmosphere long after the individuality of other central London areas had gone. It also created a social division in an area where rich and poor had, up till then, lived cheek by jowl, separating the so-called good, rich area of Mayfair from decaying Soho, which was from then on allowed to run down.

Over the next three or four decades, thousands of poor, semi-skilled or unskilled labourers moved into the cheap lodging-houses, hotels and tenements that now spread across Soho streets like a fungus. Slum clearances in the parish of St Giles in the 1830s brought in a whole new group of penniless residents. And the French Revolution and the Irish potato famine both led to large influxes of poor immigrants from overseas.

After the potato blight of 1845 and 1846, nearly two million Irish people left their country to seek a better life overseas. The vast majority braved the arduous voyage to America; but the shorter and cheaper trip to England was an easier option, especially for families with young children. In 1841, the Irish community in London had stood at a low 75,000. By 1851, the number of Irish had more than doubled. 10 years later, the figure had risen to 178,000. Mostly agricultural labourers who had never visited a city before, they now found themselves completely out of their element in what was an alien and inhospitable world. There were two main areas of the West End where the Irish poor congregated: around the slaughterhouses of the Newport Market district; and in the nearby Rookery, a notorious slum on Soho's doorstep, in the parish of St Giles.

St Giles [wrote 24-year-old Frederick Engels in *The Condition of the Working Class in England* (1844)] 'is in the midst of the most populous part of town, surrounded by broad, splendid avenues in which the gay world of London idles about, in the immediate neighbourhood of Oxford Street, Regent Street, of Trafalgar Square and the Strand. It is a disorderly collection of tall, three or four-storied houses, with narrow crooked, filthy streets, in which there is quite as much life as in the great thoroughfares of the town, except that, here, people of the working-class only are to be seen. A vegetable market is held in the street, baskets with vegetables and fruits, naturally all bad and hardly fit to use, obstruct the sidewalk still further, and from these, as well as from the fish-dealers' stalls, arises a horrible smell. The houses are occupied from cellar to garret, filthy within and without, and their appearance is such that no human being could possibly wish to live in them. But all this is nothing in comparison with the dwellings in the narrow courts and alleys between the streets, entered by covered passages between the houses, in which the filth and tottering ruin surpass all description. Scarcely a whole window-pane can be found, the walls are crumbling, door-posts and window-frames loose and broken, doors of old boards nailed together, or altogether wanting in this thieves' quarter, where no doors are needed, there being nothing to steal. Heaps of garbage and ashes lie in all directions, and the foul liquids emptied before the doors gather in stinking pools. Here live the poorest of the poor, the worst paid workers with thieves and the victims of prostitution indiscriminately huddled together, the majority Irish, or of Irish extraction, and those who have not yet sunk in the whirlpool of moral ruin which surrounds them, sinking daily deeper, losing daily more and more of their power to resist the demoralizing influence of want, filth, and evil surroundings.

Like St Giles, Soho was becoming one of the most densely populated areas in London. It was to remain that way for the next 60 years. The old decaying houses groaned under the weight of their numerous residents. In *Nicholas Nickleby*, Dickens caught their atmosphere perfectly:

> In that quarter of London in which Golden Square is situated, there is a bygone, faded, tumble-down street, with two irregular rows of tall meagre houses, which seem to have stared each other out of countenance years ago. The very chimneys appear to have grown dismal and melancholy, from having had nothing better to look at than the chimneys over the way. Their tops are battered, and broken, and blackened with smoke; and, here and there, some taller stack than the rest, inclining heavily to one side and toppling over the roof, seems to meditate taking revenge for half a century's neglect by crushing the inhabitants of the garrets beneath . . .
>
> To judge from the size of the houses, they have been, at one time, tenanted by persons of better condition than their present occupants; but they are now let off, by the week, in floors or rooms, and every door has almost as many plates or bell-handles as there are apartments within. The windows are, for the same reason, sufficiently diversified in appearance, being ornamented with every variety of common blind and curtain that can easily be imagined; while every doorway is blocked up, and rendered nearly impassable, by a motley collection of children and porter pots of all sizes, from the baby in arms and the half-pint pot, to the full-grown girl and half-gallon can.

The dreadful living conditions in parts of Soho soon matched those in the more notorious East End slums, as report after report testifies. In *Ragged London*, published in 1861, John Hollingshead gave an unforgettable picture of life in one of the crumbling Soho mansions:

> Every room is crowded with a different family, and four, if not more, landlords are interested in the rent . . . Dwellings that originally sheltered eight or ten persons are now crowded with thirty, forty, or fifty inmates. The carved wainscotings are torn to pieces, or covered, an inch deep, with black grease. The old banisters are broken down. The stairs are rugged, dark, and uneven . . . one of

the worst features of the district is a tendency to live in kitchens and cellars . . . The dirt arises partly from long-settled carelessness about domestic cleanliness, partly from the impossibility of keeping one room tidy when six or eight people have to live in it, and partly from the neglect of landlords to whitewash, paint and paper the dwellings.

Eight to a room was a conservative estimate of the West End's overcrowding problem. In 1850, eight people had been found in the Rookery sleeping in a space six foot by five, the inhabitants of one house numbered 100, and, in a picture straight out of *Oliver Twist*, 17 young thieves were discovered living in one tiny chamber.

These conditions were not to be alleviated for many years. In 1890, a lay reader of St Anne's church, visiting lodgings on the second floor of a house in St Anne's Court, recorded that 'the door was furtively opened by a half-naked girl of about 15. She was quite relieved to find it was not the "Tally-man", to whom her mother was considerably indebted. The room was almost devoid of furniture and in a horrible state of uncleanliness, and a large bedstead occupied a third of the space. Hearing some shuffling under the bed, I looked and enticed out one by one seven half starved children, clothed more with nakedness than with rags. So ten human beings existed and slept in that room!'

As late as 1897, the *Daily Chronicle* published a letter from Mr Guy Pearce, a member of the West London Mission, describing his visit to one Soho tenement: 'A space 3ft by 4ft was filled with furniture, and in a recess was the bed. On it lay a poor girl of seventeen, dying of consumption. Here lived a wife and children, and the husband, when he was at home, sharing the bed with the invalid girl . . . Here, too, all the cooking had to be done on an open grate.'

Though the Irish remained the largest group of immigrants in London until the 1870s influx of Eastern European and Russian Jews, there was a small and extremely poor Jewish community in Newport Market and Seven Dials as early as the 1830s. Writer Flora Tristan, whose *London Journal* was published in 1840, gave a graphic picture of this 'Jewish Quarter'. Like Hollingshead, she wrote of families living in dank kitchen cellars, accessible only by ladders let down from the street through grimy shutters: 'The cellars are nothing but *kennels* where the hapless people of Israel are crowded pell-mell. In each one can be seen six, seven or eight dirty urchins, thin, gaunt, lying on the bare floor among the old shoes, the filthy rags, and crawling up and down the ladder like the slugs one sees crawling on cellar stairs . . . Poor creatures! There are thousands of human beings in these cellars, English subjects who speak English and to whom no one pays any attention: one merely says with disdain: "They are Jews . . ."'

The indifference of rich and middle-class Londoners to the living conditions of the poor extended to their working conditions too. Many children worked 16-hour days, and were virtual slaves to their masters: those apprenticed to tradesmen frequently worked for eight years, only for their bed and board. Women who could not get work in service or in the tailoring industry were forced into prostitution. Unemployed Irishmen in the Rookery drank themselves into oblivion, or took to petty crime. The West End Jews scraped a living as cobblers or old clothes dealers. 'Oh, the sight of the thousands of old worn-out shoes, the rags and the rubbish,' wrote Flora Tristan of her visit to their makeshift old-clothes market near Newport Market, 'and all of it making up such an important branch of commerce gives a truer idea of the destitution of the monster city than all the findings and reports that could be published. It makes one shudder!'

Side by side with the humans imprisoned in the Soho slums were cooped up the animals on which the local inhabitants and tradesmen depended. Dickens writes of 'dingy, ill-plumed, drowsy' hens hopping 'from stone to stone, in forlorn search of some hidden eatable in the mud'. Hollingshead sighted 'nearly four hundred stables, in which are kept more than one thousand horses. Over these stables are a number of small close rooms, in which about nine hundred people reside and bring up their families, or one-fortieth part of the whole parish. Another nuisance arises from cows, of which there are at least two hundred kept at eight stations in as many streets.'

By the middle of the 19th century, Soho had become an insanitary place of cow-sheds, animal droppings, slaughterhouses, grease-boiling dens and primitive, decaying sewers. And underneath the floorboards of the overcrowded cellars lurked something even worse – a foetid sea of cesspits as old as the houses, and many of which had never been drained. It was only a matter of time before this hidden festering time-bomb exploded. It finally did so in the summer of 1854.

When a wave of Asiatic cholera first hit England in late 1831, it was thought to be spread by 'miasma in the atmosphere'. By the time of the Soho outbreak 23 years later, medical knowledge about the disease had barely changed, though one man, Dr John Snow, a surgeon and pioneer of the science of epidemiology, had recently published a report speculating that it was spread by contaminated water – an idea with which neither the authorities nor the rest of the medical profession had much truck. Whenever cholera broke out – which it did four times between 1831 and 1854 – nothing whatsoever was done to contain it, and it rampaged through the industrial cities, leaving tens of thousands dead in its wake. The year 1853 saw outbreaks in Newcastle and Gateshead as well as in London, where a total of 10,675 people died of the disease. In the 1854 London epidemic the worst-hit areas at first were Southwark and Lambeth. Soho suffered only a few, seemingly isolated, cases in late August. Then, on the night of the 31st, what Dr Snow later called 'the most terrible outbreak of cholera which ever occurred in the kingdom' broke out.

It was as violent as it was sudden. During the next three days, 127 people living in or around Broad Street died. Few families, rich or poor, were spared the loss of at least one member. Within a week, three-quarters of the residents had fled from their homes, leaving their shops shuttered, their houses locked and the streets deserted. Only those who could not afford to leave remained there. It was like the Great Plague all over again.

By 10 September, the number of fatal attacks had reached 500 and the death rate of the St Anne's, Berwick Street and Golden Square subdivisions of the parish had risen to 12.8 per cent – more than double that for the rest of London. That it did not rise even higher was thanks only to Dr John Snow.

Snow lived in Frith Street, so his local contacts made him ideally placed to monitor the epidemic which had broken out on his doorstep. His previous researches had convinced him that cholera, which, as he had noted, 'always commences with disturbances of the functions of the alimentary canal', was spread by a poison passed from victim to victim through sewage-tainted water; and he had traced a recent outbreak in South London to contaminated water supplied by the Vauxhall Water Company – a theory that the authorities and the water company itself were, not surprisingly, reluctant to believe. Now he saw his chance to prove his theories once and for all, by linking the Soho outbreak to a single source of polluted water.

From day one he patrolled the district, interviewing the families of the victims. His research led him to a pump on the corner of Broad Street and Cambridge Street, at the epicentre of the epidemic. 'I found,' he wrote afterwards, 'that nearly all the deaths had taken place within a short distance of the pump.' In fact, in houses much nearer another pump, there had only been 10 deaths – and of those, five victims had always drunk the water from the Broad Street pump, and three were schoolchildren who had probably drunk from the pump on their way to school.

Dr Snow took a sample of water from the pump, and, on examining it under a microscope, found that it contained 'white, flocculent particles'. By 7 September, he was convinced that these were the source of infection, and he took his findings to the Board of Guardians of St James's Parish, in whose parish the pump fell. Though they were reluctant to believe him, they agreed to remove the pump handle as an experiment. When they did so, the spread of cholera dramatically stopped.

At the end of September the outbreak was all but over, with the death toll standing at 616 Sohoites. But Snow's theories were yet to be proved. There were several unexplained deaths from cholera that did not at first appear to be linked to the Broad Street pump water – notably, a widow living in West End, Hampstead, who had died of cholera on 2 September, and her niece, who lived in Islington, who had succumbed with the same symptoms the following day. Since neither of these women had been near Soho for a long time, Dr Snow rode up to Hampstead to interview the widow's son. He discovered from him that the widow had once lived in Broad Street, and that she had liked the taste of the well-water there so much that she had sent her servant down to Soho every day to bring back a large bottle of it for her by cart. The last bottle of water – which her niece had also drunk from – had been fetched on 31 August, at the very start of the Soho epidemic.

There were many other factors that led Snow to isolate the cause of the cholera to the Broad Street pump. For instance, of the 530 inmates of the Poland Street workhouse, which was only round the corner, only five people had contracted cholera; but no one from the workhouse drank the pump water, for the building had its own well. Among the 70 workers in a Broad Street brewery, where the men were given an allowance of free beer every day and so never drank water at all, there were no fatalities at all. And an army officer living in St John's Wood had died after dining in Wardour Street, where he too had drunk a glass of water from the Broad Street well.

Still no one believed Snow. A report by the Board of Health a few months later dismissed his 'suggestions' that 'the real cause of whatever was peculiar in the case lay in the general use of one particular well, situate [sic] at Broad Street in the middle of the district, and having (it was imagined) its waters contaminated by the rice-water evacuations of cholera patients. After careful inquiry,' the report concluded, 'we see no reason to adopt this belief.'

So what had caused the cholera outbreak? The Reverend Henry Whitehead, vicar of St Luke's church, Berwick Street, believed that it had been caused by divine intervention, and he undertook his own report on the epidemic in order to prove his point. However, his findings merely confirmed what Snow had claimed, a fact that he was honest enough to own up to. Furthermore, Whitehead helped Snow to isolate a single probable cause of the whole infection: just before the Soho epidemic had occurred, a child living at number 40 Broad Street had been taken ill with cholera symptoms, and its nappies had been steeped in water which was subsequently tipped into a leaking cesspool situated only three feet from the Broad Street well.

Whitehead's findings were published in <i>The Builder</i> a year later, along with a report on living conditions in Soho, undertaken by the magazine itself. They found that no improvements at all had been made during the intervening year. 'Even in Broad-street it would appear that little has since been done . . . In St Anne's-Place, and St Anne's-Court, the open cesspools are still to be seen; in the court, so far as we could learn, no change has been made; so that here, in spite of the late numerous deaths, we have all the materials for a fresh epidemic . . . In some [houses] the water-butts were in deep cellars, close to the undrained cesspool . . . The overcrowding appears to increase . . .' *The Builder* went on to recommend 'the immediate abandonment and clearing away of all cesspools – not the disguise of them, but their complete removal.'

Nothing much was done about it. Soho was to remain a dangerous place for some time to come.

There were other dangers fermenting in the streets of Soho – dangerous ideas. The place had been a magnet for dissidents since 1683, when Algernon Sidney, Lord Leicester's second son, was executed for his part in the Rye House plot. As Lord Mayor Beckford had demonstrated so eloquently in front of George III, Sohoites were never afraid to speak their mind. Even today, ask a Sohoite his or her opinion of a film, or the price of potatoes, or the future of their neighbourhood and they will tell you straight out – in fact, they will probably tell you what they think whether you ask them to or not.

MP Field-Marshal Henry Seymour Conway, who, like Beckford, had lived in Soho Square during the 1760s, had been a champion of the free press. When John Wilkes was arrested for attacking Lord Bute in the newspaper *The North Briton*, Conway had argued tooth and nail against the general warrant to search for and question every writer, publisher and printer connected with the case. Eventually he had swung the House of Commons over to his opinion, and the general warrant had been declared illegal – an action that had resulted in Wilkes's release.

In 1837 number 25 Soho Square was leased by Thomas Barnes, the editor of *The Times*, who had already made his own contribution to press freedom by supporting his old school friend Leigh Hunt after he was arrested for libelling the Prince Regent in his radical weekly, *The Examiner*, in March 1872. It is not clear whether the Prince objected more strongly to the charge that he was 'a violator of his word, a libertine over head and ears in disgrace, a despiser of domestic ties, the companion of gamblers and demi-reps, a man who has just closed half a century without one single claim on the gratitude of his country or the respect of posterity!' or to being called a 'corpulent man of fifty'. Whichever, Leigh Hunt and his brother John, who were joint proprietors of *The Examiner*, were both imprisoned for two years and fined £200 each for publishing the article. As well as visiting the Hunts in prison, Barnes kept *The Examiner* going in their absence, with the help of friends Charles Lamb and William Hazlitt.

Although Beckford, Conway and Barnes were staunch supporters of democracy, they were hardly revolutionaries in the modern sense of the word. Probably the first real one of those to live in Soho was Jean-Paul Marat, one of the most prominent figures in the French Revolution. Disappointingly, however, Marat, who lodged at 31 Romilly Street in 1776, was at that time far more interested in his work as an oculist than in spreading dissident ideas. The only pamphlets he is known to have produced while living in Soho were *An Enquiry Into the Nature, Cause, and Cure of a Singular Disease of the Eye* and an *Essay on Gleets*.

By the spring of 1811, when Shelley was sent down from Oxford, Soho was the natural place for an unconventional and free-thinking 19-year-old to graduate to. Shelley may well have been attracted to the area by the existence of a radical debating society which met at the Cock tavern in Grafton Street (in the part of the Newport Market district demolished in the late 19th century to make way for the Charing Cross Road). The founder of this informal club of political free-thinkers, republicans and subversives was a land-reformer and pamphleteer called Thomas Spence. When Spence died in 1814 – his followers carried his coffin with 'due pomp' up the Tottenham Court Road to the burial ground of St James's, Hampstead Road – the debating club was kept going by one of his disciples, a political fanatic called Thomas Evans.

Under the leadership of Evans, a braces-maker from the Strand and a one-time resident of Frith Street, the Society of Spencean Philanthropists – as it was now known – flourished. Meetings were held twice weekly in Soho: at the Cock in Grafton Street and at the Nag's Head in Carnaby Market; and there were meetings in the Borough and in Moorfields as well. Speakers came from all over the country to talk to the members of London's radical underworld who congregated at these meetings, and anyone who arrived looking too smart was accused of being a government informer and thrown out. The debates were certainly not dry affairs. In fact, they were more like drunken and very ribald entertainments, and were perhaps the forerunners of today's alternative comedy revues.

A heady blend of anti-clerical blasphemy, crudeness, violent sedition and anti-monarchy was preached and sung about at the Spencean tavern clubs, where a favourite toast was 'May the last of the kings be strangled with the guts of the last of the priests.' Naturally, these goings-on attracted the attention of the government, who sent in spies to see what was happening and concluded, in a House of Lords report of June 1817, that 'the minds of those who attend their meetings are tainted and depraved; they are taught contempt for all Decency, Law, all Religion and Morality, and are thus prepared for the most atrocious scenes of outrage and violence.' That same year both Evans and his son were arrested on charges of high treason, and until their release the following January, Evans's wife Janet, an activist in her own right, was left to run the organization and keep the family business going.

Early in 1818 the Spenceans moved from the Cock tavern to Archer Street, where they established a more serious 'chapel', calling themselves Christian Philanthropists. Here Evans preached with a sailor and tailor named Robert Wedderburn, whose 'ferocious rhetoric' and 'horridly blasphemous' language caused such a split in the Spenceans that Wedderburn decamped to the corner of Brewer Street and Hopkins Street, taking the seats and a good part of the congregation with him.

In this so-called Unitarian Chapel – in reality a 'ruinous hay loft' reached by ladder – Wedderburn continued to preach revolution to audiences of male and female extremists. But though he drilled his congregation in the use of weapons, and even assembled a cache of pikes, the armed insurrection that he had planned to take place in November 1919 was a wash-out. That same month the Hopkins Street chapel broke up for good.

Karl Marx, that most famous of revolutionaries, arrived in England on 24 August 1849, having been expelled from the Continent, but leaving behind him his three children and his pregnant wife Jenny. After a few weeks his family joined him, and they moved from a small furnished room off Leicester Square to a flat in Chelsea, where their sickly son, Heinrich, was born amidst the uproar of Guy Fawkes night.

Before long, their Chelsea landlady took a dislike to them, and the Marx family moved into the German Hotel in Leicester Street, one of a number of guest-houses that had opened in Soho to cater for the foreign political refugees – mostly Italians and Germans

– who had taken advantage of the open political asylum offered by the British government. Romantic as it would be to think that the Marxes chose to return to Soho because of its reputation as a hot-bed of radicalism, they probably ended up there because it was cheap.

Before long the proprietor of the hotel, who at first gave them 'a humane reception for £5 10s a week', had had enough of Jenny, Karl and their children, and they were forced to move yet again. Eventually they found a more permanent home in the house of a Jewish lace-dealer at number 64 Dean Street, where their fellow revolutionary, Heinrich Bauer, had taken rooms.

Being the wife of a penniless revolutionary was no laughing matter. While Karl plotted regicide, collaborated with Engels on the final numbers of the *Neue Rheinische Zeitung*, and prepared a course of lectures which he gave in a room above the Red Lion pub in Great Windmill Street, Jenny and her mother's ex-maid, Lenchen, who lived with them, struggled to keep the children alive. Jenny also had to put up – and put up with – visiting Party comrades, who expected to be accommodated in the tiny flat.

The daughter of a well-off Prussian minister, Jenny was used to better things, and their hand-to-mouth existence wore her down. When in the summer of 1850 – and pregnant again – she travelled to Holland to beg help from Karl's uncle, the man barely recognized her, and she came home, as she wrote, 'empty-handed, disappointed, torn apart and tortured by a fear of death'. On her return, she found her son Foxchën dying of pneumonia – he was to be the first of three children she would lose in Dean Street.

At the beginning of 1851, Marx, Jenny, Lenchen and the four children moved down the road to a two-roomed attic flat in number 28 Dean Street – an 'old hovel', as Marx called it, also occupied by an Italian chef, an Italian confectioner and a foreign language teacher. The rooms, which had no lavatory or running water, cost Marx £22 a year. A Prussian agent who visited them there reported that they lived

in one of the worst, and hence the cheapest quarters of London. He has two rooms, the one with the view of the street being the drawing-room, behind it the bedroom. There is not one piece of good, solid furniture in the entire flat. Everything is broken, tattered

and torn, finger-thick dust everywhere, and everything in the greatest disorder; a large, old fashioned table, covered with waxcloth,
stands in the middle of the drawing-room, on it lie manuscripts,
books, newspapers, then the children's toys, bits and pieces of the
woman's sewing things, next to it a few teacups with broken rims,
dirty spoons, knives, forks, candlesticks, inkpot, glasses, dutch clay
pipes, tobacco-ash, in a word all kinds of trash, and everything on
one table; a junk-dealer would be ashamed of it. When you enter
the Marx flat your sight is dimmed by tobacco and coal smoke
so that you grope around at first as if you were in a cave, until
your eyes get used to these fumes and, as in a fog, you gradually
notice a few objects. Everything is dirty, everything covered with
dust; it is dangerous to sit down. Here is a chair with only three
legs, there the children play kitchen on another chair that happens
to be whole; true – it is offered to the visitor, but the children's
kitchen is not removed; if you sit on it you risk a pair of trousers.
But nothing of this embarrasses Marx or his wife in the least; you
are received in the friendliest manner, are cordially offered a pipe,
tobacco, and whatever else there is; a spirited conversation makes
up for the domestic defects and in the end you become reconciled
because of the company, find it interesting, even original. This is the
faithful portrait of the family life of the communist leader Marx.

This written portrait might have been faithful, but Karl certainly
was not. When Jenny was in Holland, he had an affair with
Lenchen, and there were now two pregnant women in the tiny
flat. Karl's hints that his friend Engels was the putative father did
not convince Jenny, and though she had to accept the situation out
of sheer necessity, it almost broke her heart.

Throughout their stay in Soho, the Marx family were practically
destitute, despite the small income Karl received for writing articles
for the *New York Tribune*, and the postal orders sent to them by
Engels, who had taken a job in his father's Manchester factory.
They were so poor that when their daughter Franziska died in
April 1852, Jenny was forced to beg from 'a French fugitive who
lives near us. He received me with friendliness and sympathy and
gave me two pounds and with that money the coffin in which my
child could rest peacefully was paid for.'

Lenchen was frequently dispatched to the pawn shop to raise

money to buy food or writing paper – sometimes on such dubious pledges as Karl's well-worn overcoat or shoes. At times even Marx was at his wits' end. He wrote to Engels that summer:

> My wife is ill, little Jenny is ill, Lenchen has a sort of nervous fever, I cannot and could not call the doctor because I have no money for medicine. For 8-10 days I have fed the family on bread and potatoes of which it is still questionable whether I can rustle up any today . . . I had put off until the beginning of September all the creditors who, as you know, are only paid off in small sums. Now there is a general storm. I have tried everything, but in vain . . . The best and most desirable thing that could happen would be that the landlady throw me out of the house. At least I would then be quit of the sum of £22. But I can scarcely trust her to be so obliging. Also baker, milkman, the man with the tea, greengrocer, old butcher's bills. How can I get clear of all this hellish muck?

To get away from his troubles, Karl spent much of his time studying in the peace and quiet of the British Library's Reading Room in Bloomsbury. But his family were not to escape their 'evil, frightful rooms' in Dean Street until Jenny received two small inheritances, the first from a Scottish uncle, the second from her mother, who died in July 1855. Then, 'with joyful heart', they moved into a small terraced house near Primrose Hill. 'When we slept in our own beds for the first time,' she wrote, 'sat on our own chairs and even had a parlour with second-hand furniture of a rococo style, or rather bric-a-brac, then we really thought we were living in a magic castle . . .'

Since 1926, number 28 Dean Street has been part of Leoni's Quo Vadis restaurant. The elegant ground floor dining-room gives no hint of what once went on upstairs. Patrons who do not mind the climb can, if they wish, be escorted to see the Marxes' old apartment. Anyone who has had a glass too much wine must be warned: as carpet gives way to lino, and the lino to bare boards on the steep, narrow stairs, one can easily imagine one is climbing back in time.

Dizzy from the altitude, the Marx pilgrim emerges in a small attic hall with a sagging ceiling and doors the colour of Cornish cream, each bearing the scar of a torn-off padlock. This is a Soho that has, for the most part, long since disappeared: a Soho of rooms-for-rent, where every four walls shut in another family, a Soho of cramped workshops, hungry immigrants, a Soho where wooden partition walls are encrusted with 250 years' worth of cheap paint.

To enter the door on the left is to find oneself in Karl and Jenny Marx's living-room. It is a bare room, thankfully devoid of unnecessary Marxiana, with a simple oval table, a narrow bed with an appropriately red cover, and one faded poster chronicling the life and times of Mr Marx. Through another door, at the back, is the second room, a little larger than a cupboard, but smaller than a double divan.

The windows are open, letting in the sounds of 20th-century Dean Street. But time stands strangely still in there. The two rooms are airless, and, despite the care that has been taken to furnish them, neglect festers in the corners. And the dust, oh, the dust is finger-thick everywhere, much as it was on the day when the Prussian agent came to see how the world's most dangerous revolutionary lived.

The Soho which the Marxes left behind them was a 'festering sore' of overcrowding, petty crime and prostitution. And its proximity to the smart districts of the West End made it much harder for the upper and middle classes to ignore than the equally run-down East End, which was tucked conveniently out of sight on the far side of the City. Consequently, in the second half of the century, do-gooders and philanthropists moved in on Soho in force. Six hospitals were opened to help deal with local health problems, as were a number of missionary organizations, including a soup kitchen in Leicester Square, and various temporary shelters for homeless men and women, such as the House of Charity, which opened in 1847 at number 9 Rose (later Manette) Street, and which five years later moved round the corner to Richard Beckford's old house, number 1 Greek Street, where it still is today.

In 1884, the Soho Club and Home for Working Girls, another venerable Victorian institution, was started across the road from the House of Charity by the Hon. Maude Stanley. The club, which was open every evening, organized classes in drawing, French, singing, needlework, music, gymnastics and mathematics, as well as having a library, a canteen, a Penny Bank and a low-cost medical dispensary for its members. On top of that, it provided long- or short-term lodgings for 'Young Women engaged in business, and students', who for between 3s and 7s 6d a week could rent a bed in a dormitory or even a private room, including the use of a sitting-room, gas fire and clean bed linen. In addition, the advertisement advised that 'Teachers or Students coming to London to pass Examinations can be Lodged at 1s. per night. Breakfast, Tea and Supper 2¹/₂d each, Dinner 6d.'

The Soho Club had originally started in three rooms in Porter Street, Newport Market, then at the centre of Soho's very worst slums, where a refuge had been set up in the old market buildings. The Newport Market Refuge, as this was called, also provided training and meals for young boys. One of the most distinguished members of its committee was the politician William Ewart Gladstone.

Gladstone's 'rescue work' with prostitutes was well-known, at times notoriously so. Night after night, he walked by himself through the most dangerous areas of the West End, observing first-hand the street-life of prostitutes, of which there were estimated to be about 80,000 working in the centre of town. Whenever he could, he stopped and talked to them about their lives and if possible, he persuaded them to come home with him for the night. 'What will your wife say if you bring this woman home with you?' his amazed Private Secretary asked him on one occasion when the two men were together. 'Why,' Gladstone answered innocently, 'it is to my wife that I am bringing her.'

Back at the Gladstones' house, William's wife Catherine took the girls in, gave them a meal peppered with lashings of good advice, and found a bed for them to sleep in overnight. The next day, she or William tried to secure them a place in one of the temporary shelters such as the House of St Barnabas, or the House of Mercy at Clewer, near Windsor, which the Gladstones had also helped to found. The girls were not always grateful to be whisked off the street: conditions in the shelters were often extremely depressing. As one prostitute wrote to Gladstone after running away from Clewer, 'I did not fancy being shut up in such a place as that for perhaps 12 months. I should have committed suicide.'

There were plenty of people who thought chatting up prostitutes was, to say the least, a dubious pastime for a prominent member of the government. To make matters worse, Gladstone somehow always managed 'to combine his missionary meddling with a keen appreciation of a pretty face', as MP Henry Labouchere said. Though a deeply religious Christian, there is no doubt that Gladstone deliberately 'courted evil', as he put it himself, by placing himself in a position of temptation where his will-power might fail. It was as if every encounter with a prostitute was a test of his own faith.

In 1853 the Chancellor of the Exchequer's rescue work involved him in a notorious blackmail case. While walking through Long Acre on the night of 10 May, he was approached by a woman and, after talking to her for some time, agreed to accompany her to her lodgings in King Street, Soho. When they reached her house, a young man stepped out of the shadows, and told Gladstone that he had been following him. He then made one of the most bizarre blackmail demands of all times: he threatened to tell the world that Gladstone had picked up a prostitute, unless Gladstone either gave him some money or secured him a job with the Inland Revenue – a place most people would blackmail to get out of. Since Gladstone had nothing to hide, he told the man to publish or be damned, and the case subsequently came to court. The would-be blackmailer, William Wilson, a commercial traveller from Lambeth, was sentenced to a year's hard labour. But the Chancellor, as charitable as ever, persuaded the Home Secretary to release him after he had served only six months.

Due partly to the Gladstones' efforts, rescue work eventually became a respectable, not to mention popular, hobby for the leisured classes, though there were few people who went so far as to invite ladies of the night into their homes. As the Contagious Diseases Act of 1864 clearly demonstrated, Victorian society operated a double standard which blamed women entirely for the existence of prostitution and its accompanying ills – namely, the spread of venereal disease. Yet the Gladstones were well aware that society was as much to blame for the existence of the oldest profession as any 'weakness' in the girls. As Catherine Gladstone once wrote, it was 'a common thing for [servants] to be engaged without wages or clothes and only for *food every other day*. Who can wonder at girls so situated yielding to temptation and sin?'

Not every prostitute went on the game of her own free will. Children as young as 10 years old were pushed into it by their parents; bullies (as pimps were then called) specialized in seducing 'respectable' girls and then forcing them on to the streets. There was also an active white slave trade in women and children operating both ways across the English Channel. In the 1850s a certain Mrs Jeffries, the 'madam' of a string of West End brothels, was known to be shipping English prostitutes to France, Belgium and Italy, and to be importing girls from the Continent to work in Britain. But although an action was brought against her for keeping a disorderly house, her boasts of friends in high places were not without foundation, for when her case came to court, the judge let her off with a small fine, instead of imprisoning her as he ought to have done.

But despite the work of a few upper-class philanthropists, the social conditions of Soho did not improve during the rest of the century. In the early 1880s the parish was still, in the words of one report, 'a reeking home of filthy vice', and the Newport Market district in particular was said to be 'a veritable focus of every danger which can menace the health and social order of a city. The houses, from their insanitary condition, are horribly disgusting, and can only be fitly designated as well prepared propagating ground for every kind of contagious and loathsome disease . . . The grossest immorality flourishes unabashed from every age downwards to mere children.'

It was undoubtedly Soho's darkest time.

6

Enterprise and Entertainment

Co-existing with the prostitution, crime and poverty were areas of respectability – even of wealth – like Soho Square, which remained relatively upmarket well into the 19th century, due partly to the continuing presence of the wealthy botanist Sir Joseph Banks and his family at number 32.

Banks was a born Sohoite, if not a born-and-bred one: though born in Argyll Street in 1743, he was educated at Harrow, Eton and Christ Church College, Oxford – all establishments well-suited to the education of a young member of the landed gentry. When his father, William, died in 1761, 18-year-old Joseph inherited a large estate in Lincolnshire, and enough money to indulge the passion for the natural sciences that had developed when he was at school.

It was apparently after swimming in the Thames with a group of fellow Etonians that Banks first fell in love with nature. He had never been a scholarly child, but, as he walked alone down a country lane on the way back to school in the late afternoon sunshine, the idea came to him that it would be far more interesting to study plants and animals than dead languages like Latin and Greek. His interest in botany, which started that day, was to dominate the rest of his life.

In April 1766, Banks sailed on an expedition to Newfoundland and Labrador in the *Niger*, in search of plant and animal specimens. In 1768 he set off with Captain Cook in the *Endeavour* on a dangerous round-the-world voyage that lasted three years. (During their visit to New Zealand, Banks named Botany Bay.) Soon after his return, he set off for Iceland. In 1777, the year before he was elected president of the Royal Society, he went swimming again – this time against the tide of fashion, when, with his mother, his new wife Dorothea and his sister Sarah Sophia, he moved from New Burlington Street, Mayfair, to number 32 Soho Square, where he established an extensive botanical library and museum in an outbuilding backing on to Dean Street.

What was Sir Joseph (he was created a Baronet in 1781) like? The diarist John Byng describes him as 'a wild eccentric character'. Yet Fanny Burney, who met him at a royal tea-party in Windsor, wrote that he was 'so exceedingly shy that we made no acquaintance at all. If, instead of going round the world, he had fallen from the moon, he could not appear less versed in the usual modes of a tea-drinking party.'

But Banks was not shy – at least, not in the right company. By the turn of the century, the gregarious comings-and-goings of his household had become something of an institution in the square. Scientists and students visited him all the time – as did foreigners as diverse as South Sea Islanders and Esquimaux Indians. In fact, his whole family were incredibly sociable, and held open house twice a week to the cream of London's intelligentsia. The hospitality at these literary, scientific and philosophical 'saturnalia' was so legendary that it even earned this mention in a guidebook, *Feltham's Picture of London for 1805*.

> Sir Joseph Banks, President of the Royal Society, Receives, on every Thursday morning, during the society's meetings, his friends, members of the society and gentlemen introduced by them, at a public breakfast, at his house in Soho-square. The literary, and much more, the scientific news of the day, are the topics of the conversations which then take place. New and curious specimens of subjects in antiquities, in natural history, &c., are often produced for the inspection of the persons who then assemble.
>
> On every Sunday evening, too, during the meetings of the Royal Society, the same gentleman opens his house for the reception of a conversation-assembly of his literary and philosophical friends, and of all gentlemen, whether natives of this country or foreigners, whom his friends introduce.

This makes the Sunday evening dinner parties sound a lot more high-brow than they were. In reality, they were often great fun. Guests included Omai the Otaheitan, Samuel Johnson, Fanny Burney and her father, and Horace Walpole, who recalled one occasion when a Parisian clockmaker 'produced the smallest automaton that I suppose was ever created (a singing bird springing out of a snuff box)'.

Mechanical birds were not the only animals on offer. In the mews behind the house was a goat that had travelled round the world with Banks, and when fellow scientist and future Soho Square resident Charles Bell (he moved into number 34 in 1811) attended a breakfast party at the Banks' in 1804, he reported that his host 'has a set of most absurd animals about him – living animals – German and French toad-eaters'.

The saturnalia were definitely not all-male affairs, for Lady Dorothea and Mistress Sarah Sophia, both very clever women in their own right, took an active part in them. Like her brother, Mistress Sarah Sophia was a respected natural historian. Though she had been a very fashionable lady in her youth, she became particularly bookish and eccentric over the years, especially when it came to her clothes, which even attracted the attention of newspaper caricaturists. She had three woollen riding habits (she and Dorothea shared Sir Joseph's passion for wearing only wool) which she wore on every occasion, even for dinner parties: the best of these was called *Hightum*, the second best *Tightum*, and the worst *Scrub*. It was perhaps *Scrub* that writer J. T. Smith had in mind when he described Mistress Banks thus: 'She was looked after by the eye of astonishment wherever she went. Her dress was that of the old school; her Barcelona quilled petticoat had a hole on either side for the convenience of rummaging two immense pockets, stuffed with books.'

Even though they tended to live in a world of their own, the Banks could not but be affected by the changes that were taking place around them. In 1815, their house was mobbed by rioters protesting against the Corn Bill, which proposed to limit the importation of cheap foreign grain – an action calculated to protect the interest of members of the landed gentry, such as Sir Joseph Banks. Consequently the windows of number 32 were stoned by the mob, the front door was broken down and the hall furniture, along with a number of papers, destroyed. Afterwards, describing to a newspaper correspondent what had happened, Sir Joseph was full of praise for the sang-froid of his women: 'Nothing could behave better and few persons so nobly as Lady B and my sister,' he is reported as saying. 'They sat by me without any expression of extravagant fear till the door was burst open. I then requested them to retire which they did but not out of the house.'

There was further proof of the strong-mindedness of the Banks women on 25 August 1818, when the whole family were involved in a road accident in Lincolnshire, during which their coach over-turned. 'We are all three rather heavy, and I, as you know, quite helpless,' Banks wrote to his friend Sir Everard Home two days later. 'We were obliged to lie very uneasily at the bottom of the coach for half an hour before assistance could be got to lift us out. We all bore our misfortune without any repining or any demonstration of the follies of fear; and we are all now quite recovered from the effects of our accident, except my sister, who has a cut on her head filled with lint and doing very well. But both the ladies have gone everywhere since, without an hour's confinement.'

Mistress Banks, who was then in her seventies, never did recover from the coach crash. She died four weeks later, and her private collection of coins and curiosities passed to the British Museum. When her brother died at his Lincolnshire estate in 1820, he left his house to his wife, and the use of his 'Library Herbarium, Manuscripts, Drawings, Copper plates, Engravings, and everything else that is contained in my Collections usually kept in the back buildings of my house' to Robert Brown, his librarian, 'upon this express Condition that he continues to use my Library as his Chief Place of Study in the same manner as he now does'. On Brown's death – or before it, if Brown wished – the collections were to pass to the British Museum. Lady Banks died soon after her husband, and Brown inherited the house, which he soon leased to the Linnaean Society. He continued to occupy his old rooms in the back building until he died in 1858.

Despite the presence of the Banks family and their intellectual neighbours Sir Charles Bell and *Times* editor Thomas Barnes, Soho Square was slowly but inexorably changing into a 'frankly industrial' place, as one writer described it in the 1870s. Its position just off Oxford Street made it an ideal spot for businesses such as local food manufacturers Crosse and Blackwell, who had started in King Street (now Shaftesbury Avenue) in 1830 and by the late part of the century had moved to a large factory on the north-east corner of the square, where they were to stay till the 1920s.

The commercialization of Soho Square had started as early as 1816, with the opening of London's very first department store, the

Soho Bazaar. This shopping phenomenon was opened by business-man John Trotter, who had lived in the square since 1785, and had gradually bought up the north-west corner site – numbers 4, 5, 6 and 7. One house he lived in, the others he converted into a large warehouse, from where he ran a huge business supplying the British government with all their army supplies during the Napoleonic Wars.

Trotter emerged after Waterloo with a large fortune, though apparently with a reputation for unscrupulous dealings. Before long it became clear that all his newly-made money was beginning to weigh on his conscience, and he started to devise schemes to put something back into the society out of which he had taken so much. An idea for a 'universal language' never got off the ground. But then he came up with a plan for a government-subsidized department store run on 'benevolent and patriotic principles' that would enable the widows and orphans created by the Napoleonic Wars to keep themselves by selling small, home-made goods directly to the public without having to go through a middle-man.

The government, however, showed little enthusiasm for the scheme, and refused to finance it. So Trotter decided to go ahead with it by himself, and fitted out his empty Soho Square warehouse with 750 feet of panelled mahogany counter-space, which 'persons of respectability' could rent for as little as 3d per foot per day.

In return for this low rent, Trotter was to provide not only counter-space but lighting, heating and night security guards as well. And, like the most enlightened businesses today, he built a large canteen, heated by 'a stove of a peculiar construction sending forth two distinct columns of heat', where the stall-holders would be able to buy subsidized meals.

The Soho Bazaar opened on 1 February 1816. In a publicity pamphlet, written three months later, its philanthropic aims were clearly set out: the hope was that by renting stalls there, 'the industrious . . . may hope to thrive; reduced tradesmen may recover and retain their connexions; beginners may form friends, connexions and habits, before they encounter more extensive speculations; and artists, arti-sans, and whole families, employed at home, although infirm or in the country, may securely vend their labour to advantage by proxy.'

The Reverend Joseph Nightingale, who wrote this pamphlet, added a detailed description of the premises:

The door opens out of Soho Square, the first room you enter is sixty-two feet long, thirty-six broad, and about eleven feet high. The walls are hung with red cloth from top to bottom, and around them, at a distance of about five feet from the ceiling, runs a piece of black tape, above which the tenants are not allowed, without leave, to hang or expose any of their goods, the upper part being reserved for charitable and benevolent purposes. At either end are large mirrors, and on the sides of the beams, running longitudinally along the ceiling are painted the rules of the establishment.

And, as with most philanthropic organizations, there were plenty of those. There was to be no haggling over prices. Only British-made goods were to be sold. No one 'meanly or dirtily dressed' was allowed through Trotter's hallowed doors. No dealers or middlemen were permitted to join the ranks of the 'tenants', as the 200-odd women stall-holders were called. And the tenants had to give references – up to 16 were required for each person – testifying to their 'respectability, moral character, and good temper'. Anyone who was found selling foreign goods or giving a customer a discount was to be fined and prosecuted 'with the utmost vigour of the law' – and tenants who informed on each other were to be given a five guinea reward.

There was no shortage of women willing to put up with these regulations, for the Bazaar was a runaway success from the start: the average daily attendance was over 2,000 people. Having taken a bit of a gamble by opening up without government assistance, Trotter discovered to his joy that philanthropy could pay. In fact, his Bazaar was still in operation over 80 years later, when it earned a place in the book *Two Centuries of Soho*, produced in 1898 by the Clergy of St Anne's. 'But though there remains one large room devoted, as in days of yore, to the sale of various articles, from knitted woollen goods to toys and porcelain,' the Clergy reported in the book, the Bazaar was by now 'but a shadow of its former self. The stall-holders are still of the feminine sex, for the male tenant has ever been a thing unknown, and many of the ladies are young, and fair to look at.' However, most of the building was by then occupied by a publishing house, 'a well-sized cycling school', and an employment agency for servants; 'while upstairs,' the Clergy concluded on a wry Victorian note, 'governesses are supplied with posts of responsibility, according to their capacities – and endurance, probably'.

By the late 19th century, practically every industry and retail business had a foothold in Soho: from food producers to billiard table makers; silversmiths and clockmakers; saddlers, leathersellers and curriers; carpenters and furniture makers; musical instrument makers and music printers; hat makers, tailors and dressmakers; glass-dealers and stained-glass artists; book publishers and book dealers. In Wardour Street there was even a healthy trade in second-hand books and fake antiques. 'If anybody wants the richest of books for ninepence,' Leigh Hunt wrote in 1861, 'or a piece of old ware full of bearded figures, which he does not know whether he should give twopence for, or two guineas, this is the place to look for it.' By the 1880s, the very name 'Wardour Street' had become synonymous with things unreal – from 'the pseudo-archaic diction affected by modern novelists' as one dictionary put it, to 'a perfectly modern article with a sham appearance of the real antique about it.'

Another famous name in Soho's retail world was Arthur Liberty, who opened a shop selling coloured silks at number 218A Regent Street on 15 May 1875. Mr Liberty had ideas as grand as the name of his tiny premises – East India House – and before long had turned his store into a large emporium selling Oriental curiosities as well as fabrics and clothes.

Strangely, the least glamorous of Soho's businesses had caused the most stir when it had started: the firm of W. G. Nixey, black lead manufacturers, whose factory was at number 12 Soho Square. For, as the Clergy of St Anne's testified in *Two Centuries of Soho* (1898), when Mr Nixey started up in business in the 1850s, he had found a unique way of advertising his product: he had employed a glorified sandwich-man:

This representative of Mr Nixey was dressed in complete armour, well polished with the new black lead. He was mounted on a magnificent black charger, also in a coat of mail, and carried a banner, on which was the then strange device, 'W. G. Nixey's Refined Black Lead.' His stately progress through the streets of London was attended by enormous crowds; and though his career was at length summarily stopped, yet by this time Mr Nixey's name was so well known that his new venture was fairly launched, and an enormous impetus was given to the demand for his black lead.

With street theatre like this in Soho, what need was there for conventional theatre? When Soho was already so crowded, what need was there for anything else at all? But, needed or not, the theatre industry was about to establish a firm foothold in the area. For when Cambridge Circus, Charing Cross Road and Shaftesbury Avenue were created in the 1880s, cutting their way through King Street and the Newport Market slums, Soho, on top of everything else, became the centre of London's Theatreland.

Soho has been renowned for its musicians, actors, actresses and entertainers from its earliest days. The first live theatrical performance there was probably the stunt-act witnessed by John Evelyn in Leicester Fields, where he had gone to visit Lady Sunderland 'who was going to Paris to my Lord, now ambassador there', as he recorded in his diary on 8 October 1672: 'She made me stay dinner at Leicester House, and afterwards sent for Richardson, the famous fire-eater. He devour'd brimston on glowing coales before us, chewing and swallowing them; he mealted a beere-glasse and eate it quite up; then taking a live coale on his tongue, he put on it a raw oyster, the coal was blown on with bellows till it flam'd and sparkl'd in his mouth, and so remain'd till the oyster gaped and was quite boil'd,' – a trick one can be quite sure has never been attempted since even by the staff of Wheeler's restaurant in Old Compton Street. As if that wasn't enough, Richardson then 'mealted pitch and wax with sulphur, which he dranke down as it flamed; I saw it flaming in his mouth a good while; he also took up a thick piece of yron, such as laundresses use to put in their smoothing boxes, when it was fiery hot, held it between his teeth, then in his hand, and threw it about like a stone, but this I observ'd he car'd not to hold very long; then he stood on a small pot, and bending his body, tooke a glowing yron with his mouth from between his feete, without touching the pot or grounde with his hands; with divers other prodigious feates.'

An act like that is hard for an impresario to beat, but anatomist Nathaniel St André thought he had managed it when, in December 1726, he brought an illiterate farm-worker called Mary Tofts, who came from Godalming, in Surrey, to lodge at Lacy's Bagnio, which had just opened at number 27 Leicester Fields. Though she appeared quite ordinary and performed no artistic tricks, Tofts claimed that she had been startled by a rabbit while working in a field, and had subsequently given birth to a litter of 15 of them. This claim was corroborated by St André, who, in a medical paper entitled 'A Short Narrative of an Extraordinary Delivery of Rabbets [sic]', claimed that he himself had delivered two more rabbits, or parts of rabbits, from her. George I's surgeon was sent over to the Bagnio by the King to investigate the matter, and agreed that he had seen Mary Tofts give birth to yet more rabbit parts. St André even wrote to the Royal Society's president, Sir Hans Sloane, inviting him over to Leicester Fields, 'where you may if you please have the opportunity of seeing her deliver'd'.

But Sloane did not have a chance to take up this chance-of-a-lifetime, for before long Mary Tofts was caught trying to buy a rabbit in the streets nearby, and after a cursory interrogation confessed to being a fraud. The whole, rather disgusting, affair was satirized a few years later by local artist William Hogarth, in the engraving *Cunicularii*.

For more highbrow thrill-seekers who were not turned on by watching women give birth to rabbits' paws, Soho offered a host of private museums, such as the ones belonging to Sir Joseph Banks and his friend and neighbour Richard Payne Knight, who lived at number 3 Soho Square, where he had turned his front parlour into a showcase for the fine arts. Like Banks's literary gatherings, Knight's museum earned a mention in *Feltham's Picture of London for 1805*: 'Richard Payne Knight, Esq. is the proprietor of the famous picture of the Cradle, by Rembrandt,' Feltham reported, 'of a very capital large landscape, by Salvator; and of many very capital performances by other great masters. He has also made a very large and admirable selection of antique bronzes, cameos and intaglios, which, upon application, are not difficult of access; and Mr. Knight, from having so long resided abroad, is particularly attentive to foreigners.'

Knight's and Banks's museums were predated by Sir Ashton Lever's extraordinary Holophusicon, which had opened in 1774 in Leicester Fields. Lever, an eccentric country gentleman from Alkrington, near Manchester, had started what can only be described as his mania for collecting when, fresh out of university, he acquired nearly 4,000 live birds. According to his biography, which appeared in *The European Magazine* in August 1784, 'he frequently rode from London to Alkrington, with cages full of birds, which he brought safe by holding them with a full-stretched arm, and galloping till the arm was tired, and then stopping to change hands. He had, at the same time,' the article continued, 'the best trained pack of beagles in his neighbourhood, and pointers in such perfection, that he is known to have had fifteen in the field all making a point at the same instant. He had frequently five or six hunters at the same time, all lying down and rising at the word of command, fetching, carrying, opening and shutting doors, and many other tricks.'

This forerunner of Barbara Woodhouse also had a tame bullfinch that sang on command, and a goose that waited at table 'with a napkin under its wing'. But this was not enough for him: in the early 1860s, he brought a boat-load of 'curious foreign shells' back from Dunkirk, after which he developed a passion for fossils. The birds, which he had now tired of, were ruthlessly stuffed and nailed on to perches in his museum, or were given away to friends.

Lever's vast natural history collection, exhibited at Alkrington, soon became so popular with day-trippers that he was forced to make a public announcement that he would have to refuse admission to anyone who came on foot. But when one gentleman pedestrian who had been turned away 'in order to obviate the objection, mounted a cow in a neighbouring lane, and rode back to the house, where he soon procured admission', Lever realized that something drastic would have to be done.

So, in 1774, he moved his collection to London, where he rented the grandest premises available – Leicester House, which had recently become vacant. Here, according to 19th-century historian Tom Taylor, people could see the following curiosities:

1. The staircase: weapons of war of different nations, horns, bones, teeth and heads of animals, &c. 2. Native fossils, &c., birds (5,000 in number). 3. Extraneous fossils and birds. 4. Shells and birds. 5. Birds, beasts and marbles. 6. Beasts, including hippopotamus, rhinoceros, and great ant-eater, with cases of insects. 7. Antiquities. 8. Birds, including the great bustard, penguin, birds of paradise, &c. 9. Birds of China and India. 10. Reptiles. 11. Fishes and corals. 12. Monkeys.

13. Ostriches and miscellanea. 14. Dresses of various nations. 15. Otaheite room. 16. Club room: warlike weapons of savage tribes. 17. The Sandwich Islands room, a continuation of Otaheite room; besides an outhouse with the elephant and zebra, which when alive belonged to Her Majesty.

All this for the princely entrance fee of 5s 3d – which was soon reduced to half a crown when Lever discovered that the paying London public were not nearly as interested in seeing his Holophusicon as the people back home in Manchester, who had been let in free.

Sadly, the move to London was a financial disaster for Lever, who must have been heartbroken at the public's indifference to his museum: for, as he once admitted in an advertisement, 'The pleasure of pleasing is the only true pleasure I ever knew, nor would everything the world could produce give me delight without sharers in my enjoyment.' After 12 months in Leicester House his vast collection, then amounting to some 26,000 items, was disposed of by a heavily undersubscribed lottery. The lucky (or not) winner was a Mr Parkinson, who had bought only two tickets out of the 36,000 on sale. Parkinson subsequently had to build a special museum to contain his win – the Rotunda, situated on the south side of the Thames, near Blackfriars Bridge. The Museum Leverian, as it was then called, staggered on till 1806, when every single item was sold off at an auction which lasted 65 days.

In 1783, nine years after the Holophusicon opened, Scottish surgeon John Hunter moved from Jermyn Street in Mayfair to number 28 Leicester Square, bringing with him his ever-expanding collection of medical specimens, which he housed in a large gallery at the back of the house. Behind this, and fronting on to Castle Street, was a small medical school where his pupils could study 'human and comparative anatomy' – the necessary corpses were filched from the local churchyards. Collecting, medicine and grave-robbing apparently ran in the family, for John's brother William, an anatomist, had his own dissecting theatre and an internationally-renowned museum of rare medals, minerals, shells, stuffed animals and 'specimens of rare diseases' in his house in Great Windmill Street, a mere stone's throw away.

A few years later this scientific tone dropped, if only a little, when a man called Robert Barker opened a panorama near Leicester Square. Barker, an artist, had apparently thought up the idea of reproducing a 360-degree view of nature while sketching at the top of Edinburgh's Calton Hill. In 1787 he obtained a 14-year patent on his circular, concave pictures, a 'new contrivance or Apparatus which he calls La Nature, a coup d'oeil for the purpose of displaying views of Nature at large'.

Two years later he brought his view of Edinburgh to a large room in the Haymarket. According to his first advertisement, 'The exhibition affords the spectator a complete prospect of the whole horizon as appearing from the top of the observatory on the Calton Hill, comprehending a circle of several hundred miles. The idea of this view is perfectly original (for which a patent is taken out), and the effect singular, original, and pleasing.'

In fact, this 'triumph of perspective' pleased so many people that Barker and one of his sons, Henry Aston, painted a second panorama – this time of London and the Thames – which they showed in an outbuilding behind Barker's house in Castle Street.

Barker's next project was to build a permanent rotunda to house his panorama. The new building, in Leicester Place, opened on 25 May 1793, with 'A View of the Grand Fleet regularly moored at Spithead'. This was followed by a view of the entire British and French fleets on the 'Glorious First of June', battle scenes from the Napoleonic Wars and a panorama of Constantinople.

When his 14-year patent ran out, Barker found himself with competition from an unexpectedly close source when his eldest son, Thomas Edward, went into partnership with one of the panorama's painters, and opened a rival establishment in the Strand. Robert was so furious that when he died in 1806 he made no mention of Thomas Edward in his will. The Leicester Place rotunda was left to his younger son, Henry Aston, who ran the business until 1826, when he retired on the proceeds of 'The Battle of Waterloo', and handed over the reins of power to his partners, brothers John and Robert Burford.

Burford's Panorama, as it was later known, carried on till 1861, when Robert, the last surviving brother, died. The empty drum was then converted into a church for the French Roman Catholic community which had settled in Soho since the Revolution, and though the original building was partly destroyed by bombs during the Blitz, the rebuilt church of Notre Dame de France still occupies the same circular site today.

If Burford's had been 'an educational institution of the highest and purest value', as John Ruskin described it, there was soon more low-brow entertainment on offer round the corner in Leicester Square. In 1806 'The Invisible Lady, or Delphic Oracle' appeared – or, rather, did not appear – at number 1 Leicester Square, where, according to a handbill, 'in a small Temple, impossible for [a] human being to enter, and unconnected with any surrounding object, will proceed a voice, supposed to be [in the] manner in which The Ancients Communicated with their *Gods*. And which will even describe the dress, nation, or any particular, and so completely deceiving the senses as to appear the EFFECT OF MAGIC. And there will also be produced, as if by Enchantment, MUSIC From the softest to the highest note, close to the Ear, in this philosophical and highly pleasing Exhibition. Admittance one shilling.'

Leicester House was demolished in the early 1790s, but its neighbour, Savile House, had survived two attacks by the Gordon rioters to degenerate into a multi-purpose entertainment centre. One of its longest-lived exhibitions was that of Mary Linwood's embroidered pictures. Miss Linwood, who came from Leicestershire, had started embroidering copies of old master paintings at the age of 13, and did not stop until she was 78. She had no help at all with this esoteric work except in threading her needles. According to the 1869 *Cyclopaedia of Female Biography*, in which she is the only professional needlewoman to get a mention, some of her larger pictures took as long as 10 years to complete. The *Cyclopaedia* went on to claim that 'No needle-work, either of ancient or modern times, ever surpassed the celebrated productions of Miss Linwood.'

The Linwood Gallery, which was up an 'imposing flight of steps' on the first floor of Savile House, opened on 14 March 1809. For 2s. 6d., the curious could feast their eyes on crewel-work copies of *Pigs and Dogs at Play* (after Morland), Gainsborough's *Shepherd in a Storm*, and Sir Joshua Reynolds's *King Lear*, which were among the 60-odd works on display. Most of the embroidered 'paintings' were shown in one large salon hung with scarlet drapery, and to discourage people from touching them to see if they were real, the pictures were separated from the public by high railings. From this salon, a long corridor led to a kind of 2D needlework Chamber of Horrors, where one could see an embroidered Lady Jane Grey waiting for her execution in a mock-up of her prison cell.

The years passed and Linwood's straggled on, growing dusty and moth-eaten. Dickens called it 'a gloomy sepulchre of needlework'. It did not finally close until 1845, when its creator died at the grand old age of 90. By this time, the rest of Savile House had deteriorated into the venue for a plethora of second-rate side-shows. In Linwood's day these had included an 'Astronomical Panorama', 'Miller's Mechanical and Beautiful Picturesque Representations', a shopping bazaar, the 'Saville Palace Wine, Concert and Exhibition Rooms' and William Green's shooting gallery – which achieved a short-lived notoriety in June 1840 when a 17-year-old waiter named Edward Oxford practised his aim there before attempting to assassinate Queen Victoria as she drove up Constitution Hill.

Without Linwood's to raise the tone, the standard of Savile House side-shows dropped even further to include Madame Warton's 'Unequalled Tableaux Vivants and Poses Plastiques'; a 'Lapland Giantess, 7 feet 2 inches in height', and 'Joseph Gantonio, the young Italian Giant, 7 feet 7 inches high, 5 feet 5 inches round the waist'; a comic opera, performed 'by real negroes direct from the cotton fields of America'; the ubiquitous bearded lady, this one highly educated, with a jet-black beard which reached 'from one ear to the other ear without impairing her beauty'; an egg-hatcher 'as shown by command at Windsor Castle'; and, in 1852, Mons. Auguste Reinham's 'Industrious Fleas'. By the time this last troupe of 100 little blood-suckers had arrived in Savile House, they had already 'received the distinguished patronage of the continental sovereigns', and were apparently as intelligent as the bearded lady: the handbill promised a ballroom scene 'in which two ladies and two gentlemen dance a polka. The orchestra is composed of fifteen musicians, playing on different instruments of proportionate size. Four having a game at whist. A little brunette on a sofa is flirting with a fashionable beau, while her mamma's mind is intensely engaged in the politics of a newspaper. The saloon is lighted by three elegant chandeliers. The performers in this as in all the following pieces are fleas, dressed and instructed according to their respective tasks, &c., &c., &c.'

Etcetera. The shows and exhibitions were as numerous and as ephemeral as the names given to parts of the house: the Grand American Hall; the Royal Living Marionette Theatre; the Walhalla;

the Royal Victoria Hall; the Sans Souci; Saville Hall and Hotel; the Saville House Gymnasium; the Théâtre de Variétés; and finally the El Dorado Music Hall and Café Chantant. In fact, the place became so confusing, as one contemporary wrote, that 'few could tell whether it was a theatre, a wine vault, a billiard-room, a coffee-shop, a gunsmith's, or a Royal Academy; or, if they could, they never knew, amidst the ascending and descending steps, and doors and passages, which one must take to get anywhere . . . A confusion of sounds further tends to bewilder the visitor: the noise of everything is heard everywhere else . . . and it is only by taking refuge in the lowest apartment, which partakes of a coffee-room, a cabin, and a cellar, that you will find repose.'

All this chaos disappeared with a big bang on the night of 28 February 1865, when a workman in search of the source of a gas-leak took a lighted candle down into the Wine Shades basement bar. The result was a huge explosion and a enormous fire. By the following morning, all that was left of Savile House was a charred black hole.

If the erection of Burford's panorama in the 1790s, and the gradual partitioning-off of Savile House into small galleries, had started a decline in Soho's poshest residential area, the building of the Royal Panopticon and the Wyld Monster Globe surely finished off that change.

Since Leicester Square had been part of the original Lammas pasture land acquired by Lord Leicester back in the 17th century, there had always been open access to the central garden, which had been railed off by wooden posts by the original building contractors, and planted with four rectangular lawns bordered with elm trees. In the 1720s a small wall topped with iron railings had been built around the lawns. By 1753, these had been replaced by a new set of rails, and the tree in the middle of the garden had been uprooted by a gilded equestrian statue of George I.

When the Leicester Estate was broken up and sold off in the 1780s, most of the square passed to members of the Tulk family. At the time it was still a very elegant place, which diarist Sophie von la Roche, writing in 1786, described as 'one of the many big London Squares with beautiful lawns inset; in the middle stands a statue, and there are paths all round with neatly wrought iron railings, lit up by lamps at night'. However, in 1808 the garden was sold to Charles Elms, a local dentist, who, according to reports, let it degenerate into a 'very ruinous and dilapidated' place. The lawn went to seed, the weeds ran riot, and in time the garden became a real eyesore.

By the middle of the century, when the young Liberal MP and geographer James Wyld was looking for a plot on which to build 'a great model of the Earth's surface' to celebrate 'the congregation in London of the different nations and races of our empire and the world' (presumably for the Great Exhibition of 1851 in Kensington Gardens), he decided that the overgrown garden in the centre of Leicester Square was the perfect place for it; and, after hefty negotiations with the landlords and local people, who were not at all keen on the idea of a huge building being constructed on one of the rare patches of Soho greenery, he managed to obtain a 10-year lease on the plot.

Wyld's Monster Globe went up within a matter of months, engulfing the overgrown grass and George I's rather dilapidated statue. It opened on 2 June 1851, about four weeks after the Crystal Palace. Its high brick walls and domed roof dominated the domestic architecture of the square. Inside the rotunda was a huge circular globe, 60 feet in diameter, on the inside of which were 'delineated the physical features of the earth,' cast in plaster-of-Paris panels, which sightseers could view while strolling around four viewing levels, linked by stairs. Exhibitions of maps, atlases and globes were held in four rooms projecting from the rotunda at street level.

During its 10-year existence, Wyld's Globe was the venue for a variety of dioramas, lectures and temporary exhibitions, including a moving diorama of Russia, a military museum, and a gold-mine complete with 'casts of monster nuggets'. Though Wyld would probably have left it standing for ever, it was demolished after a series of law suits in the late summer of 1862.

Meanwhile an exotic structure, destined to become one of the West End's most famous landmarks, had risen like a foreign phoenix on the east side of Leicester Square, where the Bagnio of Mary Tofts fame had been replaced by the outlandish premises of a short-lived and disastrous society called the Royal Panopticon of Science and Art.

The Panopticon – the name was derived from the Greek words *pan* ('all') and *optikos* ('sight') – was 'An Institution for Scientific

Exhibitions, and for Promoting Discoveries in Arts and Manufactures'. The brainchild of an Irish entrepreneur named Edward Marmaduke Clarke, its aims, which were set out in a Royal Charter in February 1850, were as worthy as they were numerous:

> To exhibit and illustrate, in a popular form, discoveries in science and art, to extend the knowledge of useful and ingenious inventions, to promote and illustrate the application of science to the useful arts; to instruct by courses of lectures, to be demonstrated and illustrated by instruments, apparatus and other appliances, all branches of science, literature, and the fine and useful arts; to exhibit various branches of the fine and mechanical arts, manufactures, and handicrafts, by showing the progress to completion in the hands of the artisan and mechanic; to exhibit the productions of nature and art, both British and Foreign; to illustrate history, science, literature, and the fine and useful arts, by pictorial views and representations; to illustrate the science of acoustics, by lectures, music, and otherwise; to give instructions in the various branches of science and the mechanical arts; to afford to inventors and others facilities to test the value of their ideas by means of the machinery, instruments, and other appurtenances of the Institution; and generally to extend and facilitate a greater knowledge and love of the arts and sciences on the part of the public.

After a great deal of debate about the design of the premises that would be needed to accomplish these multifarious aims, the Panopticon's Council decided to use the Moorish or Saracenic style of architecture, 'as a novelty', to the horror of their chosen architect, T. Hayter Lewis. However, as soon as Hayter Lewis realized that since 'the Saracens had not been in the habit of building Panopticon institutions', the Moorish style would allow him to 'obtain a tolerably free scope in working out the design' – in other words, that he had no precedent to live up to – he decided that it was not such a bad idea after all.

The premises duly went up at a cost of £80,000. Nothing could have been more out of keeping with the neighbouring Georgian houses. The exterior was straight out of the *Arabian Nights*, with a Moorish façade covered with glazed Minton tiles, a horseshoe-arched entrance protected by a cast-iron portcullis, and a polygonal roof topped by a railed platform and twin minarets. Inside were lecture rooms and an enormous rotunda nearly 100 feet in diameter, its walls decorated with alabaster, glass mosaics and enamelled slate, its centre dominated by a fountain which was fed by an artesian well and which shot jets of coloured water 90 feet into the air – an apparatus apparently designed to counteract the effects of the central heating. From the floor of the rotunda rose iron columns, which supported two galleries – the lower one octagonal, the upper 16-sided. On one of these galleries was a Photographic Room which could be reached by an elaborate, hydraulically powered 'ascending carriage', or by twin staircases which met over the entrance door. One side of the rotunda was dominated by an enormous organ console two storeys high, and the saucer-domed roof was inset with star-shaped windows and a large skylight.

The *Illustrated Handbook*, written by William White, a chemistry lecturer, described the rotunda as 'the most splendid room ever appropriated to scientific and artistic purposes'. It was certainly an eye-catcher. Soon after it opened on 16 March 1854, it was drawing crowds of over 1,000 visitors a day. However, the exhibitions and lectures held there were incredibly boring. The *Illustrated London News* of 18 March 1854 cited some of these 'attractions' as apparatus 'to illustrate diving; turning or planing, drilling and boring, the combustion of steel; aurora-borealis and thunder; pin-making and needle-making, and gas cookery; freezing mercury; the liquefaction and solidification of carbonic acid; ballooning under water; galvanism, magnetism, and the electric light; and a large collection of machinery, models, &c.'

As can be seen from this extract from the *Illustrated Handbook*, a day out at the Panopticon was the antithesis of any self-respecting Sohoite's idea of having a good time:

The Council . . . are determined that the Royal Panopticon shall not be a place for mere lounging and sight-seeing. Its most important feature will be profitable activity, so that, whilst the eye is gratified with an exhibition of every startling novelty which science and the fine arts can produce, and the ear enchanted with delectable and soul-stirring music, the mind shall have food of the most invigorating character . . .

Here the artisan and mechanic may learn how to avail themselves of the discoveries and inventions of the master-minds who have taken the lead in their own pursuits. The artist may take the initiative from the admirable works around him, and from the success which is shown to have accompanied talent and industry, gather fresh courage for the contest. The manufacturer, by devoting a few hours weekly to the enunciations of the chemical professor, and the oral explanations upon the models, will be better prepared to meet that competition which, though the very life of commercial enterprise, is ever fatal to the indulgence of inactivity and ignorance. The same means of instruction are available to the agriculturist, so that he may at once determine the quality of soils, and the value of the thousand-and-one species of manure offered to his notice as the acme of perfection.

In short, the Panopticon stank. In the words of *The Builder*, the Council had 'failed to produce a single illustration of their purpose', on top of which there was 'a want of proper management, or, indeed, of any management whatsoever'. And William White, the *Handbook*'s author, later did a remarkable volte-face and called the place a 'total, irretrievable failure' resulting 'from the unnatural alliance . . . of religious profession and commercial enterprise'.

The organization had lost money from the start. As *The Builder* reported, 'The opening had been postponed, not month after month, but quarter after quarter, to the great loss . . . of the shareholders.' Then, a few months after it did open, the cholera epidemic broke out in Broad Street, which no doubt put tourists off coming into town. Attendances at the Panopticon dwindled. By August 1856, the Saracenic premises were up for auction. They were sold for the cut-price sum of £9,000 to a theatrical manager and impresario called E.T. Smith.

Smith threw out the organ with the Panopticon's ideals, and installed a circus-ring in the rotunda. The Alhambra Palace, as it was now, more fittingly, called, re-opened on 3 April 1858 with a show by Howes and Cushing's American Circus. Two months later, the building was graced by its first royal visitors when Queen Victoria and Prince Albert – who had given the Royal Panopticon the cold shoulder – brought their children to see Black Eagle, 'The Horse of Beauty'.

After the royal seal of approval had been given, the Alhambra went from strength to strength, and before long Smith decided to turn his circus into a music hall. The rotunda was repainted, a stage was built on the site of the organ, the pit was filled with tables and chairs and the Alhambra Palace Music Hall opened its doors in December 1860. 'For the economical outlay of sixpence,' reported *The Era*, 'the visitor will find himself in comfortable possession of a commodious seat in a magnificently-appointed and admirably-ventilated hall, with every physical refreshment he may desire obtainable at the lowest rates, and of the best quality, and with a rational and pleasing entertainment superadded for his mental delectation.'

This was more like it. Dioramas, light opera and ballet, stuntmen like Léotard, 'the Daring Young man on the Flying Trapeze', and Blondin, the man who had crossed Niagra Falls on a tight-rope, were among the acts that appeared at the Alhambra over the next few years under the management of Smith, William Wild Jnr, and Frederick Strange, who took the building over in 1864. During the next 18 years Strange was to turn the theatre into one of London's most important ballet venues, and also to reintroduce to Soho masked balls as sumptuous as any in Theresa Cornelys's day.

In the early hours of 7 December 1882, however, the Alhambra went the way of Savile House and the Pantheon, when it was gutted by a mysterious fire. Twenty fire engines failed to put out the blaze in a scene of 'terrible grandeur'. The walls of the building and the minarets miraculously survived the destruction. 'Even when the fire had nearly burned itself out,' *The Era* reported in lyrical vein, 'and when Leicester Square and Soho had again lapsed into comparative darkness, the towers were blazing still, licked by circling wreaths of flame, and shone out like beacons from the smoky obscurity above.'

Rebuilt behind its original façade, the Alhambra later became one of London's most famous music halls, variety, opera bouffe and ballet venues. In 1919 and 1921 it hosted Diaghilev's Ballet Russe. In 1923 it made the name of Gracie Fields, who appeared there in a touring revue, *Mr Tower of London*. After a brief career as a film-set, it disappeared under the bulldozers in the autumn of 1936, and was replaced a year later by the Art-Deco-inspired Odeon Cinema.

Over the years many actors and, particularly, actresses have chosen to live in Soho – partly because of its proximity to the theatres of

Drury Lane and, more recently, Shaftesbury Avenue, and partly because of its Bohemian atmosphere. Yet not all of them have had such happy memories of Soho as Fanny Kemble, who, with her family, moved into number 31 Soho Square in 1824.

Charles Kemble, Fanny's father, was a member of the fabled theatrical family – but unfortunately he was one of its least successful members. His second-rate skills as an actor were only exceeded by his third-rate abilities as a theatrical manager: by 1829 he had let his own theatre, Covent Garden, fall into £13,000 worth of debt. It was then that 17-year-old Fanny, who had never wanted to act, saved the day by going on stage and causing a sensation as Juliet. In fact, she was such a success that before the end of the season Charles had made enough money to pay off all his creditors.

Between performances, the reluctant star cooled off in the garden, where she also learned her new lines. 'Walked in the Square,' she noted one day in her diary, 'and studied Lady Teagle. The trees are thickly cloaked with leaves, and the new-mown grass, even in the midst of London, smelt fresh and sweet. I was quite alone in the Square, and enjoyed something like country sensations.'

Actor Edmund Kean had no such happy recollections of his childhood in Gerrard Street. Born in 1787 in Gray's Inn, Kean was the illegitimate and unwanted child of an actress called Nance (or Ann) Carey. The identity of Kean's father was never really known – he was either a local tailor, an unbalanced surveyor's apprentice, or, as Kean would have it, the Duke of Norfolk. Three months after he was born, Nance abandoned her son for the first time. When he was two, she gave him up for good. Ill-fed and neglected, Kean was shunted between relatives and friends of the family, becoming in the process a sickly boy: for years he had to wear leg-irons day and night to correct his bow legs.

Eventually he was taken in by an uncle, Moses Kean, who lived in Lisle Street, and, through the charity of a Jewish neighbour, was sent to school in nearby Chapel Street. But he played truant so often that in addition to the leg-irons, a brass collar was fixed round his neck engraved, 'This boy belongs to No. 9 Lisle Street, Leicester Square.'

A few doors down from number 9 was the home of a Frenchman called Anthony Le Texier, where Kean might well have developed his own taste for drama. For *Feltham's Picture of London for*

1805 lists Texier as giving 'Readings of French Dramatic Pieces, in an uncommon style of excellence, so as to attract numerous and fashionable audiences, and excite the greatest applause'.

Kean's theatrical career kicked off just round the corner from his uncle's house, at the Sans Souci Theatre on the east side of newly-built Leicester Place. The Sans Souci, a pretty, four-storeyed building with a small colonnade of Doric columns, had been built in 1796 by song-writer, composer, dramatist and performer Charles Dibdin, a rather truculent character who had previously run his own small theatre, also called the Sans Souci, in the Strand.

'By the time I proposed leaving the Strand,' Dibdin explained in his autobiography, *The Professional Life of Mr. Dibdin, written by Himself*, 'the whole of Leicester-Place had been built up and finished, except a chasm which seemed to answer my purpose perfectly well, and which, indeed, I had almost bargained for five years before.' As there were houses on either side of this plot, he found he 'had no walls to erect, except one in front of the house, another at the back', and when he 'came to measure the ground, its dimensions were to an inch, as far as it regarded the theatre, exactly the same as those of the premises I was about to quit, so I had nothing to do but remove my materials as a frame, and refix them'.

The new Sans Souci, which opened on 8 October 1796 with an entertainment called *The General Election*, was 'fitted up in a showy style, but with very humble pretensions to what may be called classical taste,' according to a contemporary newspaper. The journalist went on to say: 'Mr Dibdin, however, if not a man of genius, is a man of much ingenuity. He writes ballads, sets them to musick, plays and sings them himself; and he now even engrosses the painter's art, and has embellished the Sans Souci with pictures from his own pencil.'

During the winter season, Dibdin gave three performances a week at the Sans Souci, between times selling his music from a small shop on the premises, and renting out the theatre for recitals, variety acts and poetry readings such as those in which the 12-year-old Edmund Kean performed at in 1799. But, talented as Dibdin was, he had made a grave mistake by leaving the Strand. As he admitted, 'I had removed too far from the city, whence I had ever drawn my most substantial support.' Heavily mortgaged, his theatre was offered for sale. In 1805 it was rented to Frederick Schirmer, who, like Texier in Lisle Street, catered for Soho's immigrant population, and staged 'Musical and Dramatical Interludes in the German Language' – many of them featuring his child-star son, Albert.

Sadly, the Sans Souci soon fell into disuse as a theatre: between 1807 and 1828 it was an army and clothing warehouse. In its last years it was used for occasional benefit performances, then by a restaurateur, and even a linen draper. It was finally demolished in 1898.

Having made his London début at the Sans Souci, Edmund Kean struggled to make a living as a provincial actor, returning to London in January 1814 to stun Drury Lane audiences with his interpretation of Shylock in *The Merchant of Venice*. Previously, Shakespeare's most famous Jew had always been played as an unpleasant character. But, like most Sohoites, Kean was not one to fall into the trap of stereotyping minorities, and he played Shylock first and foremost as a sympathetic man. 'It is an innovation,' the stage manager remarked at one rehearsal. 'I wish it to be so,' insisted Kean. The stage manager remained sceptical. 'Depend on it, it will not do.' He was wrong. Kean was acclaimed as an outstanding actor. 'No actor has come out for many years at an equal to him,' Hazlitt wrote in the *Morning Chronicle*.

With Kean and Kemble both treading the boards in Covent Garden, it would be easy to think that the early 19th century was the golden age of English theatre. But, in the opinion of one famous actress, standards of acting were definitely on the way down. To begin with, there was no proper training-ground for would-be actors and actresses. Attracted by what they saw as the glamour of the profession, young men and women simply hung around the stage-doors in the hope of picking up a job. A few of these made it: most did not; in the meantime, a number of them were lured into prostitution as a means of supporting themselves.

If anyone knew the London stage intimately, it was Frances Maria Kelly – or Fanny Kelly, as she was known. Born into a theatrical family in 1790, she had learned to recite long Shakespearian speeches by the time she was six, and made her first appearance at Drury Lane when she was only seven. Unlike many of her contemporaries, Miss Kelly knew how to act with conviction, and her unusually naturalistic style soon earned her a reputation as one of the finest actresses of her time. Unfortunately, she was far from a natural businesswoman, and the theatre which she opened in Dean Street must rank as one of the worst theatrical disasters of all time.

Though no great beauty, Kelly was an attractive and clever woman, with a vibrant personality and a lively mind. Mary Lamb, with whom she was great friends, gave her Latin lessons in her Bloomsbury flat, and Mary's brother, Charles Lamb, supervised her literary education. For years Charles was desperately in love with Fanny. In fact, he wanted very much to marry her. His infatuation with her shone through in one review of her he wrote for *The Examiner*: 'What a lass to go a-gypsying through the world with . . .!'

Though she was very fond of Charles, however, Fanny Kelly had no intention of settling down to get married. Even in middle age, she was not content with resting on her professional laurels, preferring to take on new challenges. In 1833, when she was 43 years old, she rented a theatre in the Strand where she ran a small dramatic academy and presented a revolutionary one-woman show. The most popular figure in these 'Dramatic Recollections and Studies of Character By Miss Kelly', in which she held her audience captive for two hours, was Mrs Parthian, a part written especially for her by Charles Lamb. An elderly lady, the character Mrs Parthian, simply sat in an armchair in the middle of the stage and shared a lifetime of theatrical gossip with her audience. The show was an artistic triumph, though unfortunately not a financial one: at the end of the season, she just about broke even.

Though quite small, the New Strand Theatre, as it was called, was still too large and expensive for Fanny Kelly's purposes. So when she moved to number 73 Dean Street the following year, she managed to obtain a licence to hold dramatic readings and theatrical performances in her new home. Once she had settled in, she decided to make her dearest dream into reality, and to build her very own theatre and drama school in the backyard of the house.

The house next door, number 74, which she soon acquired as well, already had its own theatrical connections, for in 1797 it had been the birthplace of a famous actress and Drury Lane manageress called Madame Vestris, who was the daughter of engraver Gaetano Bartolozzi. Behind this historic spot, and her own home, Kelly now went ahead with her plans for building an ultra-modern theatre, designed especially for her by architect and playwright Samuel Beazley, who lived up the road in number 29 Soho Square.

With the true dedication of a believer, Fanny Kelly sank most of her life savings into the venture. Building went ahead under the patronage of the Duke of Devonshire, one of her many influential friends. A manifesto was drawn up and submitted to the Duke for his approval. Among other things, this contained her reasons for opening the school:

> There is one point to which Miss Kelly has directed the most anxious consideration, and in the accomplishment of which she still is, and must continue to be, most actively engaged; namely, the necessity of providing resources for those who, whilst preparing for the Profession, are without the means of subsistence.
>
> Too many possessing considerable talent, urged by necessity, rush into humble and even disreputable positions in the Profession, from which they never rise, for want of those advantages which time and cultivation would have afforded them. Others, through some channel which commands a temporary footing, monopolize a station they have not talent to adorn; and, in either case, the result to *Female Candidates* is at least dangerous, if not pernicious, in their after course through life.
>
> To avoid this evil, Miss Kelly has devoted a branch of the Establishment to the intellectual improvement, and the industrious occupation of the youthful pupils of both sexes; affording to each a fair proportion of the funds arising from their own exertions. Thus every one will possess a power to provide against the chance of failure in the Dramatic Art, by the exercise of some ability, which, in another walk of life, may be esteemed both useful and respectable.

Due to the difficulty of installing the unique ultra-modern scene-shifting machinery, designed by engineer Rowland Macdonald Stephenson, plans to open the theatre in the spring of 1838 had to be abandoned. The first pupils at 'Miss Kelly's Theatre and Dramatic School' were not, in the end, taken on until the early months of 1840, and the grand opening of the theatre eventually took place on Monday, 25 May of that same year.

The theatre itself was a small jewel. The press described it as elegant, perfect, and 'undoubtedly the best-appointed little theatre in the country'. The opening-night audience of 200 people, who paid between 5s and 7s for each seat, was highly distinguished, though the Queen and the Prince Consort, who had been sent invitations, chose to go to the circus instead. Little did they know what a tragi-comic experience they were about to miss.

Undeterred by the royal snub, Fanny Kelly inaugurated her theatre with 'An Appropriate Address', after which there were performances of three plays: a 'trifle' called *Summer and Winter*, starring its author, Morris Barnett, and Lee Morton, a 17-year-old Irish actor, now better known as playwright Dion Boucicault; a melodrama called *The Sergeant's Wife*, in which Kelly took the title role; and a farce, also starring Kelly, entitled *The Midnight Hour!*

What should have been Fanny Kelly's most triumphant hour turned out to be her most humiliating. Though she had bragged that 'the dialogue would at least be heard' in her theatre, the much-vaunted modern machinery made so much noise that no one in the audience could hear a word that was said on stage. The actors struggled on, but their lines were completely drowned out by the clanking of heavy metal chains and the rattle of a huge crank underneath the stage. On top of that, whenever the scenery moved, the scene-shifters could be seen by the audience.

Performances on the Tuesday, Wednesday and Thursday were equally disastrous, and played in front of shrinking audiences. On Friday, Fanny was forced to dismiss the entire company and close the theatre for 'an indefinite period'. In the words of *Kidd's Journal*, the whole idea had been 'a complete failure' for the company and Kelly alike. 'The prices charged settled the business in one short week, to the injury, the serious injury of the performers and the consternation of the lessee, who thought *her* attractions alone would fill the theatre!' Kidd added cruelly. 'This insane delusion has speedily been dispelled.'

Fanny Kelly was down, but she refused to be beaten. During the next few months she poured what little money she had left into getting rid of Stephenson's expensive machinery: it was so cumbersome that the builders practically had to demolish the theatre in order to get it out. Nine months later, she re-opened with a repeat of her Strand Theatre monologues. But the strain of the whole business had broken her health, and she was forced to retire from the stage the following year.

For a time she kept the school going by renting the theatre out to various companies, including The Amateurs, the most famous amateur dramatic company in the country, of which Charles Dickens was a prominent member. On 3 January 1846, The Amateurs put on a benefit performance for her, but the money raised did not enable her to keep the theatre on, and she was evicted from the premises a few years later.

The fiasco had lost Fanny Kelly her fortune, her home and her health, yet it had not dented her fierce independence. In her new home in Moscow Road, Bayswater, she set up a new 'school' – which was in reality a genteel theatrical boarding-house, where she gave occasional lessons in the front parlour. Eventually she moved to Feltham, Middlesex, where, despite her ill-health, she lingered on till she was 92. Though she was very poor, she remained as proud as ever, and even turned down the offer of a civil list pension which was made to her in her ninety-first year.

Meanwhile, ill-luck continued to haunt the little theatre in Dean Street through various name changes. In November 1850, the first performance there of a company called The New English Opera House was denounced by *The Illustrated London News* as an unbelievable

> exhibition of incompetency and puerility. The only relief to the annoyance caused by the melancholy display, being that it presented itself throughout a three-act opera – *The Last Crusade*, by Mr. Mitchell, the blind composer – as a burlesque; and as such was laughed at by those amateurs who could not feel how much injury was done to 'native talent' by the disastrous performance; whilst, on the other hand, the 'friends' of the establishment, by a series of parodies on great lyric triumphs, in the shape of encores, re-calls, and ovations, were adding fuel to the flame of disgust and discontent. Criticism on Mr. Mitchell's pretensions is utterly disarmed by the glaring deficiency of the execution. For the future foundation, on a permanent basis, of a really National Opera House, nothing could be more fatal to art and artists than Tuesday's *Last Crusade*.

In 1860, the Soho Theatre, as it had been known, briefly became the Théâtre Français, designed to draw in the local French community, but this lasted less than a year. By November 1861, the theatre had been taken over by a Serbian dancer and actress named Albina di Rhona, who redecorated it and renamed it The New Royalty. Here was staged a ghoulish, not to say racist, revenge melodrama called *Atar Gull*. The plot, based on a Eugène Sue romance, was described in vivid detail by *The Era*'s critic on 17 November. It apparently featured 'the persevering ferocity of a Negro, who, in revenge for his father having been hanged by a Jamaican planter, devotes himself to the task of exterminating all members of the planter's family. Firing houses, poisoning his victims, and encircling a young girl with a poisonous snake, with which coiled round her body, she rushes through a verandah shrieking upon the Stage, the slave accomplishes his ends, and keeps the spectators thrilled with every kind of atrocity.'

Which just goes to show that the plot of *Rambo* is not new. Even though the show starred 14-year-old Ellen Terry, it failed to draw in the crowds, and two months later the company folded.

However, on 25 March 1875, the theatre was at last the scene of an historic success – the première of *Trial By Jury*, the first Gilbert and Sullivan operetta to be staged by born-and-bred Sohoite Richard D'Oyly Carte. Then, on 13 March 1891, reported *The Times*, 'an orderly audience, including many ladies . . . listened attentively to the dramatic exposition of a subject which is not usually discussed outside the walls of an hospital' – the first performance in this country of Ibsen's *Ghosts*.

The Royalty Theatre, as it was later known, lingered on under various managements until 1938, when it was closed down as a fire risk, due to its position in the centre of the nitrate-laden film business. Hit by a bomb during the Blitz, its derelict remains were replaced by an office block in the early 1950s.

7

Cosmopolis

When the Reverend J. H. Cardwell walked into St Anne's church for the first time, he found the fabric of the building falling to pieces, and the deserted pews littered with bills advertising the local Continental restaurants and hotels. It was 1891. Shaftesbury Avenue and Charing Cross Road, opened less than five years earlier, had swept away King Street, Hog Lane and the Newport Market slums and turned Soho into two islands – north and south – to all intents and purposes cut off from the rest of the town. At night, theatre and music hall audiences thronged Leicester Square and the new thoroughfares, and after the shows the adventurous made the occasional quick sortie into Frith Street or Greek Street in order to find something to eat in one of the many cheap Continental restaurants which had opened up to cater for the local foreign clientele.

But the respectable middle-class English seldom lingered in Soho for long. It was, after all, still reputed to be one of the most notorious red-light districts in London, 'the resort of bullies', and 'a perfect little paradise for pimps'. The streets were lined with gambling dens, brothels masquerading as restaurants, and bogus massage parlours where innocent country girls were seduced into becoming 'nurses' and performing acts of mercy that would have made Florence Nightingale leap from her sick bed. Prostitutes stood on every corner, or after 1893, congregated round the new Memorial Fountain put up in Piccadilly Circus to commemorate the philanthropic 7th Earl of Shaftesbury. It was no wonder that people soon stopped calling the aluminium statue on top of the fountain the Angel of Christian Charity and nicknamed him Eros, the God of Love.

According to Mr W. Hall – a lay preacher at St Anne's church who wrote about Soho's seamier side in *Twenty Years in Soho* (1911) – the local night-clubs were considered not only 'a source of annoyance', but a real danger to unsophisticated working girls who were lured inside by unscrupulous men, and fed drugged beverages with horrifying, and unspecified, results. In fact, the very name Soho was synonymous with moral and physical danger. It was a district 'renowned for its manslaughters, its sudden deaths, its feuds'. When Hall was first sent to work in Soho in 1891, he was warned by a friend 'to be prepared to attend my own inquest and funeral at short notice'. Anyone who took a stand against the 'vice trade', as the business had become known, was likely to meet an untimely end. 'The Vestry letter-box one morning contained a post-card on which was a pen and ink sketch of myself turning a corner,' Hall recorded, 'and a man behind me in the act of driving a long knife between my shoulder blades, while in front was a yawning coffin ready to receive what remained of me. A skull and cross-bones completed the decoration on the card, and the legend beneath the coffin was: "Spy, villain, this much good for you. Revenge."'

In the end nothing terrible happened to Mr Hall, for the threats were all talk, like most Soho villainy before and since. The leaders of the vice trade were far too busy fighting among themselves to bother with attacking Soho's respectable citizens.

To outsiders, however, everyone who lived in the district was tarred with the same brush as the vice, with the result that Sohoites in the late 19th century did not have a much better reputation than the place itself. In 1900, *Cassell's Saturday Journal* chauvinistically dismissed three-quarters of them as 'foreigners born and bred', including in their numbers anarchists who 'meet at regular intervals to discuss the most diabolical plots of revenge on society'. Another newspaper article, published in 1896, even accused the locals of speaking 'a sort of mongrel, bestial dialect, more fit for the lips of gorillas and chimpanzees . . . a sort of reeking hotch-potch of obscene, and often quite meaningless expression.' Not surprisingly, this *Planet of the Apes* language was reported to be at its worst when the local pubs closed on Sunday nights.

It is a wonder that the Reverend Cardwell did not take one look at his new parish and run straight back to the relatively rural climes of Fulham, where he had come from. But Cardwell was not to be put off so easily. A born fighter, he was as willing to take on the vice trade as he was to reform the rates or to tackle the town clerk

– who blew his top when the new rector turned the old church mortuary into a bicycle shed.

Behind the façade of brothels, restaurants and theatres, Cardwell discovered a side of Soho that revellers out for a good time did not take the time to see: Soho was a village, a village that was home to about 12,000-odd men, women and children who worked incredibly hard to scrape a living. As Cardwell wrote in the Introduction to *Twenty Years in Soho*, 'Hidden from view behind all the glare and glitter are the poor who live by ministering to the luxuries of others, and having to reside near their work must perforce pay exorbitant rents.'

Sohoites got very little in return for these high rents. Despite certain improvements that had been made since the cholera outbreak, living conditions at the end of the 19th century were still appalling. Overcrowding was so much a part of Soho life that it was common to see signs in the windows of the old houses advertising 'Part of a room to let'. In fact, in 1896, houses in St Anne's parish were found to be, on average, twice as overcrowded as those elsewhere in London.

And rents were rising all the time – due largely to the success of the vice trade. As an increasing number of outsiders were attracted into the area at night – due partly to improved public transport – the number of brothels multiplied at an alarming rate. Though some brothels were quiet and businesslike, those around Leicester Square were little more than clip joints where 'unwary men' were lured by 'innocent young girls imported from the Continent' – only to be robbed on the staircase by *souteneurs* who were 'the very incarnation of a "bounder"'.

Yet the local landlords had discovered, to the cost of Sohoites, that renting their premises to a brothel-keeper was more remunerative than renting to, say, a tailor, a chef or a milliner. As a conference at St Anne's noted in November 1895, 'our respectable workers are in many cases being literally driven out of house and home to make room for the traders in vice who can afford to pay exorbitant rents'. If Soho was not to lose the families that were its life-blood, something drastic would have to be done to put an end to the deteriorating situation: as Cardwell realized, it was time for the first 'Clean Up Soho' campaign.

What happened next was clearly summed up in 1911 in *Twenty*

Years in Soho, under the prim heading, 'Crusade against the Trade in Vice'. It may sound very familiar to those who have found themselves involved in more recent fights to save Soho from porn-shops and unlicensed sex shows.

> It is an unsavoury subject, but the story of the last twenty years in Soho would not be complete without some mention of the crusade against 'disorderly houses' which was commenced in 1892 and which has been carried on with a considerable amount of success. At that time there were a large number of these houses in the parish and the evil was growing. Respectable families were being turned out of their homes in order that the houses might be let for the higher rent which vice could pay. St Anne's Vestry determined not to submit to this invasion, and began to take vigorous repressive measures. They sought the assistance of the police, who are always willing to act energetically when they are backed up by a public body, and they also asked for the help of the Charing Cross Vigilance Society. A Watch Committee was formed which met every fortnight and was ready to hear complaints and to take action when the evidence, in the opinion of their legal advisers, seemed to be sufficient to secure a conviction against offenders. Many disorderly houses were closed, in many cases by obtaining convictions against them, and in others by threatening legal proceedings. When the old vestry was superseded by the City Council, the inhabitants of Soho determined that the crusade should not be relinquished, and elected councillors who could be trusted to carry it on, and the result is that Soho, though by no means perfect, is a cleaner and purer place than it once was.

During this first clean-up campaign, the Reverend Cardwell became a staunch supporter of Sohoites. The so-called 'anarchists' written about in the press were in reality 'decent, moral-living people', he declared publicly as he stood up for the entire population – English and foreign, Christian and non-Christian alike.

Yet to outsiders, Soho was still 'the Devil's haunt', as one journalist called it. And though the police may have supported the Purity Crusade, they had it in for many of Soho's residents. Reporting to a Royal Commission in 1906, a certain Inspector McKay claimed that 'Greek-street, Soho, is one of the very worst streets I have to deal with. In fact, it is the worst street in the West End of London.

Crowds of people gather there nightly who are little else than a pest. I will go further and say that some of the vilest reptiles in London live there or frequent it.' Cardwell retaliated to these 'slanderous insinuations' in no uncertain terms: 'I will say there is not a single disreputable character in Greek-street,' he insisted. 'I will even go so far as to say that there is scarcely one in the whole of Soho' – a statement that was probably a little over the top.

But who were these Sohoites who inspired such strong feelings in the Reverend Cardwell? What was so special about them that made him leap to their defence? They were, for the most part, ordinary working people. They included tailors, pressers, seamstresses, dairy-workers, bakers, patissiers, waiters, musical instrument makers, shop assistants and chefs. They numbered Austrians, Americans, and Africans; Danes and Dutch; Belgians, French, Italians, Irish, Hungarians, Germans and Greeks; Norwegians, Poles, Portuguese and Persians; Romanians and Russians; Turks, Serbians, Spaniards, Swiss, Swedes and Welsh. Some were Catholics, many were Protestant. A growing number of relative newcomers were Russian and Polish Jews. With the local English population, they formed as diverse, as culturally rich and as cosmopolitan a group of individuals as have ever lived together in any part of London, at any time. They were the parents, grandparents, great-grandparents and great-great-grandparents of today's Sohoites.

When Victor Berlemont and his wife Victorienne came to London from France in 1900 to visit one of the international exhibitions which were periodically held at the Crystal Palace, they were so impressed with the city that they decided to stay and learn English, in the hope that they could then go into the catering trade. Not even after a lifetime in Britain did they accomplish their first aim – to learn the language satisfactorily. But their second aim – to go into catering – they certainly did accomplish. For Victor got a job in the kitchens of London's famous Hotel Cecil in the Adelphi, working under the great chef Escoffier, and when he had learned what he could from him he transferred to the Restaurant Européen in Dean Street, where he ran the kitchen while Victorienne supervised *la salle*.

There was really no need for them to learn English when they were living in Soho, London's *quartier Latin*, where over 200 years' worth of French exiles had consolidated a world of their own,

French in language and flavour. There were French pharmacies and barber shops, French printers and publishers, French *traiteurs* selling *jambon de Bayonne* and *saucissons de Bologne*; French grocery shops displaying creamy Bries and pungent Camemberts; French bakeries where the baguettes were stacked like batons, and the croissants were every bit as buttery and melt-in-the-mouth as those in Paris; and there were patisseries selling moist sticky babas and gateaux as fancily concocted as any Parisian couture hat.

The shelves of the local bookshops were lined with works by French authors, the newspaper racks stuffed with French journaux. For the well-to-do there were French restaurants, and for the less well-off, small family-run cafés with white muslin curtains, wooden floors sprinkled with sand in the French manner, and rush-bottomed chairs, where, for a small price, you could while away the time of day or night drinking absinthe or Ricard. If you could afford the prices, you could even have your laundry washed by skilled French *blanchisseuses*, who would bring your sheets back to you pressed, folded and neatly tied with ribbons, in wide baskets which they carried through the streets on their hips.

Yes, Soho was French. Or was it? Down in Brewer Street, the locals spoke only Italian, and the shops were stocked with sacks of pasta and polenta, with fat mortadella salamis and bowls of snow-white Ricotta cheese and jagged chunks of yellowing Parmesan. The aroma of simmering minestra wafted through the courtyards of St James's Residences, which was almost exclusively occupied by Italians who worked as cooks or waiters in the West End's numerous restaurants and hotels. The Italian catering workers living in Soho were so numerous that they had even established their own benefit society, the Società Italiana Cuochi-Camerieri, which was founded in 1886 in Gerrard Street, and 10 years later moved to large headquarters on the west corner of Greek Street and Soho Square, opposite the House of Charity.

Here, the rooms which once provided shelter for a penniless Thomas De Quincey now housed the Società's 500-odd members' Sick Benefit Club, a labour exchange and a social centre. On warm days, members could often be seen standing outside in the square, where, in 1898, a journalist from Manchester's *Umpire* watched 'a sort of undress bicycle gymkhana, composed of waiters off duty. The air is full of the language of Tasso, spoken with a Central London accent. One rider, indeed an enthusiast, is tearing round the square, having wagered to drink *en route*, in two rounds, a quart bottle of Whitbread's ale. Verily a merry, laughter-loving people, these sons of Italy.'

Quite a few Italian Sohoites worked as warehousemen at Crosse and Blackwell's jam factory which had been built on the north-east side of the square, on the site of the notorious brothel, Hooper's Hotel. During the summer months, horse-drawn carts bearing consignments of strawberries and raspberries would arrive here at midday direct from the Kent farms where the fruit had been picked as the sun rose that very same morning. As they crossed Sutton Street on their way home from work, the warehousemen might well stop off to say a prayer, or perhaps take confession, at St Patrick's church, which had been built in the Italianate style on the site of Theresa Cornelys's old assembly rooms in the early 1890s.

Like their French counterparts, many of the Italians in Soho had arrived in England as political refugees in the 1860s, during Garibaldi's crusade through Italy. Though Clerkenwell was the heart of Italian London, the late hours worked by anyone in the catering trade made it essential to live near their work, and the relatively cheap accommodation in Soho had quickly become a secondary 'Little Italy'. Like the French, the Italian-speaking community had also needed their own newspapers, cafés and food shops, and before long these had sprung up, run by families such as the Parmigianas, who gradually acquired a string of delicatessens in Old Compton Street. When Severino Parmigiana married Fortunata Camisa, a young woman from Parma, her brothers Isidor and Ennio came over to England to stay with her. Like their sister, they felt quite at home in Italian Soho, and in 1940, when they had saved enough money, they opened up a shop of their own.

If Soho was Italian to the Camisas, it was Jewish to Katie Gontarski. It was also a place she had never dreamed she would see. Born and brought up in a small Jewish *shtetl* near Warsaw, she had married a cobbler called Benjamin Gontarski in 1912. Three weeks after they were married, the young groom said he needed to go to Warsaw to buy some materials for his work. Their daughter, Ettie, takes up the tale:

He didn't come back, not for days then for weeks. Thinking he had deserted her, my mother went back to live with her parents leaving his family with all their wedding presents. Then to her amazement, she received a letter from England from him containing a gold sovereign – which was worth a fortune in those days. My father said he hadn't told her he was emigrating, in case she or anyone else stopped him leaving the *shtetl*. He was now in Soho, staying with his brother who was a tailor in Berwick Street, and he would send for her as soon as he could afford to. She joined him in England the next year. First she had to pay someone to smuggle her across the Polish border. Then the boat brought her first to the Temporary Jews Shelter in the Tilbury docks. But as they sailed into the Thames estuary, my mother saw a little rowing boat coming towards them, with a man standing up in it, waving. It was my father, who had come to meet her there.

As with the Italians, the Jewish community in London was centred outside Soho – in the East End, where it staffed the sweatshops which made poor-quality garments for the lower end of the tailoring industry. But the Whitechapel tailors' strike of 1891 had driven a number of tailors' families into Soho, where, like the Scandinavian tailors already living in the area, they had found better work as high-class outdoor workers, sewing, pressing and finishing men's suits for the nearby, very posh Savile Row tailors.

The 1880s and 1890s and the opening years of the century saw wave upon wave of Jewish refugees arrive in England, pushed out of Poland and Russia by pogroms, repressive legislation and open, escalating anti-Semitism. Soho soon became an alternative starting-off place to Whitechapel. Within 30 years of the tailors' strike, the streets around Berwick Street market had become predominantly Yiddish-speaking, with kosher butchers, fishmongers, bakeries and restaurants opening up around D'Arblay Street, Wardour Street, Berwick Street and Noel Street. Before long, Soho had several small synagogues, the largest of which was the West End Talmud Torah and Bikkur Holim Synagogue, which in 1917 took over an old workhouse in Manette Street.

The French, Italians and Jews formed the three largest foreign groups in Soho. But there were other groups, too: a Swiss community living around Golden Square, many of whom worked in the woollen trade; Swedish and Greek tailors; a German community; and even an Anglo-Chinese family. And although turn-of-the-century Soho was a predominantly foreign area, there were, of course, British people living there, including a sizeable Welsh community who, like the Pugh family, ran the dairies which stood on almost every street corner.

The separate communities may have lived and worked cheek by jowl in overcrowded houses and tenement flats, yet somehow every nationality kept to its own part of Soho: Sadie Feigen, who lived near Jewish Berwick Street market, remembers that 'we didn't know the French and the Italians, because they were in Frith Street, Dean Street and Greek Street, and we never went there. What did we need to go there for when we had everything we needed where we were? So we only mixed with Jewish people, because there were only Jewish people around our streets.' To Englishman Bill Rest, who was born above his father's clock-repairing shop in Beak Street, anywhere east of Wardour Street was 'a foreign country'. A lot of the people who lived in Ingestre Place were English. And, as Rica Teagno remembers, 'Nearly everyone where I lived in St James's Residences was Italian. But,' she adds, 'it didn't matter what nationality you were – everyone got on.'

The harmonious co-existence of different nationalities and religions was something of a revelation to Soho's newly-arrived Russian and Polish Jews, who had been used to open hostility from their Gentile neighbours in their countries of birth. When they came to Soho it seemed they had arrived 'in paradise': for the first time in their lives they did not need to look over their shoulders apprehensively whenever they went out in the street.

'I have no recollection of real anti-semitism,' says Zinna Bulmore. 'Some people say there were loads of incidents. You could never go around Bateman Street, for example – people there might shout, "Bloody little Jew!" But it wasn't vicious – nobody ever harmed anybody – not in Soho. And if they did say something, we'd just say, "Oh, shut up!" We wouldn't take any notice of it. In Poland, we would have been frightened by it. But here we weren't.

'If you live in a community where there are many foreigners, you feel safe. I can remember one English family who lived about three doors away from us. They were well meaning people. But when they'd had too much to drink it was "Bloody Jews! Bloody foreigners!" It wasn't specific to Jews, it was anybody who wasn't a White Protestant British-born person. But it didn't stop us being friendly the next day.'

Any hostility between English Sohoites and the new Jewish immigrants was focused on Bateman Street. 'Going down to Bateman Buildings' became a euphemism for getting into a fight. 'My brothers would go down there armed with sticks and wood,' says Laura Phillips (née Victor), who was born and brought up in D'Arblay Street. 'My mother would say angrily, "Going down to Bateman Buildings are you? A *miesse meshina* on you!" – A curse on you! And she used to hit them if they came back cut and bruised.'

Like most Jewish families in Soho, the Victors spoke Yiddish when they were at home. Like the French and Italian adults, many newcomers found it hard to learn English when they arrived. There was really no need to, for if they stuck to their own community and their own streets, they could get by in the shops and at work without speaking a word of it. In fact, until recently many children born to foreign parents in Soho learned to speak English only when they went to school.

Though there was a Jewish school in Hanway Place, just north of Oxford Street, most Jewish Soho children went to the Pulteney school in Peter Street, or even to the church school, St Anne's in Dean Street where, by 1911, 25 per cent of the pupils were Jewish. The school authorities adapted with admirable speed and agility to the new mix of cultures: it was reported in an article called 'The Coming of the Jew to Soho' (*Twenty Years in Soho* 1911) that 'the Rabbi gives regular religious instruction to the Jewish children at the same time that the Christian children receive theirs. The Christian and the Jewish children are on the best of terms,' the report continued proudly, 'and last year a Jewish boy gained the popularity prize . . . The Jews receive the clergy very courteously, and are anxious to join any institutions of the parish which are open to them . . . They set an excellent example, moreover, of temperance, industry and family life. In social efforts we welcome their co-operation, and while we wish that they were Christians, we do not make any direct effort for their conversion.'

Children of all nationalities and religions mixed together freely at school and in the streets. French children gatecrashed Italian celebratory parties. Jewish children attended to Christmas festivities. Joan Mander, who came from an English Protestant family, had many Jewish friends, with whom she used to go to Chanukkah parties in the synagogues. As she recalls, 'No one noticed. And no one knew or cared about one child more or less.'

Once they learned a common language to communicate in, the adults, like the children, got to know each other too. A good levelling place for women was the public laundry behind the Marshall Street Baths. As Zinna Bulmore recalls, 'My mother became friendly with a lot of Italian women who she met in the laundry. It was a social event going there – the women took their washing in the morning, steeped it and put it in machines. Then they got out their sandwiches and flasks, and had a natter about their families and their different backgrounds. In the afternoon they'd dry the washing, and when we came home from school we'd help to carry it home in baskets. Women got together at the laundry – it was the nearest thing there was to a feminist movement.'

While they were happy to be friendly, the communities had no intention of merging into a whole. 'We all got on because we were all Sohoites. But it was a special community in the sense that we were so international – we kept our different cultures, different religions and different habits. And you accepted the differences.'

Despite the differences they had one important thing in common: they were poor. Like most immigrants, they had arrived in this country with nothing but a few essential clothes and, perhaps, the address of a relative or a *landsman* – a person they had known back home. From the moment they arrived, they were in the same boat as their British working-class neighbours. They had two urgent priorities – earning enough to live on, and making a decent home for their families.

Rented accommodation was not hard to find, but it was expensive and ranged in quality from merely poor to execrable. Though the worst slums of the 19th century had been swept away by redevelopment, the buildings or 'model dwellings' which had replaced them were not exactly spacious. As Lou Walters recalls, 'Six of us lived in two rooms – the kitchen and my father's workshop. And there was only one tap and one lavatory for the 28 people on our landing.' Another resident remembers, 'There were two rooms on every floor, with a family in each one. You shared a sink, if you were lucky, with the other family on the landing, and an outside lavatory with the rest of the house.'

The grand houses of 18th- and early 19th-century Soho were well past their prime, and extremely uncomfortable to live in.

> They weren't so much cold as draughty. They had high ceilings, and the windows and floors didn't fit properly. If you sat in front of the fire, your front was scorched and your back was freezing, and you had chilblains when you went to bed. We couldn't have a hot water system, even when the time came when we could afford one, because the walls weren't strong enough to fix anything to. The kitchen wall was so unsafe and flaky that my mother used to buy lining paper and pin it up with drawing pins. When the house was demolished, they found the most beautiful panelling underneath, which was sold for a fortune to America. So it had been a good house once – which was why it had an indoor loo.

Getting repairs done to houses owned by large estates or absentee landlords was almost impossible. 'You had to fight and fight, even to get a new toilet that was badly needed.' And, despite endless washing, disinfecting and scrubbing of the floors, walls and staircases, vermin were a problem everywhere: mice and rats that lived in the drains or behind the old wood panelling; and a 'Red Army of bugs' that thrived between the thick layers of wallpaper which had built up over the years.

Facilities were minimal, or non-existent. Many Soho houses had no electricity until well after the war (amazingly, Soho's last gas-lit building was not converted to electricity until 1986). Outside lavatories shared by an entire household were the norm. Having an indoor lavatory was considered a real luxury. Michael Klinger recalls how the D'Arblay Street house where he grew up had two indoor lavatories, and that 'my mother had the lavatory on the first floor all to herself. That was her sole luxury. She had the key to *her* toilet. Everyone else used the one upstairs.'

If a private tap or lavatory was a luxury in Soho, private bathrooms were unheard of. That did not mean that Sohoites did not wash, just that keeping clean was harder work. And, as one woman points out, 'In a way, people without bathrooms were more fastidious.' Some of the flats had unheated and dismal communal bathrooms in the basements. 'There were four baths downstairs in St James's Residences,' says Rica Teagno with a grimace. 'You could see from the area where we played whether the lights were on in there. If they weren't, you paid threepence to the caretaker and had your bath. The whole procedure took about an hour. The older girls used to go down there with their perfumes and bathsalts. For us children it was just carbolic, a bottle of Dettol, a flannel and soap.'

Rica Teagno's mother boarded up the small balcony outside the flat and put a small stove out there so that her children could wash in private. But far preferable to a daily scrub-down at the kitchen sink was the ritual weekly visit to the Marshall Street Hot Baths. For many children this was not so much a chance to get clean as a social outing. Armed with their soap and towel, they would all set off together in a big gang, often at four o'clock on a Friday after school. Once inside, they would pay 2d. or 3d. for a Ladies or Gents Second Class bath. There were also First Class baths, which had the added luxury of providing the bather with a towel to stand on.

They waited on the old wooden benches until a bath was free and, after the attendant called out, 'Next, please,' they would each go into a cubicle, while the woman set the small brass clock on the door and ran the bath from taps in the corridor outside. Her young customers were rarely satisfied with the temperature of the water, and their hackles still rise when they talk about her today.

> The wicked woman, she always ran it too hot or too cold for us. Each cubicle had a number so you'd call out, 'More hot water in number 1! More cold water in number 2!' But she wouldn't give you any.

> We'd drive that attendant mad by shouting 'Cold water please, I'm too hot!', then 'Hot water in number 3, please, I'm too cold!' And she'd shout back, 'You've had your hot water, number 3!' And she'd go stark raving bonkers.

> She'd scream at us kids, or she wouldn't answer us, or she refused to run us any more water.

Still, despite the attendants' angry scenes, the children used to have great fun. 'While we soaking in our tubs we used to have conversations over the top of the cubicles. And we used to sing together.'

Cramped as conditions were, the people managed to live in close proximity with little friction. 'The buildings were one big community – everybody helped each other. Everybody's door was open.' The rare flare-ups of bad feeling often erupted over noise. One woman remembers an instance when 'one of my mother's friends bought a hen and kept it on the balcony of our building. It used to start crowing at six o'clock in the morning. People complained and she became very unpopular. I mean, some of the men didn't get to bed until after midnight. Nobody would talk to her in the end, so she had to get rid of it.'

Occasionally the Italian and Maltese waiters who finished work at one or two in the morning would come home and play their radios or gramophones: 'The noise used to wake me up regularly. And it was always the same record, over and over and over again – probably because they only had one. In summer, when everybody's windows were open, it could be hell. But you accepted they had a right to play their music, and just hoped they'd turn the volume down.'

Despite the cramped conditions in the flats and buildings, it was a rare Soho child who went to bed hungry, even though their parents might have. 'We didn't starve and we didn't go hungry. We were what you would call respectable poor in Soho. Most people were careful to keep their pride. All the men worked hard, and our mothers supported them. But at the end of the week you were no better off than you'd been at the beginning. You were working to live. Conditions were hard. They were hard times. The question of a holiday, or better living conditions, was very remote.'

Though a few families were too poor to buy socks or underwear for their children, Soho children were particularly well dressed, due partly to the cheap material that could be bought in the market, and partly to the proximity of so many dressmakers and tailors who needed work. For example, even though Joan Mander insists that her family were not at all well off, she had all her clothes made to measure by a local tailor, and her hats designed by a milliner. If a young Sohoite was lucky enough to have a seamstress or tailor for a parent or neighbour, they were kitted out as well as any royal prince or princess: 'We used to watch the little princesses – as they then were – in Hyde Park, or shopping in Conduit Street. And my mother, who had a very quick eye and didn't need a pattern, would rush home and make us copies of their clothes out of remnants for next to nothing.'

Soho families were far better off than their counterparts in London's East End slums. The members of Soho's Jewish community, who had strong links with areas like Whitechapel and Shoreditch, were particularly aware of this fact. Among London Jews, the West End was generally considered to be 'more high class' than the East End. 'The people there looked up to us. We were a cut above them. And more so if we lived in Berwick Street than if we came from *the other side*.'

The other side, as any Sohoite will tell you to this day, is the district of Fitzrovia, just outside the northern boundary line of Oxford Street. Though people who lived or drank there might like to think that they were in Soho – some even called the area North Soho – real Sohoites knew that they were nothing of the kind. For to a true Sohoite, being born on the wrong side of Oxford Street was tantamount to being born on the wrong side of the tracks. If a Soho family moved north of Oxford Street, it was as if they were going into voluntary exile. And if a Soho girl married a boy from *the other side* it was as shocking as a Jewish child marrying 'out'. 'It wasn't that people there weren't as good as us. In fact, it was that they were in the main better off than we were, and there were more English people living there who weren't so conscious of the need to cling together. They lived in bigger houses, and they weren't a village community in the way we were. The market wasn't there, and that was the community's focus.'

Sohoites are usually the least snobbish people one is likely to meet. They have few airs and graces, and little time or patience for those who have. Yet they are shamelessly snobbish about the superiority of their area to *the other side*. As one octogenarian says with a shrug, 'We never went to *the other side* when we were children because there was nothing to go over there for.'

When Palmina Alalouf came to live in Soho with her Italian family in 1919 she was 15 years old, and 'a wee bit shocked' by the dirt and poverty after a childhood spent in posh Southampton. But because they were well cared for, Soho children often did not realize that they lived in slum conditions until they left the area: 'We didn't know anything different, because we all lived in the same way.' For some girls, a scholarship place to the Burlington School, or the Greycoat School in Victoria, where most pupils were much better off, brought them face to face with the reality of conditions at home for the first time.

For 13-year-old Michael Klinger, winning a place at the School of Building in Brixton forced another reality on him: 'I suddenly found I was the only Jew in a school of 500 boys. And I was very skinny and small, and very Jewish. It was a great shock to the system. I now found out what it was like to be a Jew among non-Jews. Consequently I became the champion boxer at the school.'

A school trip to see *Macbeth* at the Drury Lane Theatre proved an eye-opener for one eight-year-old, who suddenly discovered how people even worse off than her family lived: 'It was a pouring, wet, winter's afternoon. I was warmly dressed because my mother borrowed left right and centre if she needed to make sure we were warm and well-fed. But there were children playing in Drury Lane with bare feet, wearing sacks tied with bits of string. And all I could think of throughout the play were those kids. It horrified me. As soon as I came home, I started asking questions. And I haven't stopped asking them since.'

Were Sohoites really so much better off than slum-dwellers elsewhere in London? Or does nostalgia throw a veil over their memories, blunting the edges of their hardship? Almost without exception, they look back on their childhood in Soho before World War II as 'golden days', not as a time of any deprivation: 'We didn't suffer poverty. We didn't want for food or clothes. And since everyone else was at the same level we didn't notice that we were poor.'

Soho parents certainly worked hard to make sure their families were well provided for, whether they were running a restaurant, waiting at table, taking in washing or doing outdoor work for the Savile Row tailors. Waiters worked particularly unsocial and long hours for little money – sometimes for no money at all. In fact, in 1900 the Società Italiana Cuochi-Camerieri complained that waiters were actually paying 'from 1/6d to 4s per day for the privilege of waiting' at certain restaurants – presumably in the hope of making money from tips. One restaurant not only did not pay its waiters or feed them while they were on duty, it demanded that they supply their own notebooks and pencils to take down the orders with.

Life was no easier for tailors and pressers doing piecework. For a start, business was sporadic. As machinist Bessie Dowse remembers, 'If the governor had no work that day, you had no work – and no pay.' Unemployed garment workers hung around outside the labour exchange in Broadwick Street, in the hope of being offered an afternoon's work.

Life was hard enough when you were in work. Every morning the cut cloth would have to be collected in bundles from the back-doors of the Savile Row tailors (it was not done to let the retail customers know where their suits were really made), and brought to the workshops, which ranged from small factories in the mews to the front parlour of a two-roomed flat, where the work-table was also used for family meals and Christmas or Passover celebrations. Machinists worked long into the night in order to get their piecework completed. Then the suits – minus their buttons – would be handed over to the pressers for finishing off.

The tailors would bring the jackets around in the evening, [says Michael Klinger, whose father was a presser]. My father would finish work at nine-thirty, maybe ten o'clock, and fall asleep at the table while he was having supper. Then he'd get up again at two o'clock in the morning, in order to get the work ready for the tailors to take back and sew the buttons on in the morning. My father had one or two men working for him. And they also started work at two or two-thirty a.m. They'd start pressing, the fourteen-pound gas-irons would start banging, and they'd be talking, and my brother and I slept right through it all on our mattresses under the work-table. And I slept better then than I do now. Hard work is putting it mildly – for as long as I can remember, my father was working eighteen or nineteen hours a day. Saturday he'd work in the mornings – he hated that, because he was a religious man. But there was nothing he could do about it. He wore through the floorboards in that room four times, dancing up and down. They used to call him 'the dancer', because he was a very agile little man.

Soho children had their own parts to play in helping their parents to earn a living. For instance, if one of his father's workers did not turn up for the early morning shift, Michael – or his brother – would be turfed out of his bed underneath the work-table and, still in his pyjamas, sent round to the man's house to wake him up. In the morning, pressers' children like Michael or Lou Walters would have to deliver the pressed suits back to the tailors, so that they could sew the buttons on them and *their* children could deliver the finished articles back to Savile Row before going to school. On Saturday mornings, the children of outdoor workers were sent round to the master tailors to collect their parents' wages. None of this seemed strange to the kids. 'It was our job, it was part of the routine.'

Palomina Alalouf was 'plonked in the cash box' of the family restaurant, the Brice, and soon afterwards was sent off to Pitman's to learn to keep her father's books. Gaston Berlemont, whose parents acquired the licence of the York Minster pub in 1914, had a rather headier job to do: 'We imported our own wine in hogsheads, and bottled it ourselves. I could bottle a whole hogshead in three hours – and got up feeling drunk from the fumes. We kids had to do the bottle-washing down in the cellar before school. And since there was no law against it in those days, I was behind the bar in short trousers. I'd come home from school and it'd be, "Come on, serve the customers!" We were brought up to it. Even when we did twelve hours a day, we didn't think of it as work – we were simply *en famille*.'

Life was fun for Soho's children. Though they were all strictly brought up, they enjoyed the freedom of London's most varied and colourful streets. Even looking out of the window was a treat, for there was an itinerant trader on every corner.

First the cat's meat man came round [says Laura Phillips]. 'You threw him a penny, and he hurled a piece of meat into your doorway for the cat. Then the muffin man came, then at teatime a Yiddish man from the East End with cakes and biscuits in a basket and little sweet bagels on a string. Rag-and-bone carts came round, offering ornaments in exchange for junk. Then there were barrel organs. There was one organ-grinder who dressed up as a gypsy and had a parrot – when you put a penny in his tin the parrot jumped in a box and gave you a folded-up paper fortune. There were musicians, like the blind violinist and his daughter who sang.

Another man did magic tricks. The police used to make the pedlars go away, because they were collecting people round them and were a nuisance. They'd move on, but a few minutes later they'd come back. And all the time there'd be another one waiting round the corner.

Also hanging around on the street corners were Soho's many unofficial bookie's tipsters. Betting was an obsession, particularly among Jewish men, many of whom saw gambling as the only way out of the poverty trap. Since bookies were illegal they could not have offices, so they hung about in the mews where the tailors could find them and placed their bets. 'One or two men used to stand at the mews entrance, as lookouts, to make sure the police weren't coming. If they did come, they'd run into the nearest open doorway, and the people inside would turn a blind eye. Gamblers went in and out of the mews all day long. My father went and placed his bets: "Sixpence each way! A shilling each way!" All the foreign men learned to read English because of the betting – so they could buy the racing papers and find out what they'd lost or won.'

In the days before motor vehicles became common in the centre of town, the horse-drawn carts, fire-engines and buses were another source of interest. 'The horses used suddenly to fall down in their traps. The driver would have to take off the bridle and everything, and get the horse up. Then his foot would go under and he'd fall down again and we didn't know if he was alive or dead. Sometimes the horses just lay there foaming at the mouth. Sometimes someone would touch him and he'd jump up.'

A favourite game amongst Soho boys was to 'run after the carts and jump on the flap that was down at the back. People used to shout, "Look behind you, Guvnor!" and the driver would turn around and hit the boys with his strap, and they'd fall off. My cousin once went all the way to Charing Cross on the back of a Lipman's van, and when he eventually fell off he was taken to the hospital in Leicester Square, and no one at home knew what had happened to him. When he eventually turned up, all bandaged and with a broken tooth, his mother gave him a good hiding.'

The markets were open until late at night six days a week. After dark they were lit up by naphtha flares. Soho children often watched

the auctioneers sell off their goods – mainly stockings and clothes –
or played games with the orange boxes and baskets that the goods
came in. If they were hungry they bought stale cakes from the local
bakeries for a penny a bag, or walked up to Great Marlborough
Street, where, in a skip behind the Palladium Music Hall, which
had opened in Argyll Street in 1910, they might find half-full boxes
of chocolates left behind by the theatre audience the night before.
'Sometimes there were three chocolates left in the box. Sometimes
six or even twelve. We were poor, so we ate them.'

Children had no choice but to play in the streets when they were
not at school, since there was no room for them in their tiny,
overcrowded homes. Before the war, when the gardens of Soho
Square and Golden Square were still private, St Anne's churchyard
provided a rare patch of green – it was also where the schoolchildren
from St Anne's School were sent to do their physical jerks. The open
rectangle of Portland Mews, sandwiched between Livonia Street and
D'Arblay Street, doubled as an unofficial cricket pitch and football
ground – to the annoyance of residents who had their windows
broken.

Games were not limited to the boundaries of Soho. In the children's minds the whole of the West End was their playground, from
Trafalgar Square to Selfridges department store, which was topped
with a roof terrace to which entrance was free and where there was
'a big telescope through which you could see all over London'. In
summer, gangs of children, with or without their mothers, marched
to the royal parks to play on the grass or to fish for minnows in the
lakes. 'If we were too tired, we'd stay in Leicester Square and play
around the seats and flower gardens, where mothers and nannies
sat with their prams.'

Soho nights were as lively as the days, especially in summer
when people sat outside on the pavements on chairs or upturned
orange boxes and chatted to one another until way past midnight.
Sometimes the men and women paraded round the streets, perhaps
stopping at Forte's Milk Bar in Leicester Square or at one of the
many cafés or pubs for a drink. In the Russian cafés people
drank tea and gambled over chess games, dice or cards. In the
French bars they had a glass of wine or absinthe. There was even
rat-baiting in one of the pubs: Lou Walters remembers how one
family in Livonia Street would catch rats in their house and take

them to the local pub, where they let them loose and set dogs on them.

When the children were in bed, their parents felt quite safe leaving them alone at home: 'They would walk round the block and come back and listen to make sure we were still asleep.' More often than not, though, the older children stayed out as late as their parents. 'We never went to bed. We showed ourselves, then we walked up and down. So if our parents saw us and knew we were around, they'd go back to the Corner House, or to Leicester Square. We used to walk all over the place, even round Piccadilly, where we'd get talking to boys.'

The area was safe at night because 'all the people in the streets were local. People from outside only came in to the West End for the theatre and the cinemas. Afterwards they went home straight away. They didn't hang around all night like they do now. So it was quieter once the shows closed. If we stayed out too late, other grown-ups would recognize us and send us home.'

In summer, families walked together to the bandstand in Hyde Park to listen to the military bands, and afterwards strolled home down Piccadilly. During the winter, when it was too cold to stay out for long, the houses and flats were full to bursting point with family and friends. 'First there were my mother's cronies, and then my sister's friends,' Michael Klinger remembers. 'I had a stack of friends, too, and so did my brother, who was a diver, a swimmer, and a champion dancer. He even gave dancing lessons in this ridiculously small place, in the first floor parlour. He'd push the table back – it was an oval table with a plush cloth and my sister's sewing machine on it. The place was full of people. It was a very busy, active and jolly house, and everybody shouted at everybody else.'

Weekends were special. Saturday was a normal working day, but on Saturday nights the Jewish families bought salt-beef sandwiches from shops in the market. It was a night for promenading round the streets. By contrast, even as late as the 1950s, 'Sunday mornings were absolutely dead,' as Roy Harrison recalls. 'The only people you used to see were people going to church.' For Catholic families, the morning was dominated by trips to St Patrick's, Notre Dame de France or Our Lady of the Assumption in Warwick Street. But even going to church was a typically Soho-ish and cosmopolitan affair:

'When we'd received the sacraments, for a special treat we used to go to Joelson's delicatessen in Peter Street for a Jewish breakfast of cream-cheese and bagels. Then we went home for a drink – perhaps sherry or vermouth – followed by a Sunday lunch of salami and chicken. In the afternoon we'd go to Benediction, then come home for tea. Maybe we'd go to the theatre in the evening. Or sometimes a nun or a priest visited us.'

Men who did not have time to shave during the week got rid of their one week's growth of beard and dressed up in their best clothes on Sundays. They usually congregated in the pubs at lunchtime, and in the afternoon if they had families they took them out. Living in the centre of town was a huge bonus, for all the major art galleries, museums and public buildings were within walking distance, and since admission to the museums was free, families could have a great day out for very little money, and sometimes for no money at all.

At the turn of the century it was the fashion among the aristocracy to dress up in their best clothes on Sundays, and drive in open carriages down Rotten Row and through Hyde Park. Soho shop-keepers who owned horses and carts for their businesses sometimes kept open traps in their stables in the mews, and on Sundays they might harness them up and, dressed in their best clothes and hats, drive through Hyde Park with the society people. Their neighbours strolling through the park on foot kept an eye out for them. 'We used to laugh when we saw them driving through, because they acted like high society, but we knew they were only from the local fish or fruit shop.'

For the international community of Sohoites, daily life contained all the small pleasures and intimacies of living in a village at carnival time, and despite their poverty most children who grew up there enjoyed an almost idyllic life. But Soho was not a remote village – it was a tiny district in the centre of a vast and expanding metropolis that was changing fast. Like it or not, the 20th century was going to bring more dramatic changes to Soho, and to bring them more quickly, than at any other time in its history.

Outside forces, some benign and some extremely unpleasant, were about to come pouring in.

8

Bombs and Bohemians

When Britain declared war on Germany on 4 August 1914, the licensee of the Wine House at the bottom of Dean Street was a German gentleman called Herr Schmidt. 'Anybody with a name like that,' says Gaston Berlemont, 'had to go. My father, who then had the Restaurant Européen next door to Schmidt's, decided to take over the Wine House in Schmidt's absence. Because of all the *entente cordiale*-ism around at the time, he was given the licence. He became the only foreigner in England to hold a full pub licence.' That same year, Gaston was born in the Berlemonts' flat on the top floor of the pub. So, through the outbreak of war and the subsequent internment of German aliens, one of Soho's most famous pubs, known officially as the York Minster and unofficially as the French, came into being.

The first bombing raids on Belgium in 1915 brought an influx of Belgian refugees to Soho and Fitzrovia, many of whom were initially put up at the old parish workhouse in Poland Street. For a time they felt safe. Then, on 31 May, Zeppelin raids on the capital started, shocking Londoners into the realization that people at home were no longer invulnerable to foreign-based wars.

For Soho children, the raids were merely another adventure. 'We used to sit around on clear nights waiting for them to start. If there was nothing by midnight, we'd go to bed, with a parcel of food ready and our shoes beside our bed. When the Zeppelins were spotted over the coast, a policeman came out from Great Marlborough Street station on a bicycle, with a big placard hanging round his neck saying "First Warning" or "Take Cover". Whoever was up saw him and woke the others. Then we all marched to Oxford Street station. If we heard the guns, we'd start running – we couldn't get to the station quick enough.'

To children who usually walked everywhere, going into the Underground was something of a novelty. 'If it was early enough, we used to ride the trains. As soon as one came in, all us kids would jump on it, wherever it was going, and then come back again, just for the ride.'

Once men were conscripted into the army, the women who had previously worked alongside them had sole charge of running many of Soho's bars, businesses and shops. With so many army uniforms to manufacture, it was a busy time for tailors and trimmings-shops. And despite food shortages in the markets, cheap Soho restaurants soon became the popular rendezvous of off-duty soldiers and women war-workers, many of whom had money of their own to spend for the first time in their lives.

Soho was to lose many of its citizens in World War I, to the war itself and to the Russian Revolution. For in 1917, many Russian Jews, inspired by Socialist demonstrations in the streets, returned to their country of birth to fight against the Tsarist regime which had once oppressed them. Some men who went back left their wives here behind them, and were never heard of again.

By 1918, the formal order of Victorian England had been swept away for good. There was a new feeling of egalitarianism about which Soho's atmosphere suited down to the ground. With former domestic servants who had been conscripted into the army or war-work now disinclined to return to their old jobs in service, 'eating out' in restaurants became an increasingly popular pastime for the moneyed classes, who, like their servants, had been liberated from certain social conventions by the war. The bright young things of the aristocracy, hell-bent on enjoying life to the full, came 'slumming' to joints like Mrs Merrick's '43' Club in Gerrard Street, or frequented society haunts like the Hon. David Tennant's Gargoyle Club in Meard Street and the ill-fated Café de Paris in Coventry Street.

Here, as at the Berlemonts' restaurant above the bar of the York Minster, the party at the next table during the twenties and thirties might well include film stars, actresses, band-leaders, famous sportspeople, politicians or even European or British royalty – with or without their paramours. For Soho was still very much a racy place of mistresses and prostitutes, and many of its restaurants were as famous for their *cabinets particuliers* as for what they served up on the plates. 'We didn't have "rooms" on the premises,' says Gaston Berlemont. 'But it's surprising how many people asked. When the Prince of Wales said *bonjour* to my father on his way to the Gargoyle, he usually had a beautiful wench on either arm. And

Lord Beaverbrook frequently used to eat upstairs in our restaurant. He was always presenting me to *ma nièce* who was with him. He had more nieces than any man I've known.'

Though night-clubs like the Café de Paris were beyond the reaches – and perhaps the desires – of many Sohoites, the as-yet-unmarried generation of working people growing up in Soho in the twenties and thirties had as good a time as their aristocratic contemporaries. Sadie Feigen's first job may have been making sacks for curd cheese in the kosher dairy underneath her parents' flat in D'Arblay Street, but she insists that she was never short of money or the energy to go out: 'I can assure you my life was only dancing. I went out to work, and then I went out and enjoyed myself. I used to go to dances all the time – in West Hampstead and the Hammersmith Palais and the Corner Houses in Tottenham Court Road and Leicester Square.'

Since the Oxford Street gown stores were still very expensive, a whole new breed of shops selling cheap, ready-to-wear frocks opened in Berwick Street market to cater for the new working woman with a little money in her pocket. Soon nearly every front parlour from D'Arblay Street to Shaftesbury Avenue had been replaced by a shop window. As competition stiffened, a whole new breed of Sohoite was born: the 'shleppers', who stood on the pavement outside the dress-shops touting for customers. 'They were called shleppers because they used to shlep you in, that is, to drag you inside.' Soon a woman could hardly walk down the road without being enticed, and sometimes forced, into one dress-shop or another. 'There used to be murders with one shlepper accusing another of taking customers away from their shop.'

Soho's residential character was changing. Gradually, immigrants who had arrived penniless in the first decades of the century and were now prospering, or who now had working sons or daughters to help them, began to drift out to the new suburbs on the edge of town, where, for the same price as a few poky tenement rooms in Rupert Street or Dean Street, a modern house could be rented. But, as many people discovered, there were strong reasons for staying in Soho. Moving to the suburbs brought its own problems: people who worked the long hours that tailors and catering staff did were often too exhausted to undertake a long journey home. 'They ended up falling asleep at their work-tables. And before long they became ill. That's why my mother would never move out of Soho. She said, your dad is the one who's working to keep us all, so he must be the one to be considered, and to have priority.'

One person who was frequently too tired to get home from Soho at night was scientist John Logie Baird, who lived in Sydenham, Kent. In the summer of 1924 Baird rented the two-roomed attic of 22 Frith Street, where he set up a laboratory where he was to work day and night for the next 18 months. History was made in the rooms on 27 January 1926, when he demonstrated his new invention – television – in front of members of the Royal Institution of Great Britain, thus sowing the seeds for Soho's intimate involvement with the British film business.

From the start, the British film industry was dominated by the Americans. After 1927, however, British cinemas were forced to show a quota of home-produced films. Though the large studios were in London's suburbs – in Ealing, for instance, and in Elstree – Wardour Street became the centre of the British film production offices, post-production facilities and distribution companies.

To one young man from D'Arblay Street, living so close to the film industry had its bad as well as its good points: 'We were very aware we were in the centre of the film industry, because people like Gracie Fields would suddenly come to the building behind us to view her latest film. But when the Talkies came in, the film editors worked in that building, and when they were working we'd hear this repetition of terribly loud sounds. It was particularly bad in summer when everybody's windows were open. The noise was murder. It got on your bloody nerves. When they repeated it too much, we'd lean out of the window and yell at them to shut up.' Ironically, this young man was presser's son Michael Klinger, who was later to become a film producer himself.

World War I had temporarily halted the development of the British film industry. World War II was to nip the burgeoning British television industry in the bud. It was also, more importantly, to reduce large parts of Soho to piles of rubble, and, through internment, to deprive the Italian community of many of its members. For some families, the loss was temporary. For others, it was, tragically, for life.

Between April and June 1940, Denmark, Norway, Belgium, Holland and finally France, fell to the Nazis. Xenophobia ran rife in the British press. German so-called 'enemy aliens' – including

Soho in the 1950s: unemployed musicians gather at the unofficial labour exchange that operated outside the Musicians' Union in Archer Street.

Above: *Great Windmill Street in the 1950s: the early raincoat brigade queues up for the afternoon Revudeville show at the Windmill Theatre. The Theatre's motto, 'We Never Closed', just visible above the entrance, was paraphrased by some as 'We Never Clothed'. The building behind the telephone kiosks was once anatomist William Hunter's private museum.*

Right: *A striptease bar in the 1960s.*

Soho now: Rupert Street market at dawn.

Inside the House of St Barnabas-in-Soho, number 1 Greek Street. Built in the 1740s, the house was decorated in the English rococo style for Jamaican planter Richard Beckford in 1754. Since 1862 it has been a hostel for homeless people.

Window display, P. Denny and Co., Chefs' and Waiters' Outfitters, Old Compton Street.

Inside Fratelli Camisa, delicatessen. Serving behind the counter is Ennio Camisa, who, with his brother Isidor, opened the Berwick Street shop – the family's second Soho venture – in the late 1940s.

Chinese pagoda, Newport Place.

Lisle Street. The western half was built across Lord Leicester's back garden in 1682-3. The eastern half, originally called New Lisle Street, was added in the early 1790s, and still has a fine row of 18th-century terraced shops. The pediment above number 18, which is now a Chinese supermarket, bears its original tablet with the inscription 'NEW LISLE STREET MDCCXCI'.

Inside the Algerian Coffee Stores, Old Compton Street, which stocks 27 varieties of coffee and 120 different teas. In the foreground is Paul Crocetta, who joined his father-in-law's business 18 years ago.

The factory, M. Hand and Co., Gold and Silver Lacemakers. At the spindle is *Derek Hand, whose Flemish Huguenot ancestors started the business in the 18th century.*

The kitchen at L'Escargot, Greek Street.

Soho Square, from its south-east corner.

Bar Italia, Frith Street. The huge television screen shows programmes broadcast live from Italy.

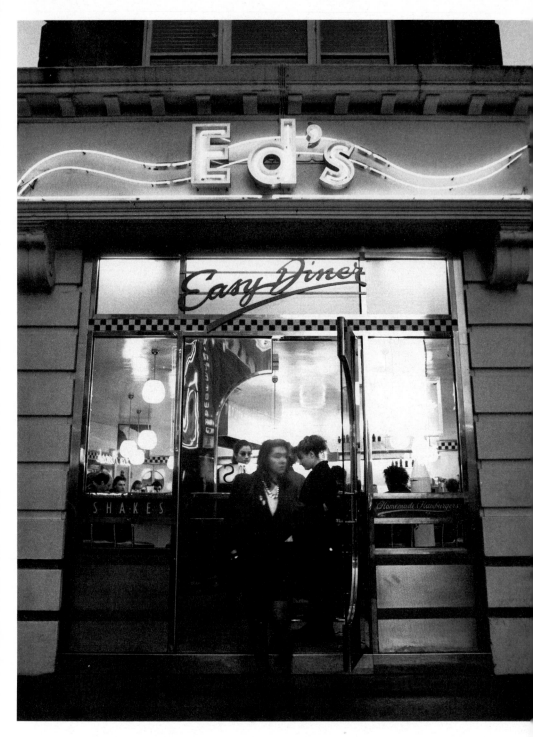

Ed's Diner, Old Compton Street: the face of the new, style-conscious Soho.

Moonrise on Brewer Street. Estate agents' boards are an increasingly common sight – a real sign of the times.

A backstreet doorway.

Jewish refugees who had sought sanctuary here from Hitler's death camps – were the first to be rounded up for internment. Then it was the turn of the Italian community to be singled out for the scapegoat treatment by the press. Newspapers published virulent attacks against the Italian community. An article in the *Daily Mirror* on 27 April 1940 claimed that 'every Italian colony in Great Britain and America is a seething cauldron of smoking Italian politics. Black fascism. Hot as Hell. Even the peaceful, law-abiding proprietor of the back-street coffee shop bounces into a fine patriotic frenzy at the sound of Mussolini's name . . . We are nicely honeycombed with little cells of potential betrayal.'

As Mussolini came nearer to joining the war, the Cabinet drew up plans for the possible, and gradual, internment of 'dangerous' members of the Anglo-Italian community. But on 10 June, the day that Mussolini declared war on England, Churchill swept these plans aside and instructed the police to simply 'Collar the lot!'

It was a black day for Soho's Italian community, who found themselves uncomfortably stranded between the land of their birth or forefathers and the country in which they had chosen to live. 'We felt very let down by Italy. We were Italian – we went back when we could afford to, for holidays – but we who had settled in England loved it here.'

Many British people, even in Soho, felt unaccountably resentful towards their Italian neighbours. The day after war was declared by Italy a group of local Soho women – all non-Italians – formed into a gang and marched angrily down Broadwick Street towards Old Compton Street, ready to take out their disappointment with Mussolini on the local Italians. As she came out of her home in Dufours Place to go shopping, Rose Blau bumped into them, and asked them what was wrong. 'When they told her that they intended to smash the windows of the Italian restaurants,' her daughter Zinna Bulmore remembers, 'she tore into them, and harangued them, and reminded them what the war was about, and that most of those Italians had been living in England for several generations and weren't responsible for Mussolini. By the time she'd finished, they looked thoroughly ashamed of themselves, and the march broke up and went home.' Nevertheless, the next night rioters from outside Soho came into the area and smashed the windows of several Italian restaurants.

A chaotic round-up of Italian so-called 'enemy aliens' had started on the night of 10 June. Breadwinners were snatched away from their families with little or no warning, often with no time to say goodbye. Within four days, 1,600 Italian Londoners had been imprisoned. Ennio Camisa remembers it all too well: 'War was declared on Monday. The police came for me and my brother on Thursday, and said, just come with us, we want to ask you some questions at the station. We shut up our shop in Old Compton Street and we didn't know what was going to happen to it.' They were not to see the shop they had worked so hard to set up for four years, by which time it had been taken over by a new owner.

In his autobiography, *I Shall Die on the Carpet*, Soho restaurateur Peppino Leoni expressed the bitterness of his unjust and incomprehensible imprisonment, through which he lost everything he had worked for:

As I walked down the corridor towards the cells, I felt a sudden hatred for the police, for the British Government which had issued instructions for my internment, and for all forms of authority. I had slaved for years, in fact thirty-three years, because I first came to England in 1907, to establish my restaurant, and a man of my own nationality had destroyed everything in an instant . . . I deeply resented the fact that after thirty-three years in England with no political or police blemish on my record, I'd be scooped up without proper consideration.

From the local police station, Ennio and Isidor Camisa, Peppino Leoni and hundreds of other local Italians were taken to Lingfield Race Course, and later to Warth Mills, a disused cotton factory in Bury, Lancashire, while their future – and, for some, their fate – was weighed up by the Foreign Office in Whitehall.

One morning soon afterwards, a list of names was read out of those due to leave England on a converted luxury cruise ship called the *Arandora Star*. The list included many Italian Sohoites, but to their surprise and sorrow the Camisas were not included. 'No one knew where the ship was going,' says Ennio Camisa. 'But we had a lot of friends going on it, and we wanted to go with them. But the authorities told us, if your name isn't on that list you can't go.'

They did not know what a lucky escape they had had. The

Arandora Star steamed out of the Liverpool docks at 4 a.m. on 1 July, on course for Canada. Including the crew and its German and Italian passengers, it held a total of 1,600 men. Just before seven o'clock that same morning it received a direct hit from a German torpedo. The huge liner sank within 30 minutes, with the loss of 730 lives, including 661 internees, of whom 486 were Italian. Many of them had belonged to the Soho community. Soho would never be the same again.

Those who, like Ennio Camisa, had escaped the fate of the *Arandora Star*, found themselves imprisoned in makeshift barracks on the Isle of Man, where, on the whole, they were treated well by their guards. Their main problem was boredom. For the first time in their lives, people who had previously worked 12 or 14 hours a day had nothing to do but twiddle their thumbs and stare at the barbed wire fences. The alternative to the unrelieved tedium of the camps was to volunteer for a job on one of the local farms.

'We were paid a shilling a day on the farm,' Ennio Camisa remembers. 'And I enjoyed it very much. The guards used to take us there from the camp at nine in the morning and leave us, then at half-past ten we stopped work for tea and toast. Later we had a three-course lunch, and then high tea. What more could we want? The Manx people were very friendly. They used to treat us like we were one of them. They didn't like the English people so much!' Such firm friendships were forged during those years that some Italian Sohoites still have links with their former Manx friends to this day.

In all, more than 27,000 men and women were interned during the war. In their absence the businesses they had been forced to abandon were kept going by women relatives, or redistributed via the Custodian of Enemy Property, who sold them 'for next to nothing'. Relatives of the Soho internees stoically swallowed their bitter feelings and closed ranks with other Londoners, drawing their blackout curtains at night and heading off to one of the many air-raid shelters which had been prepared in the opening months of the war in the Underground stations and in the West End squares.

The Underground stations were stuffy, noisy and overcrowded: as many as 4,000 Londoners slept in Piccadilly Circus station at night, lying down where they could find space on the packed platforms, escalators and stairs. Still, remarkably few Sohoites took advantage of their proximity to the Underground stations:

> I never ever went to the Tube. Lex Garage in Brewer Street was a strong building and it had been fixed up into a bona fide shelter, with a canteen, bunks, and a surgery – the lot. And very good it was too. I went there every night, regardless of whether there was a raid on. We all had our own bunks there. And before the authorities provided bunks, we brought deckchairs. Everybody from the district came. It was a good laugh. We sat and talked, and even danced. It became a very communal life. We even had visitors who were bombed out in the East End.

> We children ran wild in Lex Garage, because it was so big. We had a lovely time. But we didn't sleep very much. We played cards, and put on shows to say hallo to the soldiers and sailors. For us it was fun. But when we got home, my mother would make us wash ourselves in Life Buoy and Carbolic. Because tramps also used the same bunks as we did – they wanted shelter too.

Necessity made bedfellows of complete strangers. When the Marshall Street Baths were hit in the middle of the night, one young woman was smoked out of her home in Dufours Place: 'The people who were already in the shelter moved up and said, "Come on, get in!" And I found myself lying down in a bunk next to a man I'd never seen before. And I wouldn't have known him the next day.'

As people got used to the bombs, they began to be blasé about them. 'When the Blitz started I thought every bomb would kill me. After a few months I thought none of them would,' says Christina Foyle, who, during raids, would take shelter, with 'all the riff-raff of Soho', as she describes it, in the basement shelter underneath the family bookshop. Foyle's was nearly destroyed one night, when a huge bomb just missed it, shattering all the windows and creating a huge hole in Charing Cross Road. 'Afterwards they looked in the hole, and saw a torch light shining down there,' says Christina Foyle. 'It was a drunken American soldier, who had fallen in.'

Trying to run a business in the centre of war-time London was a nightmare. Shop windows were constantly shattered by bomb-blasts. Many pre-war customers simply disappeared. Even large, long-established businesses found themselves in trouble. Christina

Foyle, whose father William and uncle Gilbert had started the bookshop W. & G. Foyle in 1906, recalls the difficulties of the war years: 'When everyone left London in 1940, we did no business at all. We couldn't pay our bills. I never thought we'd survive it.' Mary Honeywill, who ran a leather shop in Foubert's Place with her husband, remembers how 'we sometimes had so many air raids it would have been better not to have opened at all'. Shortages and rationing began to bite in Berwick Street market: silk stockings, the staple stock of many barrows, disappeared completely; the brief appearance on the stalls of summer fruit was marked by 50-strong queues. With few frocks to sell, shleppers no longer hung about outside the boarded-up dress-shop windows.

Only one business boomed during the war, and that was Soho's night life. As the locals bedded down in the shelters, the narrow, unlit streets above them were invaded by a benign army of revellers determined to forget reality by drinking, dancing and sometimes drugging themselves into oblivion. The Shaftesbury Avenue theatres and Leicester Square cinemas filled to bursting point. Drawn to Soho's borders by the twin magnets of Piccadilly Circus and the Windmill Theatre, airmen, sailors and soldiers from all the Allied forces stumbled through blackout curtains into crowded pubs and bars, or searched for a moment's comfort in the welcoming arms of local prostitutes.

'We never closed,' Windmill Theatre owner Vivian Van Damm was able to say after the Blitz – a slogan that was soon corrupted into 'We Never Clothed'. For the variety theatre which Van Damm had managed in partnership with its owner Laura Henderson since 1931 was famous not only for its comedy acts – which over the years, would include such budding stars as Michael Bentine, Kenneth More, Jimmy Edwards, Peter Sellers, Tony Hancock, Harry Secombe and Morecambe and Wise – but for its showgirls and 'artistic' displays of female nudity.

The theatre, which was originally built as the Palais de Luxe cinema, stands on the site of the 18th-century windmill which had given its name to the Windmill Field. Appropriately, the next door house had once been occupied by William Hunter's Theatre of Anatomy – though it is unlikely that Van Damm cited this as a reason why the Lord Chamberlain should give him permission to stage nude scenes *à la française* in his Revudeville variety show.

That the Lord Chamberlain did was a shock to everyone – excepting Van Damm himself. There were, however, two provisos – that the naked girls should be seen only under subdued lighting, and that they must not move a muscle while on stage.

The 'living pictures' that were created at the Windmill were not the first such shows in Soho: they had had a precedent in the *tableaux vivants* staged at the Palace Theatre in 1896. In those days, a local vicar, the Reverend Wilton, had asked for photographs of the 'statuesque poses' to be removed from outside the theatre lest they corrupt his flock on their way to church.

Despite the inevitable criticism levelled at the nude sketches, the non-stop Windmill shows were widely acknowledged to be 'tasteful' and so discreet that critic and producer Kenneth Tynan called Revudeville 'ninety minutes of pallid concert party'. For off-duty forces deprived of female company, they were a sensation, and the stage door was besieged every night by Johnnies hoping for a date with one of the Windmill Girls or Revudebelles, as they were called. Apparently, the Lord Chamberlain's rule of non-mobility on stage was strictly adhered to, even when V-bombs were crashing down outside.

'In Soho, the people work hard and drink hard – tremendously hard,' the Reverend Cardwell had told *Cassell's Saturday Journal* back in 1900. Never had that statement – especially the second part of it – been truer than during World War II. Bohemians, society people, off-duty forces, blackmarketeers, prostitutes, pimps and local working people drank together in the pubs every evening. After the fall of France, the York Minster, already a popular watering-hole with the Bohemians, became the unofficial London headquarters of the exiled Free French. South African, Rhodesian and French Canadian squaddies who had visited the French during the 1914–18 war now returned as sergeants and officers. 'Mama, are you still here?' they exclaimed, finding Victorienne Berlemont still behind the bar, and the simple furnishings unchanged.

Meanwhile, in Macclesfield Street, the Dutch-run De Hems pub provided a base, and even beds, for members of the Dutch Resistance. Off-duty gay officers – and a frequently plastered Dylan Thomas – congregated at the Café Royal. When that closed, hardened drinkers might move on to late-night drinking clubs such as the Horseshoe in Wardour Street, the Byron in Greek Street or the

Mandrake in Meard Street, where those that could afford it might walk along the street and take the lift to the Gargoyle. In music clubs such as the Sunset and Moonglow, local girls let their hair down with the Black American troops and colonial forces who had joined the war.

Nightlife during the war was hectic, almost desperate in its intensity. But, though drinking and dancing may have been brightened up the Blitz, wartime Soho was not without its tragedies. With all the local young men conscripted into the army, or interned on the Isle of Man, life was harder than usual for those who were left behind. Bombs inflicted serious damage on the fabric of the area. Famous landmarks, such as St Anne's church and Carlisle House in Carlisle Street were soon to go. Miss Kelly's Royalty Theatre was badly damaged. On 19 November 1940 a huge bomb crashed through the roof of St Patrick's church in Soho Square, where it hit a column and buried itself in the nave but, miraculously, did not explode. Similarly, a parachute mine landed without exploding on the London Palladium, causing pandemonium in the air-raid shelter below. A firebomb crashed through the roof of Hand's Gold Lacemakers in Lexington Street, bringing the heavy ancient machinery on the top floor plummeting down through subsequent floors, and destroying most of the building. In fact, virtually every Soho street suffered substantial bomb damage. With gas and water mains being constantly interrupted, residents who had had few enough facilities to start with were soon reduced to cooking on primus stoves and queuing for water at standpipes in the street.

But far worse than the loss of buildings was the terrible loss of life. Some tragedies stick in people's memories, like the direct hit on St James's Residences in Brewer Street, which took place just before noon on Saturday, 26 October 1940. 'My mother and I were in Berwick Street when it happened,' one former resident recounts. 'Word got round very quickly that the building had been hit, and by the time we got back so had my father, who had come rushing home from the restaurant where he worked to see if we were alright. I remember seeing him run into the ruined building, shouting, "Where are my children?" In all, five people were killed by the strike, and 45 were injured. Losses would have been much heavier but for the fact that many residents were doing their shopping in the market at the time.

On the night of 8 March 1941, the basement Café de Paris in Coventry Street, advertised as 'the safest place to dance in Town', was crowded with society people and off-duty officers, who were dancing to the sound of Ken 'Snakehips' Johnson's band. 'Snakehips' himself had spent the earlier part of the evening with friends at the Embassy Club in Mayfair. Determined not to let the Café de Paris's management down, he ran through the blackout, arriving in Coventry Street at exactly 9.45, just in time for his band to go on. The band struck up 'Oh Johnny!', and more revellers crowded on to the dance-floor. Four minutes later they were blinded by a huge flash. Two high-explosive bombs had hit the Rialto Cinema above the club, and crashed down into it. One exploded at ground-floor level, the other burst on impact.

The blast was devastating. Many people had their clothes torn off them. At some tables entire parties were killed. Strangely, in the midst of the carnage, a single champagne bottle survived intact. Reeling with shock, women and men in tattered evening dress stumbled out into the street, ghostly apparitions, their faces and bodies coated with dust, plaster and, in many case, blood. Ambulances did not get through for an hour, but the local people rushed to help the survivors. A nearby restaurant – the Honeydew – was used as a temporary mortuary. In all, 34 bodies were recovered from the wreckage, including Snakehips Johnson's. An additional 50 people were seriously injured, and 30 slightly so. In time, the death toll of the disaster was to rise to 80.

But that was not the end of that night's carnage: at almost exactly the same time – 9.50 p.m. – a bomb had fallen on the Madrid restaurant in Dean Street, destroying it completely and killing another 17 people.

Perhaps the single biggest loss of local life, however, was at 3.25 a.m. on 17 April 1941, when a block of old tenement flats in Newport Place was struck by a parachute mine. A large part of the building collapsed, burying the sleeping residents, and leaving 83 casualties and 48 dead.

The threat of German invasion receded, and finally ended, leaving Soho blasted and torn. Internees who had lost their hard-worked-for businesses through no fault of their own now returned to the battle-scarred streets to start up again, sometimes from scratch.

Peppino Leoni arrived back from the Isle of Man to find that all his former customers had gone, for during the war his Quo Vadis had been turned into an Indian restaurant. Brothers Ennio and Isidor Camisa were given jobs by the new owners of the Old Compton Street delicatessen they had once owned. 'Being a boss before and then working under someone else in my old shop didn't make me very happy,' says Ennio Camisa. 'So we had to get a new licence and start all over again.' As soon as they could afford to, the brothers acquired new premises in Berwick Street where both their families could live together above the shop.

As the forces dispersed, so did many of the child prostitutes who had thronged Shaftesbury Avenue during the war. Lemons and bananas, silk stockings and nylons slowly reappeared on the market barrows in Berwick and Rupert streets. The sons and daughters of Sohoites, released from the forces, came back to Soho where they married, found jobs and had children of their own.

Gradually, daily life for most Sohoites returned to normal. However, one group of artists and writers who had gathered in the pubs and drinking clubs during the war years showed no sign of going away.

Since the turn of the 20th century London's so-called Bohemians had been associated with Soho and *the other side*, Bloomsbury and Fitzrovia. A central figure of Fitzrovian life had been Nina Hamnett, a highly talented painter who had had several individual shows in a gallery in Great Marlborough Street in the inter-war years.

Born in 1890 in Tenby, South Wales, Nina Hamnett was the daughter of an army officer, but before she had turned 20 she had renounced her middle-class background for a life dedicated to painting and the more nebulous fine art of living life to the full. This, for her, had meant dividing her time between Paris and London and befriending such notables as magician and writer Aleister Crowley (alternately called the 'wickedest man in the world' and the 'King of Depravity'), the painter Modigliani (who, Hamnett claimed, said she had 'the best tits in Europe'), and fellow artist Henri Gaudier-Brzeska, whose marble *Torso of Nina*, sculptured in 1913 and now owned by the Tate Gallery, inspired the title of the first volume of Hamnett's autobiography, *Laughing Torso*.

In the opening years of the century, the social life of London's artistic demi-monde had revolved around the Café Royal, on Soho's western border. Founded in 1865 in Glasshouse Street by an exiled Parisian wine-merchant, Daniel Nicolas Thévenon, after its move to Regent Street the Café Royal's numerous private rooms, restaurants and bars had become the haunt of Aubrey Beardsley, George Bernard Shaw, Max Beerbohm, Walter Sickert, Rex Whistler and Oscar Wilde, who in the company of Lord Alfred Douglas divided his patronage between here and Kettner's restaurant on Romilly Street.

To the young Nina Hamnett, as to many aspiring artists, the chief attraction of the Café Royal had been the Domino Room, a French-style café with *fin de siècle* gilded décor, large mirrors to see and be seen in, and the earthy, very French touch of a sawdust-strewn floor. Here the painter Augustus John had held court, buying glasses of créme de menthe frappée for the less successful acolytes who flocked round him. Hamnett, a tall and striking figure with bluntly cropped hair and a personality and a mouth to match, had quickly become a close friend of fellow Tenbyite John, and an integral part of a social circle which had included society rebel Nancy Cunard, East End painter Mark Gertler, Bloomsbury artists Roger Fry, Duncan Grant and Dora Carrington, and writer and artist David Garnett, who, in 1923, opened an antiquarian bookshop in Gerrard Street.

Hamnett and her circle had divided their time between the pubs and restaurants of Fitzrovia, the Café Royal and the drinking pubs and clubs of Soho. In the late thirties, their circle had expanded to include writer Julian Maclaren-Ross (the author of a book of short stories entitled *Nine Men of Soho*), painters Lucian Freud and John Minton, and a beautiful and exotic Sinhalese poet, Tambimuttu, who was editor of a magazine called *Poetry London*. During the war, they were joined by poet Dylan Thomas, who was working with Maclaren-Ross as a script-writer for Strand Films in Golden Square.

If Soho during the forties had provided an escape from the realities of war, Soho during the fifties was to provide an escape from post-war austerity. At a time when unusual social or sexual behaviour was frowned on, not to say condemned, elsewhere, Soho's inherent tolerance offered the unconventional, the eccentric, the rebellious and the merely different a chance to be themselves.

'To the young especially, Soho is irresistible, for it offers a sort of freedom,' wrote Daniel Farson in *Soho in the Fifties*. 'When I arrived there in 1951, London was suffering from post-war depression and it was a revelation to discover people who behaved outrageously without a twinge of guilt and drank so recklessly that when they met the next morning they had to ask if they needed to apologise for the day before.'

This, in a nutshell, sums up Soho life for the small constellation of artists, photographers, writers, refugees from suburbia, general hangers-on and 'characters' who congregated there between the end of World War II and the beginning of the sixties. Like the earlier Bohemians, few of them actually lived in Soho. Twenty-four-year-old Farson stumbled into the area almost by chance. Others came because they were introduced by a friend in the know, or because they worked in the area. Whatever brought them in, they all found its tolerant cosmopolitan atmosphere so perfectly suited to their temperament, and its landlords, landladies and restaurateurs so congenial to their impecunious states and their inversely large drinking habits, that they were to stay for years, sometimes for ever, and to adopt Soho as their second home.

Like Hamnett and her contemporaries, they were drawn together by a love of good talk, good champagne and outlandish behaviour, as well as a need for company, by their artistic interests and, in some cases, by their homesexuality. They numbered among them people who are well-known, even world-famous, in their fields today: painters Lucian Freud, Frank Auerbach, John Minton, Rodrigo Moynihan, Robert Colquhoun, Robert Macbryde, and Francis Bacon – undoubtedly the most talented painter of his generation; photographer John Deakin, who worked for *Vogue*, which then had offices in Shaftesbury Avenue, and Daniel Farson, who had come to London to work for *Picture Post*; the Bernard Brothers – Oliver the poet, Bruce the painter, and writer Jeffrey, whose column in *The Spectator* still regularly features the Coach and Horses in Greek Street, where he continues to have a permanent seat at the bar; musician and writer George Melly; writer Colin MacInnes and playwright and ex-convict Frank Norman, whose play *Fings Ain't Wot They Used T'Be* caused a sensation in the early sixties; and David Archer, gentleman bookseller extraordinaire and the founder of a small but fine imprint, Parton Press.

The planets around which these stars revolved were, naturally, the pubs: in particular the Coach and Horses and the York Minster, where Gaston Berlemont, sporting the same handlebar moustache as his sportsman father, had taken over as landlord when Victor died in 1950; the Fitzroy on *the other side*, which was still frequented by Augustus John and the by-now alcoholic Nina Hamnett; and the Golden Lion on Dean Street, which was a magnet for gay soldiers and sailors passing through town. Dean Street now also boasted two famous drinking clubs: the French-run Caves de France; and its neighbour, the Colony Room, which was owned by a beautiful but formidable Birmingham-born Jewess, Muriel Belcher.

The Colony Room, which opened in late 1948, was Muriel Belcher's second Soho club: the first had been a society and the-atrical haunt of the late thirties, the Music Box in Leicester Place. It is for the Colony, however, that Muriel Belcher is remembered, for she presided over its shabby bamboo-clad bar like a monarch over a small, tightly knit kingdom, her strong Sephardic profile reminiscent of a canny, watchful hawk.

Under her discreet but firm orchestration, life in the Colony Room became a non-stop verbal concert of good conversation, with the parched throats of the participants moistened by copious amounts of drink. To people she liked, Muriel Belcher could be warm-hearted, charming, loyal, witty, caring, generous and indulgent. She referred to her favourite male customers as her 'daughters', and greeted them from her bar-stool with her warmest expression, 'Hallo, dearie!' However, unwary strangers who climbed the dark flight of stairs to what was in reality her *salon* were greeted with the warning cry of 'Members only!', followed, if they persisted, by an unanswerable 'Fuck off!' Her language was legendary. If she took a dislike to someone, she could be monumentally rude and insulting. She had no time for anyone who was mean with money, and she could not tolerate bores.

In fact, being a bore was one of the few cardinal sins members of the Soho drinking set could commit, and being mean ran a close second. Conversely, it was more of an honour than an embarrassment to admit to being poor. In a manner prophetic of sixties' radicalism, anyone from a respectable background went out of their way to escape his or her bourgeois origins – though, strangely, being a member of the aristocracy was quite acceptable. People who were in the money – due either to a private income, an unexpected inheritance or the sale of a painting – were expected to treat those who were penniless to a drink, a champagne lunch (preferably at Wheeler's in Old Compton Street) or even a night out at the Gargoyle Club. Money lent was seldom repaid by the borrower; a careless attitude to money was obligatory, particularly when it belonged to someone else.

So the fifties passed, in drunken evenings followed by hung-over mornings which bled into drunken afternoons, the same small circle of friends meeting, talking and laughing about their drunken exploits in the same darkened, smoke-filled bars. It is a time that has been much written about, and much romanticized by the participants, some of whom are still to be found on their Soho bar-stools. It is almost a legend. But like all legends it had its dark side. Though some thrived in the 'play now, pay later' atmosphere, as Tambimuttu had once warned Julian Maclaren-Ross, Soho was 'a dangerous place'. Addiction to it took its toll in the form of alcoholism, suicide, early death and dissipated talents.

Painter Robert Macbryde was killed in a road accident in Dublin in 1966, after watching his partner Robert Colquhoun die four years earlier. David Archer took a lethal overdose at the age of 64, having frittered away his inheritance on his friends and on running the most delightful but unbusiness-like bookshop that Soho has seen. John Deakin gave up photography for an unsuccessful career as a painter. Like Colin MacInnes, he died of cancer – Deakin in 1972, MacInnes in 1976.

Nina Hamnett, the long-lasting Queen of the Bohemians, ended her days as a chronic alcoholic who was often to be seen demanding drinks from regulars in the French and the Caves. In her sixties she was penniless, incontinent, and in constant pain after fracturing her thigh bone in a drunken fall in 1953. The fracture had healed badly, with the result that, during her last years, one of her legs was substantially shorter than the other.

She had written two volumes of autobiography – the second, *Is She a Lady?* came out in 1955 – but her talent as a painter had never been fully realized. At the beginning of December 1956 she was brilliantly impersonated in a radio play about Fitzrovia in the thirties. The portrayal was too close for comfort. Eleven days after the broadcast she was dead, having fallen from the window of her room in Westbourne Terrace and impaled herself on the iron railings beneath. Though most people who knew her believed she had committed suicide, the coroner recorded a verdict of accidental death.

'Soho in the fifties? That wasn't our Soho,' says one life-long resident of Berwick Street firmly. 'It had nothing to do with the local residents. We weren't remotely involved.' For, as in the past, most Sohoites paid little attention to the people who invaded their neighbourhood. Bohemians, socialites, sailors and soldiers, drunks, dead drunks and mere drinkers – they were used to the lot of them, and took their presence in Soho in their stride.

For most locals life in the early fifties continued much as it had before the war. The scruffy, run-down streets, blighted by bomb damage, were slowly patched up. St Anne's church had gone – the vicar would no longer pop out of the sacristy door and run across the road into the French for a quick drink during the middle of Sunday morning service as he had once done. The remaining cracked walls of the church were demolished in 1953, leaving only Cockrell's ungainly steeple of 1801 standing rather forlornly at the west end of the empty site. The damaged part of St James's Residences in Brewer Street was rebuilt, and when the occupants moved back in, they found that the new flats had the unheard-of luxury of their own small bathrooms. Railings were replaced round the central gardens of Soho Square and Golden Square – the old iron ones had been salvaged during the war – and, thanks to a motion put forward by Zinna Bulmore, the first Soho-born Labour councillor on Westminster City Council, public access to what had formerly been private gardens was maintained, giving the local population two village greens. In the daytime children were sometimes entrusted to the care of local bookie's tipster, Prince Monalulu, who, dressed in his African robes, watched over them while he held court for his customers in Soho Square.

Lily Walters, who had been brought up in East London, moved to Soho in 1946 when she married Sohoite Lou Walters, whom she had first met in the swimming pool of the Marshall Street Baths. Lily recalls the advantages of bringing up her children in Soho: 'The suburbs can be so boring. But the children here were fortunate. They had the squares and Hyde Park, St James's Park, Regent's Park and Lincoln Inn Fields. And look at all the wonderful things they could see on the way to these places! There was so much to interest them. After school, we used to take them to Soho Square, where all the mothers gathered until the children's bedtime. But we never let our children play in the street, and you never saw them out late at night.'

Soho children had always come first in their parents' lives, with the result that young people, local or not, had always been treated with an indulgence that was frowned on elsewhere in Britain. But in the growing post-war affluence, attitudes towards the young – and, more importantly, attitudes of the young – were changing dramatically all over the country. Children who had grown up knowing only the depravations of rationing were now getting jobs and coming into their own. Suddenly they had money in their pockets, and time on their hands in which to spend it. The moment had come for them to shake off the shadow of the war which had hung over their childhoods. The youth revolution was happening, and its cradle was to be – where else? – Soho. After all, people had been letting their hair down and having a good time there since the days of Mrs Cornelys. Now it was the turn of every teenager in southern England to have his or her share.

Nowhere was Britain's youth revolution more evident than in the coffee bars which sprouted up during the fifties in every town centre and suburban high street. For the price of a cup of frothy coffee, Teddy-boys, Rockers and skiffle fans could sit for hours behind a steamed-up window listening to the latest Elvis or Chuck Berry hit on the juke box, accompanied by the loud hiss of an espresso machine. But for fans of home-grown heroes like Terry Dene, Tommy Steele and Adam Faith, there was nothing to beat a trip Up West to Soho. As one former jiver puts it, 'There were coffee bars in Ipswich and Bermondsey – but you couldn't see Cliff Richard performing there, like you could in the Soho coffee bars. Soho was simply the Mecca. It had the best skiffle, the best rock, and the best jazz.'

Not all the locals were disinterested in what was going on in their area. For Soho youngsters, living in 'Mecca' was a dream. Rica Teagno, who had been working as a dressmaker in Hanover Square since the war, watched the coffee bars open with growing excitement: 'Each place had slightly different décor, or pastries that were a bit more expensive instead of the fish-and-chips or steak-and-kidney-pie which the old caffs used to serve. Now they had sandwiches, and coffee made by machines, which was a real novelty. I used to go to each one that opened, just to see how they'd done them up.'

It was not long before Rica handed in her notice at the dress factory and followed her father into the catering business by becoming a waitress in one of the local coffee bars. 'It was hard work, but you met interesting people,' she recalls. And being a local girl was an added bonus: 'Other people were tourists. I belonged there. It was my domain. When all the people started to come in, I was very proud, actually. I thought, they're coming into my place.'

Not every Soho coffee bar had a décor that was worth a detour. To the hero of Colin MacInnes's novel *Absolute Beginners*, to whom Soho was a place where 'all the things they say happen, do', its coffee bars were of 'the pig-sty variety . . . What you do is, rent premises that are just as dear as any other, rip up the linos and tear out the nice fittings if there happen to be any, put in thick wood floors and tables, and take special care not to wipe the cups properly, or sweep the butts and crusts and spittle off the floor. Candles are a help or, at a pinch, non-pearl 40-watt blue bulbs. And a juke-box just for decoration, as it's considered rather naïve to *use* one in these places.'

If it was not considered hip to turn on a juke-box, live music was essential. As established musicians looking for jobs congregated outside their union in Archer Street, all but blocking the road ('You couldn't get a car up there on Monday afternoons because of them,' Roy Harrison remembers), teenagers clutching their first guitars and skiffle boards travelled into Soho from the provinces to watch Terry Dene, Billy Fury, Wee Willie Harris and Adam Faith and the Worried Men. Favourite dives were Russell Quay's Skiffle Club in Greek Street, the Top Ten in Berwick Street, and Heaven and Hell and the Two I's in Old Compton Street.

Paul Lincoln, an Australian wrestler who worked under the professional name Doctor Death, had bought the Two I's from the Irani Brothers, from whom the place took its name. Beneath the coffee bar was a tiny cellar where would-be rock'n'roll and skiffle stars congregated in the hope of being discovered by local impresarios such as Larry Parnes.

Merchant seaman Tommy Steele only played once at the Two I's

– and it was a memorable occasion, both for him and the club. He had come along to lend a hand, or rather a voice, to some friends who had a band called the Vipers, were desperately trying to get a recording contract and had invited a Decca record producer to come and hear them that night. In the event, Tommy's voice stole the show, and Decca signed him up instead of the band. A mere 10 days after the release of his first record, 'Rock with the Caveman', Tommy Steele had become the first British teenage pop idol, and the national press had turned the Two I's into the most famous music venue in the country.

It was after reading a newspaper article about Steele that a 16-year-old Geordie called Bruce Welch decided to come to Soho for a weekend to find out what all the fuss was about. A few months later, in April 1958, he was back at the Two I's, this time with his guitar and his best friend, Hank Marvin, another Newcastle lad.

The Two I's was *the* place to be discovered [recalls Bruce Welch 30 years on]. 'If it was good enough for Tommy Steele it was good enough for us. Between April and September, Hank and I almost lived there. We had a one room flat in Finsbury Park, but we hung around the Two I's every day. If we were lucky, we'd play downstairs four nights a week, from seven till eleven – mostly Buddy Holly and Everly Brothers numbers. It was a small place, very hot and very sweaty, with a tiny eighteen-inch high stage at one end, a microphone and a few old speakers up on the wall. It wasn't exactly salubrious, but it was always packed. Other people would come up to us and say, Can I sit in? And they'd get up and play with us. It was like a big jam session. All these would-be musicians dreaming of being rock-stars.

The manager was a guy called Tom Littlewood. He basically ran the place, told you whether or not you'd work that day. When we weren't playing, Hank and I worked the coffee and the orange machines, for which we were paid the princely sum of exactly eighteen shillings. Years later we figured out that it should have been one pound, and that Tom was taking ten per cent commission. Lincoln also used to put on wrestling shows, and he'd hire me to help put up the wrestling rings in places like the Wimbledon Palais. It nearly killed me. But I'd have done anything for two or three quid.

The late fifties was an austere time. London was very grey in general, full of bomb sites which had been turned into car parks. Hank and I found Soho terribly exciting. It seemed to attract characters. It was full of Greeks and Italians. And it had a very happy atmosphere. It wasn't glamorous, but it didn't seem seedy, because it was all so new to us. It was certainly a lot different from life back home.

Among the young hopefuls who came to the Two I's that summer were Jet Harris and Tony Meehan, who would later join 'the Geordie boys', as Hank and Bruce were known at the Two I's, in forming the Shadows. Another would-be star was the still unknown Cliff Richard, who played there one night with the Drifters, his current backing band, while Bruce Welch looked on from behind the drinks machine.

By the end of that summer, the two Geordies had made 'quite a little reputation for ourselves', says Bruce Welch . . .

. . . especially Hank, who could copy Buddy Holly guitar solos note for note. In September, a man called John Foster came down to the cellar looking for a very good guitarist he'd heard about – and that was Hank. He said that he managed an artist called Cliff Richard, who he'd booked for a tour starting in October. Would Hank be interested in the job? Hank said he would, if I came along too. Foster walked us round to Dean Street, where we climbed a flight of stairs to a tailor's workroom, where we first met Cliff Richard, who was having a pink jacket fitted at the time. We went back from there to his council house in Cheshunt, and did a sort of audition/rehearsal. And that was it. We joined the Drifters, and we later became the Shadows.

The excitement of rock'n'roll drew the pioneers of British pop music to Old Compton Street. For George Melly, however, the excitement of Soho in the fifties 'was very much the excitement of jazz', which for him meant first and foremost the rediscovery of the jazz of the twenties. When Melly first came to London in 1948, 'I didn't know these Revivalist bands existed. But I soon found out. . . . Jazz in London had two homes at the time: in the pubs on the outskirts of London, which implied a tube and a bus journey, and in Soho. If you wanted to get to Finsbury Park to hear a band, you practically needed major bearers to get you there. But Soho was convenient, it was in the middle of the West End. And it was a sympathetic place. You didn't get neighbours banging on the wall.'

One of George Melly's first ports of call was a large room upstairs in an NSPCC building in Leicester Square, where Humphrey Lyttleton regularly played. Eventually 'Humph', as he was known, moved to 100 Oxford Street – a jazz club run by the Willcox brothers – and his fans followed. Humph played on Mondays and Saturdays. 'There were queues round the corner,' George Melly recalls. 'First we'd drink in the Blue Posts, in what they called North Soho, and later we'd go and eat, in particular at the Rex in New Compton Street, where they served up stodge, the kind of food you needed when you were young, a plate of spaghetti served with bread and butter and chips. It wasn't a very hygienic place – they kept tins of peeled potatoes next to the lavatory.'

Another favourite Melly haunt was the Marquee Club. Though it moved to premises in Wardour Street in 1964, where it become a legendary rock music venue (Jimi Hendrix, the Who, Eric Clapton and the Yardbirds were among literally hundreds of famous acts who played there), when the Marquee first opened in 1958 in a room under the Academy Cinema in Oxford Street – the club apparently took its name from the tent-like décor of the cinema – it was strictly a trad jazz place. So was Cy Laurie's, a small club in the dark smoky basement of Mac's Rehearsal Rooms in Great Windmill Street. When Cy Laurie instituted 'Al-nite Rave-ups' at Mac's, the ever-vigilant tabloid press sprung to the attack. 'People did neck a lot, and stay up all night,' George Melly remembers. 'I suppose it was quite wild by the standards of the time, but now it would be considered very mild.'

Another jazz-fan who went to Laurie's 'rave-ups' remembers them for his first flirtation with drugs. 'We used to take Dexadrine or Benzadrine, feel really great and stay up all night jiving and smooching. It was licensed anarchy. And all the time, there'd be someone reading Sartre in the corner. About six in the morning you'd go out into the street, find a caff and have breakfast with all the prostitutes, who were just knocking off work.'

For fans of modern jazz there was the Metro, a tunnel-like basement in Old Compton Street which was packed with French students; Club Eleven, which, like Cy Laurie's, was situated in

Mac's Rehearsal Rooms, and later moved to Carnaby Street; and the now-legendary Ronnie Scott's Club, which started up in 1959 in the basement of 39 Gerrard Street, moving to its present Frith Street premises in December 1965. Late at night, musicians gathered for impromptu jam sessions at the Mandrake in Meard Street, which during the day was a club for chess enthusiasts, or at two clubs off Charing Cross Road: the Cottage and the A & A – the Artists and Actors Club – which served cheap Greek food and, because it was open till the small hours, was the hang-out of taxi-drivers, crooks, the odd prostitute and anyone waiting for the first Tube home.

By the late fifties, the young had well and truly taken over Soho. As Colin MacInnes wrote in _Absolute Beginners_ (1959):

> . . . in this Soho, the headquarters of the adult mafia, you could everywhere see the signs of the un-silent teenage revolution. The disc shops with those lovely sleeves set in their windows, the most original thing to come out in our lifetime, and the kids inside them purchasing guitars, or spending fortunes on the songs of the Top Twenty. The shirt-stores and bra-stores with ciné-star photos in the window, selling all the exclusive teenage drag I've been describing. The hair-style saloons where they inflict the blow-wave torture on the kids for hours on end. The cosmetic shops – to make girls of seventeen, fifteen, even thirteen, look like pale rinsed-out sophisticates. Scooters and bubble-cars driven madly down the roads by kids who, a few years ago, were pushing toy ones on the pavement. And everywhere you go the narrow coffee bars and darkened cellars with the kids packed tight, just whispering, like bees inside the hive waiting for a glorious queen bee to appear.

MacInnes's queen bee turned out to be Swinging London, which appeared, or rather exploded, on the Soho scene in Carnaby Street, a quiet and rather dingy lane just behind Regent Street. According to one local resident, pre-war Carnaby Street was 'one of the filthiest streets in Soho'. By 1953, when Peter Anderson came to work at the long-established Soho tobacconists, Inderwick's at number 45, the street was a respectable backwater occupied by ironmongers, a saddler, a chess-piece maker and between 40 and 50 self-employed tailors who ran up suits and officers' coats for the Savile Row stores.

Then, in 1960, a young man called John Stephen opened up a

small retail shop at the top of Carnaby Street, selling scarves. It was the beginning of a clothing revolution – particularly for men. Before long he had established a chain of trendy boutiques in the street and the local shop-keepers had realized that they were sitting on a gold-mine. As Peter Anderson recalls:

> By 1962 it was a retailer's dream. The street was packed with teenagers, and all of them were ready to spend. We were closing the door on them. We were coining it. We were literally standing on money because we couldn't get it in the till. And everything we sold had to have Carnaby Street written on it. Before long every retailer had a Rolls Royce or a Lamborghini. There was a beautiful atmosphere here – all the staff of the shops were chatty and friendly. Everyone came here, from Long John Baldry to the Small Faces.

While the youth culture was invading Kingly Street and Carnaby Street, the area south of Shaftesbury Avenue was being colonized by a new group of immigrants who, over the next 20 years, would imprint their own strong cultural character on Soho, just as their French, Italian and Jewish predecessors had done before them: the Chinese.

Chinese immigrants had first come to Britain during the late 18th century as seamen in the employ of the East India Company, when they had settled mainly in the dockland areas of the country's two main ports, Liverpool and London. Though links between Britain and China were strengthened after the 1840–42 Opium Wars, for well over 100 years the number of Chinese living in Britain remained extremely small. At the turn of the 20th century there were only 545 Chinese people in the entire country, a number almost entirely composed of men, whose shops and cafés catered mainly for the transient Chinese population of seamen. Still, by 1914 there were about 30 Chinese businesses in the Limehouse area of London, a district that was widely known as Chinatown.

The British, who had in the past shamelessly exploited the Chinese in order to ensure a good supply of tea for themselves, were far from welcoming. Chinese sailors were considered a direct threat by their British colleagues, who in May 1908 massed in the East India Dock to prevent Chinese crews from signing on for work.

All Chinese people were suspected of being lawless opium addicts who were by nature unclean – a smear belied by the fact that, up to the fifties, some of the most successful laundries in London were run and staffed entirely by Chinese. In 1919, racist bigotry against the Chinese was challenged by D. W. Griffith's epic film, *Broken Blossoms*, in which a desperate young English girl, played by Lillian Gish, is befriended by Cheng Huan, a Chinese poet, who attempts to save Gish from her murderous father.

The Limehouse streets, re-created in Hollywood for the filming of *Broken Blossoms*, were all but wiped out during the Blitz, along with much of the East End, and the part of Limehouse formerly occupied by Chinese people was rebuilt during the fifties. At the same time, the Seaman's Union brought in rules which made getting work more difficult for non-British seamen, and the introduction of launderettes and domestic washing machines put paid to the Chinese laundry business. Suddenly the British Chinese community – which in 1950 amounted to some 2,000 people – was faced with a double problem: finding new sources of income and finding a new area to live.

The post-war years had seen an upturn of interest in Chinese cuisine – probably due to the return of British soldiers who had been stationed out in the Far East. Consequently, the handful of Chinese restaurants in London's West End, which had previously catered mainly for Chinese students and businessmen, began to enjoy a boom in more local trade. If the future prosperity of the community lay in catering, where better to open Chinese restaurants than in Soho, where there were already one or two Chinese businesses which had been established well before the war.

Gerrard Street in the late fifties was one long line of shabby brothels, seedy night-clubs and faded restaurants which had seen better days. Its houses and shops were very run down and very cheap. In fact, short leases could be picked up for next to nothing in the whole area between Shaftesbury Avenue and the back of Leicester Square. Because of this, Chinese entrepreneurs began to acquire premises in Gerrard Street and Lisle Street in order to set up restaurants of their own.

At the same time, thousands of agricultural workers from Hong Kong's New Territories, forced out of their traditional occupations by changes in the world rice markets, began to arrive in England looking for work through the traditional grapevine of *t'ung heung shuk pak* (village uncles) and *t'ung heung hing-tai* (fellow villagers). As fast as they arrived, the burgeoning labour-intensive catering industry – which, during the sixties, spread to every country town and village in England – swallowed them up.

It was an extremely hard life for the new, predominantly male, immigrants, whose sole purpose in coming to Britain was to earn money to send to their families back home. Despite the fact that they were British citizens, many of them had come from small rural communities and did not speak a word of English – and working 17 hours a day as a waiter or a chef did not give them the opportunity to learn. In order to save as much money as possible, they lived in extremely basic and overcrowded hostel accommodation which was often tied to their jobs – some Chinese waiters still live in this kind of tied accommodation today.

By the early seventies, a host of local Chinese businesses had opened up to cater for the restaurant workers' needs. Gerrard Street became London's new Chinatown. Now some of the men brought over the families from whom they had been separated for many years. Mrs Sohing Pang's husband, for instance, came to England from the New Territories in 1956, but she did not join him until 1974. When she arrived, he was working in a Chinese restaurant in New Milton, Dorset – not an area renowned for the size of its Chinese community. Consequently, Sohing Pang, who spoke no English, found the town so alien and frightening that she did not leave their accommodation for a whole year. So cut off did she feel that a couple of years later the family moved into a tiny two-roomed flat in Soho's D'Arblay Street. It was a move that came as a great relief to Mrs Pang. 'Soho was much less frightening than New Milton,' she says now, 'simply because there were more Chinese people nearby.'

A worker from the Chinese Community Centre in Gerrard Street explains the feelings of isolation that Chinese people – whether from Hong Kong, Singapore or Malaysia – can feel in a city like London:

Life here can be so lonely and boring compared to back home. It's a harder life here. People work longer hours, and when they go home they just tend to watch videos or the TV. Otherwise there's no place to go out, unless you go dancing. Back home in Singapore or Hong

Kong, the shops are open until late, so you can go out shopping or just window-shopping after work. The weather's nice and you can stay outside. It's a totally different lifestyle, much more casual. For example, if you wanted to see a friend, you'd be nearby and you could just drop in. But in England, you'd have to phone up first.

As Chinese immigrants and their British-born children – or BBCs as they are known to each other – began to prosper in the seventies and early eighties, so they moved out into the suburbs, and Gerrard Street became more of a cultural and business centre than a place where Chinese people lived. But for Sohing Pang, who, after 14 years in England, had still mastered only a few words of English, living in Soho is still a necessity. 'I am very happy here,' she insists. 'If I went to live with my son in the suburbs, he and his wife would go out to work, and I'd be alone in the house all day. It would tie me up completely.'

English-speaking Sohoites have always been very helpful to Sohing Pang, and her Chinese neighbours are extremely sociable. All the facilities of Chinatown are on her doorstep. Within its Chinese-speaking world, she can enjoy full independence. A staunch Roman Catholic, she goes to Father Chung's Cantonese services in St Patrick's church every Sunday. Whenever she feels like company, which is almost every day, she walks down to her local clansman's club, the Pang Association – there is a club for almost every Chinese surname – for a cup of tea and a chat. On the way back home she can do her shopping. She will usually meet someone she knows whenever she is out in the street. Besides, she insists, there is another reason for her not wishing to give up her independence: living with one's children was a custom that belonged to her parents' generation; young and old do not necessarily get on together nowadays.

Sohoites have always been gamblers. So too have the Chinese, to whom gambling is a serious business. In fact, it is almost a way of life. Chinese men will bet on roulette, horses, cards, or on traditional games like mah-jong, pai-kau or fan tan. The first illegal Chinese gambling clubs in Soho probably opened when the first restaurants did – in the mid-fifties. There are still about half-a-dozen such clubs today.

The clubs cater to an exclusively Chinese clientèle. They do not open until the afternoon, for their first punters are usually off-duty restaurant staff who come there to pass their one-hour midday break. Chinese tea is served, and fruit juice and beer, though nothing stronger: the punters need their wits about them, for the stakes are high – a week's wages, a month's wages, even a restaurant, can frequently change hands during a single game.

From time to time, the Metropolitan Police's Clubs Squad raid the illegally run, unlicensed gambling dens in Chinatown. But it is accepted that the clubs can be useful – if only to help the police keep tabs on any organized crime that might be going on. On the whole, Chinatown is an extremely law-abiding district. Most crime which is committed there consists of young, and often prosperous, British people becoming racially abusive towards Chinese restaurant staff, and sometimes refusing to pay their bills.

Yet organized crime – in the form of prostitution and drugs and protection rackets – does exist within the underworld of Soho's highly competitive Chinese community, and from time to time violence spills out on to the otherwise peaceful Chinatown streets. In 1982, seven people were killed in the fire-bombing of an illegal basement gambling den in Gerrard Street. In 1985, a Glaswegian-Chinese businessmam who had opened a restaurant in Soho was hacked to death, as were the wife and children of another Chinese businessman. In April 1989, four employees at a Gerrard Street amusement arcade were burned alive during a night-time raid. There is little – sometimes no – direct evidence linking these murders with the Mafia-style secret societies from Hong Kong known as Triads, who may, some fear, have infiltrated Britain's Chinese community. But the police have their suspicions. Certainly, British gangs using Triad-inspired tactics do exist.

However, far from introducing crime into Soho during the seventies and early eighties, the Chinese presence south of Shaftesbury Avenue had the opposite effect of keeping corruption out. The impact of a handful of Chinsese crooks was negligible compared with that inflicted on the rest of the district by the thugs and criminals who ran the burgeoning sex industry – and by the forces of law and order themselves.

9

In the Grip of the Vice

Soho's unjust reputation as a high-crime area probably dates back to Tuesday, 18 September 1683 when a strange metal coffin was discovered near Soho Square. It was inset with a glass panel, through which could be seen a human corpse, floating 'in some Liquid Matter as clear as Cristal'. Rumour, spread by a broadsheet, had it that this was the murdered body of either the Duke of Monmouth, the Earl of Shaftesbury or Lord Grey, all of whom had been involved in the recent Rye House plot. When the metal coffin was eventually opened, however, the local coroner found that, far from being the victim of a murder, 'the Corps was a person deceased 7 or 8 days ago; his Brother, with whom he dwelt, being a Chyrurgion, had Enclosed it, in the manner as you have heard, to satisfy his Curiosity; and the Body is removed to a Shed in St Martin's New Church-Yard, where it lies at present, in Order to await its Internment.'

Naturally, there has been the odd murder or two in Soho during its long history. The most gruesome was the killing of Anna Millicent King, who in 1757 moved into number 36 Leicester Square. Four years later Miss King made the biggest, and last, mistake of her life by taking in a lodger, a Swiss miniature painter and drinking companion of Hogarth's by the name of Théodore Gardelle. Whether it was while under the influence of the demon gin that Gardelle did in Miss King is not known. What is certain is that he hacked her to pieces, 'carried bits of her about in parcels' and, having left her entrails 'in the boghouse', burned the remains.

Despite isolated events such as this, however, Soho has never been a violent district. As the local police admit, an innocent bystander is nowadays more likely to be attacked in a quiet suburban street than in its busy thoroughfares. Even in the past most dark deeds attributed to Soho actually took place elsewhere. 'If there was a murder, say, in Northumberland Avenue,' claims Gaston Berlemont, 'the newspapers would come out with a headline like "Another Murder in Soho!" Because a murder in Northumberland Avenue didn't sell newspapers, but a murder in Soho did.' Crimes which did take place in Soho were singularly unsuccessful, like the abortive plot by French Papists to poison the Earl of Essex while he was dining at Leicester House on 11 January 1642, or the French Ambassador's plan to drug the Chevalier d'Eon and dump his body in the Thames.

Yet another failed crime was dreamt up by Lord Berkeley, First Lord of the Admiralty and a resident of Soho Square. Berkeley suggested to George I that, given the go-ahead, he would kidnap the Prince of Wales on the King's behalf and transport him to America, where the young man would be kept under such close observation that he would never bother his father again. The King, in a temporary flash of paternal feeling – or, more probably, diplomacy – decided to draw the line at actually getting rid of his loathed son and heir. But he probably gave the matter some serious consideration; certainly, Berkeley was never punished for dreaming up the treacherous affair.

Berkeley's neighbour in Soho Square was one Thomas Parker, the Earl of Macclesfield and George I's Chancellor, who in 1725 was impeached for receiving bribes for the sale of official offices. Since crimes against property were treated far more harshly than crimes against the person in Hanoverian England, it was no surprise that his trial in the House of Lords reduced Parker, who was a lawyer by profession, to a state of 'abject despair'. At the end of the 24-day hearing Parker was found guilty, fined £30,000 – an unheard-of sum in those days – and thrown into the Tower of London for six weeks. As it turned out, however, he was so rich that he managed to pay off the entire fine – less a £1,000 donation from the King – without having to sell either his Soho house or his country castle. Still, the embarrassment of being found out broke his spirit, and a few years later he died in Soho Square after a bad attack of strangury, feeling, so he claimed, as if he was 'drowning inwardly and dying from the feet upwards.'

With a few exceptions – and what community does not have those? – the people of Soho have always been remarkably law-abiding, and it was, and is, widely acknowledged that practically all crime which takes place in the neighbourhood is committed by people who live elsewhere. Nevertheless, Soho's reputation as a hot-bed of vice lingers on to this day, no doubt fed by the fact that, since the mid-19th century, it has been the most famous red-light district in Britain.

The residents of Soho do not consider its prostitutes to be a problem. For anyone born or brought up in the neighbourhood they are simply a fact of life. Their presence is more than tolerated – it is accepted as an intrinsic part of the village and an added thread to the rich tapestry of cosmopolitan life.

'We never thought anything of it,' says one septuagenarian who grew up in the village. 'There was no bad feeling. The women used to mix with us, and we knew them all. We didn't fraternize, but we weren't unfriendly. We even had them living in our house.'

'It was rather nice living in a red-light district,' recalls another long-term resident. 'It wasn't vulgar. It never bothered me. Why should it? They kept themselves to themselves in those days. People criticized them, but they didn't know why they did it. They might have been starving! They had to do it for the money. If they'd had money they would never have done it.'

To immigrant women from small, often deeply religious communities, suddenly finding themselves living in a red-light district could come as a shock. There was a marked difference in the attitudes of immigrant parents and Soho-born children. 'When I was growing up I knew all the girls who were on the street. They used to say to me, "Hallo, Curly, do you want a sweet?" But my mother, who was brought up in Italy, would say, "Don't touch that sweet unless it's wrapped. You don't know where it's been!" She thought they were terrible women.'

In the days before legislation pushed prostitutes into the nether regions of bare, dimly lit staircases, the profession was much harder to ignore than it is now. Still, some people did manage to pretend that it did not exist. 'My father never mentioned prostitutes to me, and I never talked about them to my children or even to my grandchildren,' says an elderly Italian resident. 'In fact, my grandchildren didn't know anything about them at all. Of course, they asked questions. One day, one of them, who had been looking out of the window, said to me, "Grandma, that lady's been waiting on the corner for a long time – what's she waiting there for?"'

Other early immigrants were more broadminded: 'My mother, who was from Poland, was very progressive, so my sister and I knew by the age of ten what the prostitutes were there for. I also knew about an unofficial brothel in Broadwick Street, where on a Monday evening at eight o'clock along came a policeman who knocked at the door and, when it was opened, was given a bag of money. Then off he'd go. It was a convenient arrangement all round.'

Until World War II many of Soho's prostitutes were professional Frenchwomen – the Fifis, as they were called. They could be recognized by their immaculate clothes ('They weren't ladies, but they looked like it,' recalls one gentleman), their immaculate houses (many employed cleaning ladies, and those that could not afford to were forever polishing their door furniture or washing the stairs), and sometimes by the distinctive gold chains which they wore round their ankles. The French, or York Minster, was a second home to the Fifis. Gaston Berlemont remembers them as 'lovely girls – the best in the world. They used to come in here and have a half bottle of champagne, a Pernod or a Ricard. And if anybody approached them, they'd yell for help. They might promptly leave here and go and stand on their corner, or wherever it was they worked. But in here was sacred. I'd tell the men to hop it. They'd say, "But . . ." And I'd say, "But nothing! Those women are entitled to have a drink without being bothered by people like you!"'

There were also, of course, English prostitutes, particularly young girls who had had illegitimate children and had been thrown out by their parents, and so forced on to the game. 'They were the cheap ones, who operated around Lisle Street, in a doorway for half-a-crown a time. The professionals resented them, not because they were rivals but because they didn't know or care about health matters, so they put the professionals at risk.'

One thing was clear, the prostitutes always came from outside the area. The villagers had a proud boast – never a local girl. 'If you lived in Soho, you were either a prostitute or you didn't have sex until you were married. There was nothing in between. At least, as far as we knew.'

Living in a red-light district had its entertaining side. 'One girl came into the shop and said, "Trade is so bad at the moment I think I'll go on hire purchase."' There were sometimes cases of mistaken identity: 'I was standing on the corner of Dean Street and Oxford Street one day waiting for a couple of friends, and one of the prostitutes came over and said, "What's business like up this end, love? Is it any good?"'

For a Polish family living in Peter Street, one particular evening turned into a nightmarish farce:

There was a brothel next door to our house, and it seemed that a man who had gone there had had his wallet stolen. The next night he came back to try and claim it, but he forgot which number the brothel was, and started banging on our door instead. The door was locked, so he broke in and rushed upstairs to the second floor where he'd been with the prostitute and started beating on what he thought was her bedroom door. My parents were already in bed in that room. My mother was so terrified that she completely lost her speech. My father flung open the window and called out, 'Police! Police!' But there weren't any police around that night. Luckily, someone down the road had a telephone, and he called them up. They came round and talked to the man, and found out what had happened, and explained it to my father, and asked him if he wanted to charge the man for breaking in, and he said no. But the next morning he dressed up in his Sabbath best and marched down to the police station in Savile Row where he demanded to see the inspector. 'I've come to launch my protest!' he said. 'I am a decent citizen! People don't do that to me in my own home.'

When prostitutes were openly soliciting for business there was always something to watch in the street. Would this one get that man to come home with her? Would that one get nabbed by the police? And which MP or Lord would come out of that brothel doorway? 'Did important people come here? Not half!' Christina Foyle remembers. 'We used to see them hanging around at the bottom of the staircases. I once saw one of my uncles. And I was so naïve that I went up to him and asked him what he was doing there.'

The prostitutes' clients were no problem to the local women. In fact, what little trouble there was came from the girls themselves. 'I can remember when there was a girl on every corner. That was a nuisance,' Christina Foyle continues. 'Because when I was young they often thought I was competing with them. They were extremely rude to you sometimes. There was one, in particular, who used to solicit in Manette Street where I lived. We had a roof garden outside our flat, and I used to put pots of flowers all along the edge of the balcony. One day a pot of geraniums fell down on this poor girl's head. And she took us to court and sued us for loss of earnings – I think it was about £25.'

On the whole, relations between prostitutes and the rest of the local women have been extremely amicable. After all, they were all women, sharing many of the same joys and the same problems: 'When my son was born in the early fifties, the girls all threw money in his pram for good luck when I brought him home from the hospital,' remembers one Soho woman. 'Then one day, a few years later, I remember coming home very tired and very fed up, and one of the girls just came up to me and put her arms round me and gave me a big hug.'

But one must not romanticize the Fifis, insists Paul Raymond, the owner of Raymond's Revue Bar: 'When people say now that the girls 30 years ago were a much better class of girl, it's a load of tripe. Because at that time people were saying exactly the same thing about the girls 20 years before.'

Though most Sohoites would disagree with him, mourning the days when, as one retired clock-repair puts it, 'you accepted the prostitutes as fellow tradesmen', the sex business has always had its darker, and more worrying side: organized crime.

The five Messina Brothers did not introduce the idea of vice rings to England, but they certainly helped to consolidate them in Soho. Salvatore, Alfredo, Eugene, Carmelo and Attilio Messina were the sons of a Maltese mother and a Sicilian father, Giuseppe Messina, whose vice-racketeering had taken his family from Malta, where they had claimed British citizenship, to the shores of North Africa. The boys were brought up in the slums of Alexandria, Egypt, where Giuseppe ran a string of brothels which provided the boys with all the education they would need in their future careers.

When they arrived in London in the early thirties, the brothers quickly established a network of brothels in Soho and Mayfair staffed both by British prostitutes and by women whom they imported from the Continent under the guise of arranged marriages, and who were often kept in the country against their will and forced to work the streets by a potent mixture of coercion, beatings, razor-slashings, terror and threats. Rival gangs were similarly dealt with by hired foreign assassins and a string of runners and henchmen, including one man called Bernie Silver, who would later earn himself the nickname 'the Godfather of Soho'.

Despite one early charge against them, the Messinas' vice empire became so large and so all-powerful over the next decade that in 1947 the Home Secretary, Chuter Ede, would admit in a House of Commons debate that nothing could be done to stop them. It was left to a single crusading journalist, Duncan Webb of the *People*, to chase them from the country and pursue them into Europe.

The underworld of crooks, pimps and thugs established in Soho during the Messinas' reign might have been cleaned up when they fled. It was not. Incredibly it was allowed to get worse. Englishman Bernie Silver teamed up with another Maltese gangster, 'Big Frank' Mifsud, and the two men stepped into the Brothers' empty shoes, establishing a new, even larger network of prostitutes, gambling dens and striptease and illegal drinking clubs throughout the West End which they ran from an office in Romilly Street.

By the late fifties, Silver, Mifsud, and another rival gangster called John Mason had the Soho underworld well and truly within their control, with the help of high-up local police officers and Scotland Yard detectives whom they bribed on a massive scale. Their businesses flourished, expanding to include what were initially discreet shops selling erotica and pornography. Due to the confused state of the laws on obscenity, officers of the Obscene Publications Squad (the OPS, or 'Dirty Squad', as it was known) had a great deal of power over what was sold, by whom, and where. They were kept 'happy' with huge sums of money, in return for which they raided or scared off competitors and turned a blind eye to the Mason, Silver and Mifsud dealings. It was not just a matter of police protection but police protectionism on a vast scale.

Liverpudlian-born theatrical impresario Paul Raymond made his name from running nude touring shows in the provinces. In the late fifties, he decided to set up a nude theatre-cabaret in London. 'I was looking for premises for 18 months,' he says. 'People always told me "Whatever you do, don't go near Soho. It's an appalling place, and you won't last two seconds there because of the gangs, and you won't be allowed to survive".' Raymond ignored their advice, rented a building in a seedy alleyway called Walker's Court and opened what was to be the first of many Raymond clubs in Soho.

Over 30 years later, Raymond's Revue Bar is still very much a going concern – for many people its very name is synonymous with Soho – and despite the fact that he has bought up many properties used by the porn trade which, he insists, he 'could not do a thing' about, Raymond prides himself on being the sex business's Mr Clean. 'The whole time I've been here,' he insists, 'I've never been approached for protection money, never. I think the only people who are bothered that way are people who have something to hide.'

Michael Klinger agrees that 'part of running a club in Soho is keeping your nose clean. If you're not careful, you can find yourself in the hands of gangsters or corrupt policeman.' In 1955, he and a partner, Jimmy Jacobs, bought the old Gargoyle Club in Meard Street. After a disastrous beginning ('A single customer turned up on the first night,' he admits, 'a writer, who was drunk when he arrived. And he only ordered a jug of water') they brought in the Harry Roy Band, turned the luncheon room into the risqué Nell Gwynne Revue, and the club became as successful as it had been in its early days.

Growing up in Soho, Klinger had always been aware of gang warfare: 'I remember seeing a man killed on Frith Street when I was a kid. But the gangs were always fighting each other. The people who lived in Soho were never interfered with. We felt no fear.'

Once he had a club of his own, the situation was rather different:

There was a famous West End character called Tony Mella who was eventually shot in Dean Street. He came into the Gargoyle one night with two guys, and one was a heavyweight fighter. They just stormed in, and sat down at a table. I told the waiter not to serve them, and when they refused to go I called the police, so they ran out the back. A week or so later, I was on my way to the car park at the top of Dean Street, and these two guys are walking towards me, saying 'We're going to get you, you f. . .ing b . . .' So I said to them, 'If you want to come after me, you'd better kill me. Because if you touch me, I'll come after you wherever you are. Because that club's my business and my livelihood, everything I've got in the world is up there. And I'm not going to put it in jeopardy because you fancy a night out. If you want a drink now, it's a pleasure, come and have a drink.' That was it. End of story. The same thing with corrupt police – you don't tolerate it.

Nineteen fifty-nine marked a turning point for Soho and the British sex industry, for it saw the passing of two important pieces of legislation: the Obscene Publications Act, the aim of which was to straighten out the hitherto unworkable obscenity laws; and the Street Offences Act, which sought to clear prostitutes off the streets. The Street Offences Act succeeded in doing this, but at the expense of forcing prostitutes into the arms of pimps and organized criminals. The way this worked was simple: unable to solicit for customers on the streets, prostitutes now had to rely on pimps to tout for them, or to meet their clients in special 'hostess' bars, strip clubs, saunas and bogus massage parlours set up expressly to bring prostitute and client together.

The new Act, aptly nicknamed a 'pimp's charter' by its critics, had yet another beneficial effect on the vice industry. Men who wanted a prostitute were prepared to pay a lot of money to get into a club where they might meet one, and when there, they could be forced with very little pressure to spend again, well over the odds, for the beverages which they and their hostess consumed. In addition, by making sure that no sex act took place on the premises, and by observing the alcohol licensing laws and serving only mock-champagne, non-alcoholic wine and 'near-beer' to the punters (the non-alcoholic content of the drinks was usually written in tiny letters on the back of a tariff card, well out of sight) they could stay well within the law while raking in profits which made those taken down the road in Carnaby Street look like peanuts. The government had virtually presented the vice barons with a licence to print money.

Ironically, at the same time that real sex was going underground into dingy basement near-beer bars and striptease clubs, the pornography business, which had been discreetly tucked away in the back rooms of a handful of Soho shops, was at last coming out into the open.

The 1959 Obscene Publications Act was brought before Parliament under pressure from the Society of Authors, who were anxious to protect Britain's bona fide literary writers and publishers from prosecution under the existing muddled obscenity laws. What exactly was the definition of an 'obscene' publication? It had previously been taken to mean any publication that had a tendency 'to deprave or corrupt those whose minds are open to such immoral influences, and into whose hand a publication of this sort may fall' – a definition in which the intention of the writer or publisher was deemed to be irrelevant. The new Act added small but crucial changes: 'For the purposes of this Act an article shall be deemed to be obscene if its effect or (where the article comprises two or more distinct items) the effect of any one of its items is, if taken as a whole, such as to tend to deprave and corrupt persons who are likely, having regard to all relevant circumstances, to read, see or hear the matter contained or embodied in it.' The clause 'if taken as a whole' was deemed to be of paramount importance. The intention of the author now had to be taken into account in a judgement on obscenity: a book or article could be defended on the grounds of being for the public good. At last it seemed that there was a clear-cut answer to the age-old question, 'Is it pornography, or is it art?'

The Act's intentions may have been good in theory. In practice, it was a nightmare. It had done little to clarify the situation, as publishers Penguin Books found out less than a year later in the *Lady Chatterly's Lover* obscenity trial, when D. H. Lawrence's literary intentions were dismissed as grounds for defence. Neither did amendments added to the Act in 1964 sort out the muddled situation. Works of art which had been on sale for years – sometimes for hundreds of years – were now seized and declared obscene, while soft-core pornographic magazines were openly displayed on the shelves of newsagents' shops. With the powers for the initial seizure of obscene material lying firmly with the police, radical publishers like Gay News found themselves in court accused of crimes such as blasphemy or conspiring to corrupt public morals, while, down in Soho, handouts from the porn merchants to crooked OPS officers like Detective Chief Superintendent Bill Moody and Commander Wallace Virgo of the CID – among others – ensured that their openly pornographic stock was untouched.

Meanwhile the shopkeepers, skilled artisans and restaurateurs of Soho got on with the business of making a living, as tolerant as ever of the changes in their midst. On the surface at least, Soho was still very much a residential area of families and children. Boy scouts still flocked to Madame Floris's chocolate factory during bob-a-job week, asking to lend a hand in the hope of taking home a bag of sweets. Children on their way to school may have giggled when they went past the bookshop windows and hostess bars, but as yet there was nothing explicit to see outside the premises. No one bothered much with the strippers who tripped down Brewer Street on their way from club to club (most of the strip-clubs were organized in chains, and worked by the same few dancers). Their needle-sharp stilettos, fish-net tights, mini-skirts, nylon wigs and vanity cases containing the tools of their trade – feather boas, whips and corselets – had become as common and unremarkable a sight as the film-company gofers who staggered between the cutting-rooms and viewing theatres of Wardour Street under the weight of film cans.

But the situation was about to change dramatically. Relaxation of censorship laws in Denmark and Sweden during the mid and late sixties sent wave upon wave of hard-core pornographic magazines into England, along with films that were a far cry from the innocuous naturalist films such as *Naked as Nature Intended*, which was made by Michael Klinger and Soho-based photographer George Harrison Marks. Before long, Soho was flooded with explicit sexual material. For the next decade and a half it was to seem to the local population that all the most tawdry flotsam and jetsam in Europe had been washed up on their streets.

The number of sex establishments mushroomed, and their displays became notably explicit. But with powerful figures like Moody and Commander Virgo – who was by now in charge not only of the OPS but of Scotland Yard's entire Serious Crimes Branch – still in the pay of the porn barons, nothing was done to stop them spreading. Since the OPS had to be seen to be doing their business, premises were periodically raided, but, as in the past, prior warnings were always given so that offensive material could be safely hidden beforehand. Sex had become a multi-million pound business, and the police, like the porn men, were creaming off the profits. Thousands of pounds' worth of pay-offs were changing hands every week in Soho's pubs, coffee bars, clubs and mews, often in full view of the public on the street.

As the sixties drew to a close, Silver, Mason, Virgo and Moody were so overconfident, and the net of police corruption so widespread, that it was inevitable that people would become suspicious and that the whole machine would collapse. After allegations made by two *Times* journalists, Scotland Yard started an enquiry into suspected corruption within their ranks. Within a few months of the investigation starting, Moody was appointed on to it, which guaranteed that it would have no success. It was not until 1976 that Virgo and Moody were finally arrested, along with 10 other top officers from Scotland Yard. Moody and Virgo were tried in March 1977, found guilty, and both sentenced to 12 years in prison. Less than a year later, Virgo was released 'on medical grounds'.

But corruption was not confined to Soho, or to Moody and Virgo. Nearly 400 officers either resigned or were dismissed when under investigation during the course of Commissioner Sir Robert Mark's four-year campaign to clean up the Metropolitan Police. The result, however, was not to clean up the streets of Soho. Now that the top porn barons were out of action ('Godfather' Silver had been sentenced to six years in 1974 for living on immoral earnings, and Mason, who had given evidence at the OPS trials, was living in the Channel Islands) and the police protection racket was over, the small men who had been scared off before could move in.

The business became even more cut-throat, more undisciplined and even more competitive. The strip clubs disappeared, to be replaced by a lurid rash of video booths, peep-shows, topless bars, sexual 'toy' shops and nude encounter parlours. Clip joints which promised the punters everything, took their money and gave them nothing became commonplace. Planning regulations were blatantly defied. Property values for suitable sex-business premises shot up in relation to demand – and many local shop-keepers found their rents rising accordingly.

Sohoites who had co-existed peacefully for so long with prostitution, now felt as though they were being taken over. To them, the spread of the 'plastic vice', as they called the sex shops, was not a moral issue but a purely environmental one. Walking through the village had become frankly unpleasant. Touts hung about on the pavements as the shleppers had once done, trying to coax punters into their video bars and sex shows. Photographs displayed outside clubs and cinemas were so omnipresent and so blatantly pornographic that visitors and residents literally did not know where to look. Soho had become ugly, sleazy and sordid. Outsiders who had previously frequented the food shops and restaurants stopped coming into the area. The sex industry might have been a flourishing concern, but it sounded a death-knell for other businesses.

'The only good thing about the porn shops,' says Alberto Camisa, 'were the shop-fitters, who could change one shop to another overnight. Otherwise it was embarrassing, particularly when uncles, aunts and friends came over from Italy to see where we lived and worked. It was the centre of London, yet there was rubbish and litter everywhere, and people peeing in doorways.'

The local council, Westminster, proved curiously indifferent to their blighted city centre, perhaps because there had been plans to rebuild Soho, with the rest of London, since the end of World War II. By the early seventies, most of Soho had been zoned for comprehensive redevelopment. Demolition of the 18th-century buildings which had seen so much was due to take place on a massive scale. The council itself had already pulled down terraces of fine Georgian houses in St Anne's Court and Livonia Street. As the current chairman of the Soho Society, Bryan Burrough, remembers, 'There were plans passed for 300,000 square feet of offices around Piccadilly Circus. That meant 20- or 30-storey tower blocks, with pedestrians walking across concrete walkways 60 feet up in the air and six lanes of traffic whizzing away below.'

The most bizarre plan to rebuild Soho was surely the Pilkington Glass proposal for Soho in the year 2000, which was drawn up as early as 1954. This involved glassing over the entire area at roof level, building six 24-storey blocks of flats, each with 60 'heligarages' for helicopter parking, and constructing five miles of boating canals and a glass-floored swimming pool at roof level.

Kemp House in Berwick Street, a 17-storey block of council flats built at the beginning of the sixties, was a single component of one such scheme to build a Brave New Soho. Today it stands as a permanent, brutal reminder of what the village might have become. The merits or faults of the building itself are unimportant. What is relevant is that it is quite out of touch with what has always made the streets of Soho special – their small, essentially human scale.

Bryan Burrough is a descendant of a family of Huguenot silk weavers who settled in Soho in the 18th century. Though he was brought up in Sussex, he first came to Soho when he was 18. 'I found Soho very addictive, in that it was a very friendly place. It was the one place where I felt at home. It was generally sleazy and run down, but the residential community was incredibly long-lived. Very few people left the neighbourhood. Most people who lived here had lived here all their lives, and had relatives who lived here. Many were married to people who were born here.' Though his presence in Soho was often to be interrupted by postings abroad, Burrough quickly became an accepted and valued member of the community, and worked part-time in a local French restaurant run by the Martelli family, Le Petit Savoyard.

In November 1972, Bryan Burrough attended a historic meeting of local people in a small room above Kettner's restaurant. The meeting had been called by local councillor Thelma Seear. 'The Martellis, who lived above their restaurant in Romilly Street, said you'd better go across, Bryan, something's going on. So I went, and instead of a handful of concerned locals, there were over 200 very angry locals.' Their anger stemmed from the imminent threat of destruction which hung over their neighbourhood, and over a community that had been evolving for nearly 300 years.

The Soho Society, born that day, has become a tribute to that much-devalued notion, 'power to the people'. Through hard lobbying, its members managed to get the whole of Soho declared a conservation area, and so prevent it from being bulldozed into the ground. 'In the process,' Bryan Burrough says, 'it meant that Soho became politicized – not in a party political sense, but in the sense that we realized that because we were a tightly-knit community we were able to speak with one significant voice which couldn't be ignored.'

Having prevented their village from being demolished, the residents realized that something had to be done to discourage people from leaving it. Since living conditions were so primitive, with many flats still having no electricity or bathrooms, quite a few people – particularly young families – had had enough of living cheek by jowl with the sex industry, and were moving out to housing estates in Pimlico or to the suburbs. If Soho was to survive as a working community, the young people who were its future life-blood would have to be encouraged to stay. So, with the help of a £700 loan, the free use of a room in the renovated tower of St Anne's church, and two people working for a year for no wages, the Soho Housing Association was formed, with the aim of rehabilitating the area's dilapidated housing stock. By 1986, the last flat lit by gas had become a memory.

Once the Soho Society had realized their power, there was no stopping them. The next item on their agenda was to get rid of the plastic vice. This was no moral crusade, but a matter of the community's survival. As Bryan Burrough explains, 'We weren't trying to drive all sex out of Soho. We've never regarded individual prostitutes as a problem, and we have never suggested that they were. We were talking about the plastic vice, the nude encounter parlours, topless bars and sex cinemas. We lobbied to change the legislation regarding the licensing of sex premises, but we were not supported by Westminster City Council, who in May 1976 approved the change of use to 11 sauna and massage parlours. That meant that by 1977 there were 185 Soho buildings in use by the sex industry.'

To try and enlist the support of the council, the local people put up two independent councillors for Westminster's Soho and Mayfair ward. Brigadier Gordon Viner and Lois Peltz were both voted on to the council with an enormous majority. Once there, they brought up local issues at each and every council meeting, battling against the council's reluctance to get involved in what they saw as the moral issue of driving vice out of the centre of town.

'For them, it was a matter of censorship,' says Councillor Lois Peltz. 'For us, it was purely environmental. Soho had become a travesty of a place. Children were ashamed of admitting that they lived there. We were helped in our fight to clean up Soho by MPs of both parties, and by Members of the Lords. The local council, however, were hardest to change, because the City Solicitor was fearful of the disrepute that Westminster could be brought into.'

Trying to enforce what laws there were – town planning and licensing laws and health and safety regulations – was virtually impossible. In order to bring a prosecution against a particular business, the owner had first to be found. With premises closing down or changing hands overnight, and with most owners operating from an administrative and legal distance, finding the right person to prosecute was a bit like trying to grasp a bar of soap in the bath. No sooner did they seem to be caught than they slipped through the fingers.

In 1982 and 1986, after heavy lobbying and a change of heart by the City Council, new licensing laws were brought in for sex shops and places of entertainment that virtually forced the illegal vice operators to run legitimate businesses. Under the new legislation, local councils could fix the number of sex shop premises they would allow in their district. Anyone who wanted a licence to run one could apply only by filling in a long and comprehensive application form, proving that they were of 'good character' – and few operators were able to do this without incriminating themselves. If the vice tried to operate unlicensed premises, the police could now move in and close them down.

When operators did apply for licences, members of the Soho Society pursued them into the courts, where they themselves soon became as knowledgeable and as devious as the men they were fighting. 'We were just as clever as they were,' admits Bryan Burrough. 'We had people sitting in the court galleries who would look shocked if the appellant so much as said damn. We would surreptitiously 'by mistake' slip something in about a prior conviction for Grievous Bodily Harm. We pursued cases into the Crown Court and High Court on points of law. We persuaded witnesses to come along and testify against every applicant. Once we had the community involved, we were simply unassailable. The vice lost case after case. It was a marvellous thing.'

In a matter of months the shutters came down on the district's most sordid premises. The local artisans and residents breathed a sigh of relief. Their fight to live in a decent area was over at last. Yet to out-of-towners, the change in Soho was disappointing: football fans descending on the West End for an erotic night out found only streets of unlit neon and padlocked doors. As one resident said, 'They all came to Soho looking for excitement, but there was no excitement here any more. They could have got more excitement by going into W. H. Smith and looking at the magazines on the top shelf.'

For a brief moment it seemed to outsiders that the heart of the district which people had loved to hate for so long was dying. The reality was quite the opposite. Soho was about to be reborn.

Quo Vadis?

Soho has now come full circle. No longer the social pariah of London, it is once again the in place to be. A few years ago no one but a handful of die-hards wanted to work, eat, drink or run a business there. Some Sohoites were even too ashamed to admit to outsiders where they lived. Now, says Roy Harrison, 'I've stopped telling people I grew up there because it sounds so trendy.' Soho is no longer synonymous with sleaze but with style. 'Soho' is the new buzz-word on everyone's lips.

In the morning Patisserie Valerie is packed with young executive breakfasters. At lunchtime, style-conscious post-punks gather outside the French or at the window tables of the Soho Brasserie. The streets are jammed with VW Golf convertibles, drivers clutching the inevitable car-phone. Every bar, club, restaurant and street is crowded of an evening – ironically, the only place that is now deserted is St Patrick's church, on the site of Mrs Cornelys's 'Temple of Festivities'.

There has been an outbreak of designer restaurants. The Braganza has gone black, white and wrought-iron; potted palms and halogen lights have even hit the once-cheap Chinese cafés on Lisle Street. There are designer dress shops, designer shoe shops and scores of designer hairdressers; there are Filofax shops and shops selling useless but attractive *objets d'art*, and there are designer sandwiches to eat. In fact, Soho now has everything for a total designer lifestyle, including newly paved and cobbled designer streets.

Times have certainly changed since there were 186 sex establishments in the seediest half square mile in London. A decade on, there are a mere 35 licensed strip joints, hostess bars, peep shows and sex cinema clubs, concentrated around the Brewer Street/Rupert Street/Walker's Court junction, and in the eastern reaches of Old Compton Street. Since the introduction of compulsory licensing the plastic vice has not so much left town as been bound and gagged with its own handcuffs and harnesses. With window displays reduced to a discreet minimum, the near-beer bars must rely on young receptionists to lure in their customers. The girls, sometimes no older than school-leavers, stand in the narrow entrances of the cellar bars in heavy make-up and thin T-shirts looking cold and lack-lustre and usually about as sexy as a quick dip in the Marshall Street Baths.

'Pick your own Purr!!!fect Pussy to relax with. Most of our Pussies are Bi-lingual', is the double-edged boast of one bar in Brewer Street. 'Into the 80s with sensual erotic experience' promises a sixties survivor striptease bar, the Sunset Strip, which now keeps a lone vigil in Dean Street. Video and bookshop windows are blanked out discreetly like plain-wrapped parcels, their doors guarded by signs limiting entry to the over-18s.

Despite the occasional thwarted punter stalking the neighbourhood, the local residents still think prostitution is less of a problem than, say, the disappearance of a local launderette or ironmonger shop. As one resident of Kemp House put it, 'An old lady came round the other day with a petition because someone had put a red light bulb in the window across the street. I said, I'm not signing that! What, one red light in Berwick Street? I can think of far more important issues I'd like to sign for!'

The change from vice area to nice area has happened incredibly quickly. When would-be restaurateur Nick Lander first visited the old L'Escargot Bienvenu on Greek Street back in 1980 with a view to buying it, the Soho streets were as seedy as the restaurant's kitchens, which had been closed down by Westminster City Council on 44 different counts. But neither the proximity of the local brothels nor the state of the ovens put Lander off. 'I fell in love with the building,' he says now. 'I thought it had great potential and charm. And it was an enormous challenge.'

While the old kitchens were being torn out and the restaurant was being revamped, Nick Lander would wander through seedy Soho wondering if he had done the right thing. 'I watched everyone walking around, and told myself they had to eat somewhere. I'd often stand at the railings outside St Martin's School of Art on Charing Cross Road and count the people who walked past – that was very consoling.'

Though L'Escargot re-opened to great acclaim, that did not stop potential customers from being put off going there by the proximity of the sex industry. 'People would make up lots of excuses for not coming in,' says Lander. 'But they'd never talk about their real reasons – they'd say, we'd love to come, but it's so hard to park. Which was nonsense, because parking was difficult throughout the West End.'

Nick Lander's initial risk paid off. With Soho's most famous and warm-hearted manageress, Elena Salvoni, installed in the quiet upstairs dining-room, and the talented Stephen Chamberlain presiding over the art exhibitions and cabaret in the cheaper brasserie downstairs, L'Escargot turned out to be the vanguard of a new breed of fashionable Soho restaurants whose numbers multiplied as the sex industry declined. That did not stop its owner from worrying about the burgeoning competition – Alistair Little's, started by his original chef, and the private Groucho Club, a media and literary retreat on Dean Street, which was opened by several of his best ex-customers in 1985. Lander's fears that L'Escargot would lose out were, however, unfounded: 'The population of Soho expanded, and there were just more places to take care of it.'

Undoubtedly, there have been huge improvements in Soho. Many long-term residents have a new, benign landlord, the Soho Housing Association (SHA), and, under its aegis, enjoy refurbished and renovated accommodation, and a degree of security they have never had before.

Soho's residential community is still a tremendously stable one: it is not unusual to find second- or third-generation Sohoites being educated at the Parish School, which is a direct descendant of the original St Anne's Church School founded in 1699. Only 12 years ago, the declining numbers of children living in Soho threatened the future of this school. Now numbers have doubled, and the school is full again, with 120 children and six teachers on the roll. Three hundred years ago, its pupils were mainly French and English Protestants. Thirty years ago, the bulk of them were Russian and Polish Jews, or Italian Catholics. Six years ago, they were mainly Chinese. Many Chinese families have now moved out to the suburbs, and the school now enjoys Moslem, Hindu, Christian as well as Buddhist pupils. The so-called problems of running multi-cultural schools, much talked about by educationalists, are not regarded as such in Soho, but as a distinct benefit: as David Barton, headmaster until the summer of 1988, puts it, 'We got over those particular panic reactions a hundred years ago.'

Sixteen years after it was founded, the Soho Society – an entirely voluntary organization – is as active as ever. Its chairman and driving force is Bryan Burrough. Quiet, charming and unassuming, his energy and his determination not to be beaten know no bounds. Like the Reverend Cardwell in the 1890s, he has become the champion of his neighbourhood and of his neighbours. As they all acknowledge, without him Soho might not have existed today.

Having saved the fabric of the district, Burrough and his fellow Soho Society members still vigilantly vet every plan that is submitted to Westminster City Council, and strongly oppose any they do not consider are in the area's interest. Their progress, or otherwise, is faithfully charted in the *Soho Clarion*, a free newspaper which they produce and circulate to a readership of 6,000 people. They also organize a children's party every Christmas, a weekend festival in July, and an active history group run by Kathleen Gibson, an ex-warden of the House of St Barnabas. The monthly meetings of the History Society are packed, reflecting local people's pride in their home. There is much kissing of cheeks and shaking of hands when people assemble for the lectures, for the evenings also provide an opportunity for born-and-bred Sohoites to get together, as well as to meet some of the people who have recently moved in.

Nearly 50 years after it was bombed, St Anne's church is being rebuilt, a symbol of Soho's regeneration. The Rev. Fred Stevens, the vicar of St Anne's, has no idea when it will be finished, but the old church vaults have been excavated in readiness for foundations to be laid. In the process, about 4,000 corpses have been exhumed from the crypt and reburied in the East London Cemetery. There are at least another 10,000 late parishioners buried in the old churchyard – it is for this reason that the garden's level is six feet above the rest of Wardour Street.

As well as a purpose-built chapel, the new building will contain a community hall – Soho's first – a small museum, permanent headquarters for the Soho Society in the restored church tower, and 22 SHA flats. Part of the new building will be built with bricks made locally in the 17th century, when Brewer Street was a brick-field called Knaves Acre; these were salvaged from the original church. The whole rebuilding scheme is being brilliantly financed, in what is now typical SHA style, by a small commercial development of 4,000 square feet of office space and three shops fronting on to Dean Street, opposite the French pub.

The French itself continues to be a monument to the old Soho as well as a focus of the new. As always, it is crowded with people. At the time of writing, Gaston Berlemont still presides over the bar himself. Little, if anything, has been altered downstairs. The walls are still covered with photographs of politicians, boxers, aviators, cyclists and movie stars. De Gaulle's call to arms, now brown with age and nicotine, is still pinned to the staircase banisters, reminding one of days when the pub was a meeting-place for the Resistance. Only the name outside has changed – after years of misdirected postal deliveries which ended up at the York Minster Cathedral, Dean's Yard, York, Soho's own York Minster, Dean Street, is now officially known as 'The French'.

Though past clientèle has included celebrities such as Wyndham Lewis, Amy Johnson, Vivien Leigh, Brendan Behan, Dylan Thomas, Aleister Crowley and Salvador Dali, Gaston Berlemont is as welcoming to unknown newcomers as to Auberon Waugh, Francis Bacon and Anthony Burgess, some of his present regular stars.

> The customers change, but they stay the same [Berlemont insists]. Characters are replaced by other characters of the same ilk. The crowd we have now is just a carbon copy of the same crowd that was coming in forty or fifty years ago when I was a boy. They are the same type of people. Our type. People who like life, who like to drink wine and enjoy each other's company. They themselves create an atmosphere. It's no use putting up a couple of plastic onions and saying that you're creating a French atmosphere, it doesn't work like that. Atmosphere is a human thing, concerning hearts and souls.

It was to stop the atmosphere of Greek Street patisserie Maison Berthaux from changing too much that Michelle Wade bought it in 1988 from Monsieur and Madame Vignon, who had run it since 1923. When the patisserie went on the market Michelle and her French-Austrian partner Johann Steinecker faced heavy competition from outside interests all too ready to turn the building into offices or even into another designer boutique. To the relief of traditionalists, Maison Berthaux's future is now in safe hands.

Michelle Wade was well-known to the patisserie's 10-strong staff when she took over, for she had already worked there, on and off, for eight years. To her, it is much more than a business. 'I just love it,' she says. 'I knew if someone else bought it, it would change. Actually, I have made certain changes. I've added flowers and a few pictures, and I've run up new net curtains. But no one seems to have noticed,' she adds with relief.

Another Soho eatery which seems to defy time is the legendary Frith Street Greek restaurant, Jimmy's, which was opened by Jimmy Christodolous in August 1949. Whitewashed walls, wooden chairs and faded seersucker tablecloths serve as a plain backdrop for wine served out of kitchen tumblers, and huge platters loaded with substantial quantities of moussaka, salad and chips. Chairs nearest the counter are often occupied by elderly Greek men drinking tiny cups of thick sweet coffee or smoking cigarettes. 'I come here every day,' says one. 'I'm a senior citizen, and they're relations, so they don't chuck me out.' In atmosphere the place feels less like a West End restaurant than a family taverna in a small Mediterranean town.

Sadly, Jimmy died in the summer of 1988. He is much mourned by everyone who knew him. 'He was a simple family man and businessman,' says his cousin John Koiza, 'but he was respected. He always helped people who needed help. Even the crooks had respect for him. No one came here just to make trouble.' The traditions he established during nearly 40 years as a Soho restaurateur are being kept up by his son and other members of the family, who find, as John Koiza admits, that Soho's renewed popularity is 'very good for business. But our aim is not just to make money and get out – our business is to look after our customers,' he insists.

Nowhere is Soho's regeneration more noticeable than in the portion of Soho south of Shaftesbury Avenue, where the streets built on the former Military Ground and Lord Leicester's back garden are now officially recognized as Chinese. Apart from the countless Chinese restaurants and tea-rooms, there are Chinese solicitors, Chinese accountants, Chinese banks, Chinese doctors, Chinese beauty parlours and a Chinese newspaper. There are herbalists selling Chinese medicines, and a Chinese Community Centre patronized by elderly locals and young British-born Chinese.

John Dryden's old house in Gerrard Street is now a supermarket overflowing with woks, porcelain bowls, chopsticks, pickled plums, packets of noodles, deep-frozen scallops, preserved kumquats and milky white sweets. Newport Place and Newport Court, which once skirted the shambles of Newport Market, have a Chinese pavilion, video shops selling Hong Kong imports and fish shops stocked with sabrefish, abalone, whiskered cat-fish, and live carp and eel. Boxes of fresh knobbly ginger, lettuces and garlic are stacked up on the pavement alongside baskets of juicy longan, prickly durian fruits as big as footballs and Thai-grown lychees.

On Sunday afternoons, or late on weekday evenings, London's Chinese community flock to Gerrard Street from the suburban areas where most of them now live to do their shopping, to buy a Chinese newspaper, to meet friends, and to eat *en famille*. They also come for another, less tangible, reason: to touch base. For the area holds an important symbolic value for the whole Chinese community: it is a place where young people brought up in Britain can enjoy their own culture, and enjoy a few hours' relief from the isolation they sometimes feel.

Chinatown is also big business now. It has become a major London tourist attraction, on a par with Carnaby Street. Oriental arches, pagoda-like telephone kiosks and stone lions have been recently added as part of Westminster City Council's plans to recognize the importance of this. The team behind these cosmetic changes – and behind all other such changes in the area – is Westminster City Council's Soho Project, which was launched in 1984 with the aim of smartening up the shabby Soho streets.

In their offices in Westminster City Hall, Victoria, the Soho Project designers plot such tangibles as traffic management, street furniture, land use, and the creation of new pedestrian precincts. Cobbles are coming back in, as are high-quality York stone pavements and the kerbside bollards removed in the late 18th century that will, it is claimed, stop drivers from parking on the fragile pavement lights. The Broad Street pump is to reappear in what is now Broadwick Street as a fountain – minus, it is to be hoped, the cholera germs. Trees are being planted, though not too many, and a proposal for having hanging flower baskets has been thrown out as too twee. Driving through and parking in Soho are to be made even more difficult than they already are, if that is possible. Rupert Street and Berwick Street are to receive smart wall-to-wall paving, and it is proposed that the present market stalls should be redesigned and repositioned back-to-back, instead of being on either side of the street. Soon the markets, it is claimed, will be as attractive to tourists as pedestrianized Gerrard Street and Argyll Street.

With so many improvements going on, it seems that everyone must be happy. But are they?

Soho's streets are altering faster than they can be walked. As the village rockets up-market a whole host of small family businesses are being replaced by refurbished offices and fashionable boutiques. A few years ago, rent reviews in nearby Covent Garden – a favourite haunt of advertising and marketing companies – sent dozens of businesses into neighbouring Soho because it was cheaper. With most of the TV and film facilities companies in London on their doorsteps, not to mention the best restaurants, they discovered what Sohoites had known for many years – that no other district could be as convenient to work in.

As a result, Soho has enjoyed a sudden rush of popularity, and commercial rents, which were artificially depressed by the existence of the vice for so many years, have risen dramatically. Speculators who bought up property in the bad old days are now laughing: legitimate business, they find, pays even better than the sex industry used to do. Long-established Soho firms such as violin dealers and restorers J. & A. Beare, who bought their own premises 10 or 12 years ago, when local morale was at its lowest, discover that they are sitting on a potential goldmine.

But there is a dark side to the boom in prices. Long-established businesses which occupy rented premises now find they are being pushed out by the rent rises. As a direct consequence, the network of individual shops and workshops which was an integral part of Soho's atmosphere is vanishing like a thin tissue of ancient material exposed to the 20th-century air for the first time. Local shops – the kind where you could buy half a dozen nails, or get your watch repaired – are disappearing so fast that it is not a question of 'here today and gone tomorrow', but of 'here yesterday and gone today'. The casual, haphazard feel of the district is disappearing as 'Closing Down' becomes as common a sign in Soho windows as 'Monique French Model' used to be on the stairs.

With every gain there inevitably comes a loss, and Soho's traditional craft industries are proving to be the main victims of the village's renaissance. Sadly, they have been threatened as much by government legislation as by anything else. The Use Classes Order, passed in May 1987, abolished the classification of property for Light Industrial use. Now, when old leases come to an end, landlords can turn light industrial workshop space into offices without obtaining permission – and office space commands much higher rents. Between May 1987 and October 1988, 50,000 square feet of light industrial space in Soho was turned into offices.

One need only look at a single company to measure the scale of the potential loss to Soho. Take, for example, the family firm of M. Hand and Co Ltd., Gold and Silver Lacemakers, which is run by a husband and wife team, Derek and Bunty Hand. Derek Hand is a direct descendant of a Flemish Huguenot weaver called Hans who set up the business in Bethnal Green in the 1760s, making gold lace and embroidery for the aristocracy and the military. At the turn of this century, the company moved from the East End to Lexington Street, near Golden Square, where, while the family worked in the factory, a Berwick Street child-actress called Jesse Matthews played with her dolls on the stairs.

Hand employs a full-time staff of seven, as well as 16 outdoor-workers who live as far afield as Cornwall. It is not unusual for the firm to keep its staff for 60 or 70 years – its oldest outdoor-worker is currently 82 years old, and its designer and draughtsman, Mr Miles, joined the company in 1940, the same year that their premises were bombed.

Hand undertakes the finest hand-worked lace and embroidery – epaulettes, badges, cap peaks, sword sheaths, the gold-work on the Lord Chancellor's coat – 'the top stuff', as Derek Hand says. The business is snowed under with orders. Its customers range from individual American collectors to entire armies. 'The British Army is our bread and butter,' says Bunty Hand. 'The Middle East armies are the jam on the bread. The Sultan of Oman is our best customer. But we don't work directly for him, or for English Royalty – we work for the tailors who make their clothes.'

Running a long-established family business is hard work and, they admit, a great responsibility. 'It's a bit like riding a tiger: we can't get off because there's nobody to follow.'

Sadly, the tiger may have bucked them off first. In March 1989, Hands' lease with the Sutton Estate came to an end. A few months beforehand the fate of the firm lay in the balance, for Bunty and Derek Hand had no idea what the outcome of their next rent review would be. 'We've been trying to buy the building, we've saved up all our money and made an offer on it, but our landlords won't sell. We feel very much under siege – as do many so many people round here. This business with the premises has been haunting us for years. Our sons went into other professions, because it wasn't fair to bring them in when the situation was so dicey. If we could buy the premises now, our grandsons might come in with us. But if we lose the building, we'll close down. We won't look for other premises at our age.'

As Bunty and Derek Hand know, it is not easy to move a business such as theirs elsewhere, for, like many local firms – especially those in the tailoring or film industries – it depends on the proximity of other, related businesses. 'We used to boast that, if a diplomat had to present his credentials at St James's Palace, we could whip round and get all his essentials and trimmings from Soho and Mayfair within 24 hours. Miss Rule curled the ostrich feathers for his hat, we made the gold cord and braid, the tailors made the suit – it was all done round here.'

With Miss Rule, another Soho artisan, about to be evicted from her premises, and the Use Classes Order threatening some of the Savile Row tailors as well as themselves, this kind of service will soon not be possible. By the time this book is published the firm of M. Hand and Co, in existence since the 18th century, may well have been forced to close its doors for good, despite having full order books. 'This is what infuriates us,' says Bunty Hand. 'We had the depression in the thirties, we had the war and the bombing, we had the pornography, and we survived all that – and now it's the landlords.'

The sharp rent rises which have become a fact of life in Soho are affecting all local businesses. Small film facilities companies are slowly having to leave the area. Even long-established restaurants are being threatened by demands for doubled, tripled and quadrupled rents. The market people are worried that they, too, will be pushed out once Rupert Street and Berwick Street are smartened up by the council. 'They'll just pave them over and put up our rent,' fears Berwick Street greengrocer Bill Bean. 'It's always been a hard market to work, it's very competitive and getting harder all the time. We used to store our stuff overnight in Covent Garden or in the local mews – but they are turning them all into studios now. At the moment, we've got a bit of grace to park our vans on the empty site at the end of Peter Street. Soon that'll be built on, and turned into boutiques. What'll we do then?'

The kind of changes that are now happening in Soho are to a large extent inevitable. They have already happened in every local high street in the land. The only way to stop them would be to hold back change – the very thing that has always been an intrinsic part of life in Soho. Nothing could, surely, be less desirable. Besides, when one considers what the area has gained, the losses should not matter too much.

Somehow, though, they do matter. One cannot help feeling that in the process of gentrification, something extremely valuable is being lost – a richness and a depth that has taken 300 years to evolve. For as the shutters come down on yet another corner shop, it seems that it is not just another business which is going – it is the end of an era, and a whole way of life.

For Soho is a very special place. Since the days of the Huguenots it has been a springboard for immigrants of all nationalities, and a place of opportunity for ordinary working-class women and men. It is probably the last district in central London which still has a stable residential and business community – a community whose members have, over the years, learned the value of helping each other as much as helping themselves.

Bryan Burrough tells a story. It sounds apocryphal, but it is true. He was round at Mr and Mrs O'Shea's, the clockmakers in Dean Street, when Isidor Camisa of Camisa Fratelli came in clutching a metal ring from one of his pasta machines. The ring had broken, and Mr Camisa was in urgent need of a replacement part. There and then, Mr O'Shea ran up a replica ring on his metal lathe. Mr Camisa thanked him profusely and took the new ring back to the family delicatessen in Berwick Street. Ten minutes later, a delivery boy turned up at the O'Sheas' bearing a crate of Chianti. It was a perfect business transaction. Everyone was happy, and not a penny changed hands.

The O'Sheas have now retired, and their old premises, a fine 18th-century mansion on the corner of Dean Street and Meard Street, stands empty and forlorn and, as they say in the trade, ripe for refurbishment – probably into yet more luxury offices. And as other craftspeople like the O'Sheas leave the area, the kind of transaction Bryan Burrough witnessed, which is still relatively common in Soho, will become increasingly rare.

The Soho Society is fighting tooth and nail to prevent Soho from being turned into an office monoculture. If Soho is not to have the heart knocked out of it, they argue, light industry needs to stay. Without protection, companies like M. Hand and Co. will disappear for good, and with them will go the area's special character. With a little intervention, what is left of it could remain. If so, Soho could enjoy a golden renaissance.

But at the time of writing the future looks grim for the traditional businesses as well as for the residents. The growing number of offices command top-whack rents, and tiny private flats which were sold five years ago for a pittance now fetch prices comparable to those in Hampstead or Belgravia. With the Soho Housing Association's help, the existing residential population is secure – at least for the time being. Whether a fourth generation of Sohoites will be able to afford to stay in the future remains to be seen. Young adults who follow their parents into traditional local catering and tailoring jobs could never afford to pay the kind of market prices which are now being asked for private rented accommodation in Soho, nor could they afford to buy into the area. If they leave, the existing community will remain – but preserved in aspic. Soho will become an ersatz village of working-class pensioners and wealthy yuppies, like many a picturesque Cotswold hamlet today.

In 1926, Peppino Leoni opened a restaurant in Karl Marx's old house in Dean Street. He decided to name it Quo Vadis, as he did not know whether it would ruin him or make him a rich man.

It is time to ask that same question of Soho. Where is it going? Will its vitality and individuality survive this latest up-turn in its fortunes? Or is it destined to become a victim of its own success?

Soho Update

As this book goes to press, M. Hand and Co., Gold Lacemakers, have just negotiated a new lease on their Lexington Street factory.

A proposed rent increase has persuaded Gaston Berlemont to retire as patron of The French House. He is to leave, appropriately, on Bastille Day, 14 July 1989. Though his regulars are outraged at the prospect of his departure, Gaston says stoically, 'After 75 years here, I don't know whether to be sad or relieved.'

Bibliography

Angelo, Henry: *Reminiscences of Henry Angelo*. Henry Colburn, 1823.

Arblay, Madame D': *Diary and Letters of Madame D'Arblay (Fanny Burney)*. Edited by Charlotte Barrett. Macmillan, 1904.

Battiscombe, Georgina: *Mrs Gladstone, the Portrait of a Marriage*. Constable, 1956.

Bentley, G. E.: *Blake Records*. Oxford University Press, 1969.

Bushell, Peter: *London's Secret History*. Constable, 1983.

Casanova: *My Life and Adventures*. Translated by Arthur Machen. Joiner and Steele, 1932.

Creichton, Charles: *The History of Epidemics in Britain*. Cambridge University Press, 1894.

Cox, Cynthia: *The Enigma of the Age: The Strange Story of the Chevalier d'Eon*. Longman, 1966.

D'Oyley, Elizabeth. *James: Duke of Monmouth*. Geoffrey Bles, 1938.

Edmonds, Mark: *Inside Soho*. Robert Nicholson Publications, 1988.

Francis, Basil: *Fanny Kelly of Drury Lane*. Rockliffe, 1950.

Gaunt, William: *The World of William Hogarth*. Jonathan Cape, 1978.

Gillman, Peter and Leni: *'Collar the Lot!': How Britain Interned and Expelled its Wartime Refugees*. Quartet Books, 1980.

Goldsmith, Margaret: *Soho Square*. Sampson Low, Marston & Co., 1947.

Graham, Stephen: *Twice Round the London Clock*. Ernest Benn, 1934.

Hamnett, Nina: *Laughing Torso*. Constable & Co., 1932.

Hartup, Adeline: *Angelica: Portrait of an Eighteenth Century Artist*. Heinemann, 1954.

Hooker, Denise: *Nina Hamnett: Queen of Bohemia*. Constable, 1986.

Jahn, Otto: *Life of Mozart*. Translated from the German by P. D. Townsend. Novello, Ewer and Co., 1882.

Kingsford, Charles Lethbridge: *The Early History of Piccadilly, Leicester Square and Soho*. Cambridge University Press, 1925.

Lees, Lynn Hollen: *Exiles of Erin: Irish Immigrants in Victorian London*. Manchester University Press, 1979.

Leoni, Peppino: *I Shall Die on the Carpet*. Leslie Frewin, 1966.

Leslie, Charles Robert Taylor: *The Life and Times of Sir Joshua Reynolds*. John Murray, 1865.

Lewis, Chaim: *A Soho Address*. Victor Gollancz, 1965.

MacInnes, Colin: *Absolute Beginners*. Macgibbon and Kee, 1959.

Macnamarra, N. C.: *The History of Asiatic Cholera*. Macmillan & Co., 1892.

Mander and Mitchenson: *The Lost Theatres of London*. Rupert Hart-Davies, 1968.

Melville, Lewis: *Mr Crofts, The King's Bastard: A Biography of James, Duke of Monmouth*. Hutchinson & Co., 1929.

McCalman, Iain: *Radical Underworld*. Oxford University Press, 1988.

McCormick, G. D. K. *The Private Life of Mr Gladstone*. Frederick Muller, 1965.

McLellan, David: *Karl Marx: His Life and Thought*. Macmillan & Co, 1973.

Peters, H. F.: *Red Jenny*. Allen and Unwin, 1986.

Proctor, B. W.: *The Life of Edmund Kean*. Edward Moxon, 1835.

Norman, Frank: *Soho Night and Day*. Secker and Warburg, 1966.

Rimbault, E. F.: *Soho and its Associations*. Dulau, 1895.

Scott, Ronnie: *Some of my Best Friends are Blues*. W. H. Allen, Allen, 1979.

Smith, Edward: *The Life of Sir Joseph Banks*. John Lane, The Bodley Head, 1911.

Smith, John Thomas: *Nollekens and His Times*. Edited by Edmund Gosse. Richard Bentley, 1895.

Snow, John, MD: *Snow on Cholera*. Oxford University Press, 1936.

Summerson, John: *Georgian London*. Pleiades Books, 1946.

Taylor, Tom: *Leicester Square*. Bickers and Son, 1874.

Telfer, J. Buchan: *The Strange Career of the Chevalier d'Eon de Beaumont*. Longmans, Green and Co., 1885.

Tomkinson, Martin: *The Pornbrokers: The Rise and Fall of the Soho Sex Barons.* Virgin Books, 1982.

Tristan, Flora: *Flora Tristan's London Journal: A Survey of London Life in the 1830s.* Translated by Dennis Palmer and Giselle Pincetl. George Prior, 1980.

Van Damm, Sheila: *We Never Closed: The Windmill Story.* Robert Hale, 1967.

Walpole, Horace: *Letters.* Edited by Mrs Paget Toynbee. Clarendon Press, 1905.

Young, Sir George: *Poor Fred: The People's Prince.* Oxford University Press, 1937.

Letters of Mozart and his Family. Edited by Emily Anderson. Macmillan & Co., 1938.

Survey of London. General Editor F. H. W. Sheppard. The Athlone Press, Vols XXXI & XXXII (The Parish of St James, Westminster) 1963, Vols XXXIII & XXXIV (The Parish of St Anne, Soho) 1966.

Twenty Years in Soho. By the Clergy of St Anne's. Truslove and Hanson, 1911.

Two Centuries of Soho, Its Institutions, Firms and Amusements. By the Clergy of St Anne's. Truslove and Hanson, 1898.

Index

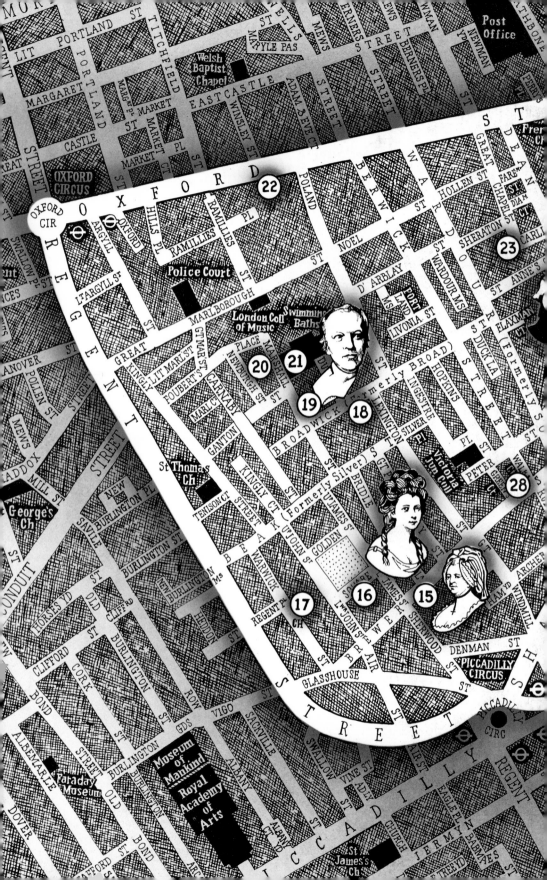